Data Analysis Using SPSS for Windows Versions 8 to 10

A Beginner's Guide

JEREMY J. FOSTER

SAGE Publications

London · Thousand Oaks · New Delhi

© Jeremy J. Foster, 1998, 2001

First published 1998, reprinted 1999
This edition first published 2001. Reprinted 2002.

SAGE Publications Ltd
6 Bonhill Street
London EC2A 4PU

SAGE Publications Inc.
2455 Teller Road
Thousand Oaks, California 91320

SAGE Publications India Pvt Ltd
32, M-Block Market
Greater Kailash – I
New Delhi 110 048

British Library Cataloguing in Publication data

A catalogue record for this book is
available from the British Library
ISBN 0 7619 6026 8
     0 7619 6927 6 (pbk)

Library of Congress catalog card number 133951

Typeset by Photoprint Typesetters, Torquay, Devon
Printed in Great Britain by The Cromwell Press Ltd,
Trowbridge, Wiltshire

SUMMARY OF CONTENTS

CONTENTS

21 Obtaining neat printouts and tables 240

References 248

Index 249

PREFACE

This book is designed to teach beginners how to operate SPSS for Windows using versions 8 to 10 of the package. You have some data and some questions such as 'How do I get a frequency table, an average, or a histogram?'. The book gives you the answers, explaining the commands you need, and showing you the output the commands provide. It is not a text in statistical analysis; I have assumed that the person who comes to SPSS is likely to know, at least in general terms, what statistical analysis they want to do. What they do not know is how to get SPSS to do it for them!

The book is intended for the individual student or researcher who has access to a PC with SPSS for Windows installed; moving between the computer and the written explanation is the only way to develop skill in using the program. A set of hypothetical data is used in explaining how to obtain the results you want from SPSS. Do please carry out the various examples and exercises: it is only by having hands-on practice that you will develop an understanding of the way SPSS works, and become its master.

SPSS is very efficient, but it is complicated. Do not become discouraged if at first you find it confusing: we all do! Once you have mastered the general principles, you will soon find that it is comparatively straightforward to obtain the results you want. And remember that when you are able to drive SPSS, you have enormous power at your disposal.

Jeremy J. Foster

ACKNOWLEDGEMENTS

Thanks are extended to SPSS UK Ltd for permission to use copies of SPSS for Windows screens.

SPSS is a registered trademark of SPSS Inc.

For information about SPSS contact:

SPSS UK Ltd, St Andrew's House, West Street, Woking, Surrey GU21 1EB.
Tel: 01483 719200; fax: 01483 719290.

USING THE DISK

A disk is provided with this book. It contains a number of files which illustrate the analyses described.

There are three main types of file within SPSS: data files which contain the data to be analysed, syntax files which contain the commands telling SPSS which analyses to perform on the data, and output files which contain the results of applying the commands to the data.

Data files on the disk

There are a number of data files on the disk, each ending in the filename extension .sav. These files can only be opened when SPSS is running, using the File Open Data procedure described in section 5.10. They cannot be listed or printed except within SPSS.

The data described in chapter 4 and section 5.1 is in file salesq.sav. The file salesq2.sav comprises the same data as salesq.sav, but after the Compute and Recode operations described in sections 12.2 and 12.6 have been run. There are two additional variables, totatt and custrc, added to the data. The file jfch16.sav contains the data used in section 16.13 to explain how to carry out an analysis of variance with two within-subjects variables. The data file jfch20.sav contains the data used in chapter 20 on factor analysis.

Syntax files

Syntax files, which contain the commands you have chosen and are described in chapter 8, end with the filename extension .sps. How to open syntax files within SPSS is explained in section 8.6. Syntax files are text files, and can be opened in a word processor for inspection, editing and printing.

The syntax used in each chapter from 9 onward to analyse the data in the file salesq.sav has been saved in the file jfsyntax.sps.

Some of the example analyses use a different data file from salesq.sav. The syntax to carry out the within-subjects analysis of variance described in section 16.13 is in the file jf16syn.sps. It analyses the data in the file

jfch16.sav. The syntax used to carry out the factor analyses described in
chapter 20 is saved in the file jf20syn.sps. It analyses the data in the file
jfch20.sav.

Note that if you want to run any of these syntax files, the appropriate
data file must have been opened in SPSS. At the top of each syntax file
there is a comment line which states the data file needed. Comment lines
begin with an asterisk and end in a full stop (period), and the syntax files
contain a number of comment lines which explain what the syntax
does.

It is possible to run a syntax file without having the appropriate data
file open, so long as the syntax file contains the command to open the
data file. An example is provided in the file openf.sps, which is otherwise
identical to the file jf16syn.sps. It contains the lines

```
GET
  FILE='A:\jfch16.sav'.
EXECUTE
```

These two commands instruct SPSS to open the data file jfch16.sav which
is on the disk. Before trying to run the file openf.sps, you would have to
make sure a floppy disk containing the data file jfch16.sav in the root
directory is in the disk drive, drive a: If the file jfch16.sav is on a CD, you
would need to have the CD in the CD drive. This drive may be drive D,
but depending on the way your system is configured, the CD drive may
have a different name: it could be drive E or some other letter. (You can
find out which letter is used to denote the CD drive if you use Windows
Explorer to list the directories and drives on your system.) Whichever is
the letter for your CD drive, note that you will have to edit the file
jf16syn.sps so that the line shown above is changed to

```
GET
  FILE='D:\jfch16.sav'.
EXECUTE
```

with the letter D altered (if necessary) to correspond with the letter
which your system uses to refer to the CD drive.

If you want the syntax to be printed in the output, as in the examples
given in the book, you need to go to the Edit /Options /Viewer as
described in section 7.1 and check the Display Commands in Log
option.

Output files

A major benefit of using syntax files is that the output can be created by
running the syntax without having to select the commands from the
menu system. Since running the syntax files provided will generate the
outputs illustrated, the disk does not include all the output files used in
the book. But two examples are provided.

The file fig7_7.spo contains the output illustrated in Fig 7.7, which is obtained by running the Frequencies procedure on the variable cust in the data file salesq.sav. Output files ending in .spo are generated by the Output Viewer, and these .spo files can only be opened within SPSS as explained in section 7.6.

An alternative to the Output Viewer is the Draft Viewer, which produces output less neatly formatted. Files produced in Draft Viewer are saved with the filename ending in .rtf. On the CD, the file fig7_7df.rtf is, like the file fig7_7.spo, produced by running the Frequencies procedure on the variable cust.

By opening both of these output files you will be able to see how the formats of the Output Viewer and the Draft Viewer differ. Draft Viewer files ending in .rtf can be opened in a word processor. But inserting the contents of an Output Viewer .spo file into a word processor is more difficult, as is explained in section 7.12.

It is possible, as described in section 5.12, to import into SPSS data which has been prepared in a spreadsheet. To provide the opportunity to practise this, two Excel version 4 files are included on the disk. Both contain a small spreadsheet of data: the first column is the respondent's identification number (id), the second column is age, the third is sex (coded as 1 or 2), the fourth is a measure of performance (perf). In file import1.xls the names of the variables are given in the first row of the table. File import2.xls is the same, but variable names are not included.

Files contained on the disk

- Data files
  salesq.sav
  salesq2.sav
  jfch16.sav
  jfch20.sav
- Syntax files
  jfsyntax.sps
  jf16syn.sps
  jf20syn.sps
  openf.sps
- Output files
  fig7_7.spo
  fig7_7df.rtf
- Spreadsheet files
  import1.xls
  import2.xls

1

AIMS OF THIS BOOK

Summary

- This book is based on versions 8, 9 and 10 of SPSS for Windows.
- The main differences between the versions are described in section 1.1.
- Before starting to use SPSS, read chapters 3 to 8.

1.1 Versions of SPSS for Windows

This book is designed to teach you how to use SPSS for Windows, versions 8, 9 or 10. (To find which version you have, use the Help /About entry of the menu when you have SPSS running.) The descriptions of how to drive the package refer to versions 9 and 10, but version 8 is very similar: the major differences are listed in section 1.1.1, and if you are using version 8 you should refer to that section regularly.

Version 10 operates in the same way as version 9, but some improvements have been made to the Data Editor, which is the screen shown when you are entering the data to be analysed. They are explained in section 3.9.

The original edition of this book was written for SPSS/PC+, a DOS-based predecessor of SPSS for Windows. SPSS for Windows implemented a much simpler interface so that it became much easier to learn how to drive the system. With the introduction of the Windows 95 operating system, new versions of SPSS were produced. The most recent version is number 10, which like versions 7, 8 and 9 operates under Windows 95/98. Those familiar with the now obsolete version 6, which ran under Windows 3.x, will find that the Windows 95/98 versions appear rather different; but, assuming you are familiar with Windows 95/98, there should be little difficulty in making the upgrade: most of the procedures are unchanged, it is the interface that has been updated. In some areas, especially creating, viewing and editing graphs, and producing neat tables of output, the improvements are more pronounced. The appropriate chapters in this book show you how to use these improved facilities.

1.1.1 For users of SPSS version 8

The major differences between versions 8 and 9 are:

1 Version 9 has a menu entry Analyze. In version 8 it was entitled Statistics.
2 Version 9 has under the Analyze menu the submenus Reports and Descriptive Statistics. In version 8 the entries in these submenus were together under the submenu Summarize.
3 Version 9 has under GLM an entry entitled GLM Univariate. In version 8 it was GLM General Factorial.
4 Version 9 has an entry OLAP Cubes. In version 8 it was called Layered Reports.

1.2 How to use this book

This book is intended to show you how to operate SPSS for Windows so that you can analyse data which you want analysed. The fact that you are reading it means that you are thinking of using SPSS for Windows, and are probably aware that SPSS is a set of programs that allows you rapidly to analyse huge amounts of data, and that it lets you carry out in a few moments statistical analysis that would be impractical without the aid of a computer.

This is not a book on statistics. Although there are now a number of books which combine teaching statistics with teaching SPSS, this one assumes you know the analyses you want, if not how to obtain them. I have taken the view that learning statistics and SPSS together is risking overload, and that it is easier for the student to learn them one after the other. If you need a simple text on basic statistics, there are a number of excellent ones available (e.g. Hinton, 1995). There is a brief account of the basic principles of statistical analysis and various statistical procedures in chapter 2, but this is intended as a refresher rather than a statistics course for beginners. Sections 8 and 9 in chapter 2 are intended to help you decide which analysis you require.

This book covers most of the facilities offered by the Base module of SPSS for Windows and some of the more advanced procedures which are provided by optional extra modules. I have structured the text by considering the questions that the user asks, moving from the simpler to the more complex procedures. (Manuals are often written the other way round; they explain the various commands one after the other, giving you the answer before you understand the question.)

Even the Base modules of SPSS offer you a very wide range of options when analysing your data. Saying that this book covers the facilities of the Base module, does not mean that I have attempted to describe every possible feature. There are thousands of different options which one can choose, and many of these can be explored at leisure once the basic mode of driving the package is understood. As in the previous editions, I have tried to explain the structure of the system and describe very fully how beginners can obtain the analyses they are likely to require. Once you have gained the fundamental skills, you can explore further facilities for yourself.

This book assumes you are sitting in front of a PC that either has SPSS for Windows installed on it or is connected into a network that makes the package available to you. The Windows environment has become so dominant in the PC world, that I have assumed that the reader is already familiar with it and with how to operate the mouse by pointing, clicking the mouse button, double-clicking (clicking twice in rapid succession) and click/dragging, which means you press the mouse button and while it is depressed move the mouse.

The first part of the book deals with general issues that are essential before you can use SPSS effectively. Chapter 2 is a summary of the principles of statistical analysis and can be skipped if you feel confident about what you want to do and why. In explaining how to use the package, I employ a set of hypothetical data, described in section 4.3, and referred to as salesq.

You need to acquire some basic information before you begin to use the package. I strongly urge you to read chapters 3 to 8 before doing anything else.

Chapters 14–20 deal with various types of statistical analysis, and provide an explanation of how to obtain them and how to read the printout. For this edition, all the examples have been re-analysed using SPSS for Windows version 9.

1.3 Conventions used in the printing of this book

Pressing the Enter key (also known as the Return key) is shown as ↵.

The Alt and Ctrl keys are rather like shift keys in that they modify the meaning of pressing an ordinary key if that key is pressed while Alt or Ctrl is depressed. When you need to press two keys together, for example the Alt and E keys, press down the Alt key and while it is depressed tap the E key, then release the Alt key. This is shown in the text as Alt+E, but remember it does not mean that you press the Alt key followed by the E key, and certainly does not mean that you press the + key: the Alt key must be held down when you press the E key.

1.4 Using floppy disks

Once installed, the various programs that make up SPSS are stored on the hard disk in their own directory. It is perfectly feasible to store the data that you want analysed and the results of the analysis on the hard disk, but hard disks can 'crash' (i.e. fail) so whatever is stored on them is lost. Furthermore, if you store your files on the hard disk they are not portable. But when stored on a floppy, they can be taken to any PC that has SPSS for Windows installed on it, and used on that machine. So you are not tied to one PC, and can make copies of your data and command files so that you have a back up copy in case disaster strikes and your floppy gets damaged. I shall assume that you have a formatted floppy disk for storing your data, commands and the results of your analyses. As any computer user knows, ALWAYS keep at least one copy of your work on a floppy – and if it is really important keep two copies in separate locations, so if one burns down you still have your files!

2

THE BASICS OF STATISTICAL ANALYSIS

Summary

This chapter provides a rapid revision of basic statistics.

- Descriptive statistics are used to describe sets of data.
- Inferential statistics are used in generalizing from a sample to a wider population and in testing hypotheses.
- Some variables are continuous, others are categorical or discrete.
- There are four types of measurement scale: nominal, ordinal (rank), interval and ratio.
- The type of scale determines which type of statistical analysis is appropriate.
- If scores on two or more variables come from the same respondents, you are dealing with related (within-subjects) comparisons.
- If the scores being compared were obtained from different respondents, use independent groups (between-subjects) procedures.
- Directional (one-tailed) hypotheses predict the direction of any observed difference in scores.
- Ensure you understand how to interpret the outcome of a significance test.
- Use Figure 2.3 at the end of this chapter to help select the appropriate test.

The main body of this book assumes that the user knows the statistical analyses that are needed, and describes the procedures for getting SPSS to provide particular statistics and apply specific statistical tests. The aim of this chapter is to remind readers of the principles of statistical analysis, so that they can decide which statistics they need for their particular sets of data. It is not intended as a substitute for a text on statistics, but should be seen rather as an aide-memoire for those who have temporarily forgotten what the various statistical procedures are used for.

2.1 Fundamental definitions

2.1.1 Population and sample

A population is an entire set of objects or people, such as the residents of France or Australian nine-year olds. A sample is a subset of a population, and in the majority of research analysis one works with a sample of a population. Usually one hopes to generalize from the sample to the population, as in opinion polls where perhaps 1000 people are asked for their opinion, the results obtained from this sample are generalized to the whole voting population of the country, and statements are made about the popularity of political parties in the country as a whole.

Whether it is valid to generalize from the sample to the population depends upon the size of the sample and whether it is representative of the population: does it have the same characteristics as the population of which it is a subset?

2.1.2 Descriptive and inferential statistics

Descriptive statistics are used to describe and summarize sets of data. They answer questions such as 'What was the average age of the patients who were admitted to the local hospital with a heart attack in the last six months?'.

Inferential statistics are used in generalizing from a sample to a wider population, and in testing hypotheses, i.e. deciding whether the data is consistent with the research prediction.

2.1.3 Scales of measurement

NOMINAL SCALES are where the numbers are used merely as a label. For example, we may code sex of respondent as 1 or 2, with 1 meaning male and 2 meaning female. The size of the numbers is meaningless, and 2 is not bigger or better than 1 (we could just as easily have used 1 to indicate female and 2 to indicate male).

Bear in mind that SPSS will happily give the mean of a variable measured on a nominal scale even though this is meaningless. There are examples in the scientific literature of eminent researchers making this mistake and reporting that the mean score on sex was 1.5. With nominally-scaled data such as sex, where respondents are 1, 2 or 3 (representing sex unknown), the mean of the scores is literally nonsense. But SPSS does not know that; it only knows there is a set of figures, so it does not object when it is asked for the mean even if it is not appropriate to do so. It is the user's responsibility to look at the results of the analyses intelligently!

ORDINAL (RANK) SCALES have some correspondence between the size of the numbers and the magnitude of the quality represented by the numbers. A common ordinal scale is position in a race. One knows that the person who came first (position 1) was faster than the person who came second (position 2), who was in turn faster than the person who came third (position 3). But the numbers 1, 2 and 3 do not tell you anything about the size of the differences between the three people. The winner, number 1, may have been well ahead of numbers 2 and 3, or number 1 may have just beaten number 2 with number 3 trailing far behind.

INTERVAL SCALES are where the numbers represent the magnitude of the differences. A frequently-cited example is the Celsius temperature scale, where the difference between 20 and 30 degrees is the same as the difference between 30 and 40 degrees. But note that the Celsius scale is not a ratio scale: something with a temperature of 40 degrees is not twice as hot as something with a temperature of 20 degrees.

RATIO SCALES are where there is a true zero point and the ratio of the numbers reflects the ratios of the attribute measured. For example, an object 30 cm long is twice the length of an object 15 cm long.

The type of scale used in measuring a variable relates to other attributes one needs to bear in mind. Some variables, such as age, are continuous in that they can at least theoretically take any value between the lowest and highest points on the scale. They contrast with categorical or discrete variables which can only take a limited number of values. An example of a categorical variable is sex, since there are only two possible values.

Similarly, one can distinguish between different types of data: quantitative data is the result of measuring some variable on an ordinal, interval or ratio scale whereas categorical or frequency data involves categorizing things and counting how many cases there are in each category. Many of the statistical procedures which apply to quantitative data cannot be used meaningfully with frequency data, and you need to decide which type of data you have before starting statistical analysis.

2.1.4 Parametric and non-parametric data and tests

The distinction between types of scale is important, as the type of scale determines which type of statistical analysis is appropriate. In order to use the parametric statistical tests, one should have used an interval or ratio scale of measurement. If the data is measured on an ordinal scale, use non-parametric tests. For nominal or categorical scales, some of the non-parametric tests, such as chi-square, are appropriate.

2.1.5 Dependent and independent variables

In experiments, the experimenter manipulates the independent variable, and measures any consequential alterations in the dependent variable. If the experiment has been designed and carried out properly, it is assumed that the changes in the dependent variable are the results of the changes in the independent variable.

The distinction between dependent and independent variables is not restricted to experiments. When correlational studies are performed, one also has a dependent variable and independent variables. For example, there has been a considerable amount of research into the factors associated with students' success and failure at their courses. This research has correlated students' study habits and personality to their course grades; the grades form the dependent variable and the study habits and personality are independent variables.

2.1.6 Within-subjects and between-subjects comparisons

If scores on two or more variables come from the same respondents, comparing the scores involves related (within-subjects) comparisons. If the scores being compared were obtained from different respondents, they are compared using independent groups (between-subjects) procedures. In some studies, both related and independent comparisons are needed. For example, one might have data on men and women's ability to drive when they have had no alcohol and when they have had a certain amount of alcohol. If one used the same people in the no-alcohol and the with-alcohol conditions, alcohol would be a related-subjects variable, while sex of course is an independent-groups (between-subjects) variable.

Different statistical tests are appropriate for within-subjects and between-subjects comparisons, and it is important to ensure one is using the proper test for the data being analysed.

2.2 Measures of central tendency: mode, median, mean

Given a set of scores or readings, one usually requires a single figure which indicates the 'typical' value of the set. There are three alternative figures one can use: mode, median and mean. Table 2.1 shows the scores of 22 respondents on an attitude-scale question, where the possible responses were coded as 1, 2, 3, 4 or 5.

The *mode* is the most frequently occurring value, in this instance 4.

The *median* is the value that divides the distribution of scores in half: 50% of the scores fall below the median and 50% fall above it. When the scores are in ascending order, if there is an odd number of scores, the median is the middle score. If there is an even number of scores, average the two middle scores. In Table 2.1, there are 22 scores, so the median is obtained by taking the average of the 11th and 12th scores; in Table 2.1 these are both 4, so the median is 4.

The arithmetic *mean* is obtained by totalling the scores and dividing the sum by the number of scores. In Table 2.1, the total of the scores is 75, and the mean is therefore $75/22 = 3.41$.

Table 2.1   *Scores on an attitude scale question*

Respondent	Response
01	1
15	1
19	1
02	3
06	3
08	3
11	3
17	3
21	3
22	3
04	4
05	4
09	4
12	4
13	4
14	4
16	4
18	4
20	4
03	5
07	5
10	5

2.3 Measures of variability

2.3.1 The concept of variability

An important feature of a set of data is the spread or variation of the scores in the set. We need to be able to express the variation within a set of scores as well as the central value (mode, median or mean) of the set. Table 2.2 shows the number of customers visited by male and female sales personnel.

2.3.2 Range; interquartile range

The *range* of a set of scores is simply the difference between the highest and lowest scores. So for the males in Table 2.2, the range is $83 - 28 = 55$ and for females the range is $79 - 33 = 46$. Range gives an indication of the spread of the scores, but of course it depends completely on just two figures from the whole set, the highest and the lowest. One very low or very high score will produce a large increase in the range, and this might be quite misleading.

One alternative measure is the *interquartile range*. As mentioned earlier, the *median* is that score which divides the set into two halves, with half the scores falling below the median and half the scores falling above it. The median is the 50th percentile, which means 50% of the scores fall

Table 2.2   *Customers visited by male and female personnel*

Males		Females	
Respondent number	Number of visits	Respondent number	Number of visits
2	46	1	43
3	48	6	72
4	83	7	42
8	28	11	39
9	41	14	33
10	76	15	36
12	30	16	79
13	68	18	48
17	38	19	58
21	39	20	60
		22	40

below it. We can also have a 25th percentile, which is the score below which 25% of the scores fall, a 75th percentile, a 90th percentile etc. The interquartile range is the difference between the 25th and 75th percentiles. The values of interquartile range for the two sets of data shown in Table 2.2 are 34 for males and 21 for females. The semi-interquartile range is the interquartile range divided by 2.

Unlike the range, the interquartile range is not affected by a single score which is much greater or much less than the others. But it does use only two figures from the set to express the variability in the set, and so ignores most of the numbers.

2.3.3 Variance and standard deviation

A better measure of variation would be one that used all the numbers in the set, not just two of them. This problem is tackled by looking at the mean of the set of scores, and taking the difference between each score and the mean. If one adds these deviations from the mean, the total is zero: so this figure is not going to be very helpful as an indication of the variation in the set of scores! The way round this is to square each of the deviations, which gets rid of all the negative numbers, and then add them up to obtain a sum of squared deviations. In order to get an idea of the variation in the set, it is sensible to take the average of the squared deviations. If n is the number of values in the set, then the sum of the squared deviations divided by n is known as the *variance* of the set of scores.

(Note: If you are using data from a sample as an estimate of a wider population, then divide by $n - 1$ to obtain a better estimate of the population variance.)

The square root of the variance is the *standard deviation*, and is the number used to express the variation in the set of scores.

2.4 Frequency distributions

2.4.1 Histograms and barcharts

A frequency distribution shows the number of times each score occurs in the set of scores under examination. Figure 2.1 shows as a histogram the frequency distribution of the scores in Table 2.1.

Histograms and barcharts are graphical displays of the frequency distribution of the scores. A histogram is used for a continuous variable, and a barchart for a categorical variable. In a barchart the bars are separated to indicate that they represent different categories. In SPSS, any category which is empty (has a frequency of zero) will not be shown in a barchart.

A frequency distribution can be symmetrical or skewed. Figure 2.1 is skewed – the scores tend to be piled up at one end of the scale. If a distribution is roughly symmetrical, the mean can be used as the measure of central tendency, but if it is skewed the median should be used rather than the mean. A normal distribution, which is symmetrical, has a skewness statistic of zero. Kurtosis measures the extent to which observations are clustered in the tails.

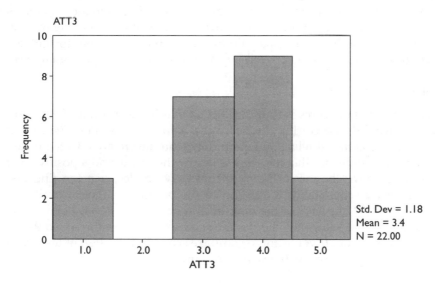

Figure 2.1   *Example of a histogram showing distribution of scores on a variable*

2.4.2 The normal distribution curve

The normal distribution curve, illustrated in Figure 2.2, is fundamental to statistical analysis. A perfect normal curve is symmetrical, with the 'middle' being equal to the mean. The skewness is zero and the kurtosis statistic is also zero.

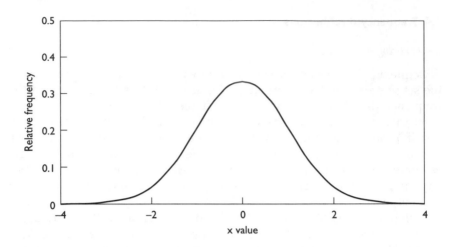

Figure 2.2   *The normal distribution curve*

One can measure off the horizontal axis in standard deviations (sd) from the mean. Very nearly all the distribution lies between -3 sd and $+3$ sd from the mean. Tables of the normal curve, found in most statistics texts, give the proportion of the curve falling above and below any position on the horizontal axis. From such tables, it is easy to find the proportion of the curve between any two points on the horizontal axis.

2.4.3 z scores

When a series of scores is transformed so that it has a mean of zero and a standard deviation of 1.00, the scores are known as z scores. The benefit of a z score is that it tells you where that score lies relative to the mean: a negative z indicates that the score is below the mean, and a positive one that it is above the mean. From normal curve tables, one can find just where any z score stands in relation to the population. For example a z score of $+1.50$ has 5.9% of the distribution above and 94.1% below it, so this means that someone who has a z score of $+1.5$ has surpassed 94.1% of the population. If you want to compare scores from different tests, you can do so if you express the scores in z units.

2.5 Standard error and confidence limits

Inferential statistics involve estimating the characteristics of a population from the data obtained from a sample of that population. For example, one uses the mean of the sample to estimate the population mean. If one took a large set of samples from the population, the means of the samples would form a normal distribution. The standard deviation of that distribution is given by taking the standard deviation of the sample and dividing it by the square root of n, the number in the sample. This is the *standard error*.

The standard error allows one to state the probability that the true mean of the population is within specified limits. From the properties of the normal distribution, it can be deduced that there is a 95% probability that the true mean of the population is within plus or minus approximately 2 standard errors of the sample mean. Suppose you have taken a sample of 100 subjects from a population and found that the mean of the sample is 50, and the standard deviation is 15. The standard error is 1.5 (15 / square root of 100). One can conclude that the true mean of the population has a 95% probability of being within the limits 50 ± two standard errors = 50 ± 3, i.e. between 47 and 53. So the 95% confidence interval means that there is a 95% probability that the true mean is between the limits specified.

2.6 Statistical significance and testing hypotheses

2.6.1 Statistical significance of the difference between means

The data in Table 2.3 shows the number of customers visited by the sales personnel of two employers (labelled 2 and 3). The question that the

Table 2.3   Customer visits by sales personnel from two employers

Employer 2		Employer 3	
Respondent number	Number of visits	Respondent number	Number of visits
2	46	4	83
5	71	6	72
8	28	10	76
11	39	13	68
14	33	16	79
15	36	19	58
20	60		
21	39		
Mean:	44.00	Mean:	72.67

researcher asks is: is there a statistically significant difference between the mean number of visits of the two groups of sales personnel?

In Table 2.3, employer group 2 has the smaller mean, and so you might wish to conclude that these people made fewer visits. But look at respondent number 5 in employer group 2 and respondent 19 in group 3: the group 3 member has a smaller score than the group 2 member. So if you took just those two scores, you could not say that group 2 had the lower score.

If there were no difference between the two groups, their mean scores would be the 'same'. This does not imply, of course, that they would be identical, because responses almost always show some variance (variability). This random, unexplained variation is due to chance. For example, the variation in the scores for employer group 2 in Table 2.3 is variation due to chance. The mean for respondents 2, 5, 8 and 11 in group 2 is 46 and the mean for respondents 14, 15, 20 and 21 from the same group is 42. The difference between these two means is simply due to chance, random variation. It arises even though both these subgroups come from one 'population' (the complete set of scores given by employer group 2 respondents).

Our question now is: is the difference between the means of group 2 and group 3 also simply due to chance? If the difference between the means of group 2 and group 3 is the result of chance, then groups 2 and 3 are samples from the same 'population', just as respondents 2–11 and 14–21 of employer group 2 are samples from one population.

To decide whether groups 2 and 3 are samples from one population or are 'really' different and come from different populations, one applies a test of statistical significance. The significance tests let you estimate how likely it is that the data from the separate groups of respondents come from one population. If it is unlikely that they came from the same population, you can conclude that they didn't, and that they came from separate populations.

In the significance testing of differences we look at the difference between the sets of scores and compare it with the amount of variation in the scores which arises from chance. If the chance variation is likely to have produced the difference between the groups, we say the difference is non-significant, which means the difference probably did arise from chance variation. We have to conclude there is no 'real' or statistically significant difference between the groups, and they are both from the same underlying population.

2.6.2 Significance level

If the difference between two groups is likely to have arisen from chance variation in the scores, we conclude there is no real 'significant' difference between them. On the other hand, if the difference between the groups is unlikely to have been brought about by the chance variation in scores, we conclude there is a real, statistically significant difference between the groups.

But what do we mean by likely? It is conventional to use the 5% probability level (also referred to as alpha-level): what does this mean? If there is a 5% (usually written as 0.05) or smaller probability that the difference between the groups arose from chance variation, we conclude it did not arise from chance and that there is a 'real' difference. If there is more than 5% (0.05) probability that the difference arose from chance, we conclude the difference is not a real one.

You may well ask why we use 5%; and the answer is that it is merely convention. We could use 10% (0.10), 1% (0.01), 0.5% (0.005).

2.6.3 Type I and type II errors

A significance test allows us to say how likely it is that the difference between scores of groups of respondents was due to chance. If there is a 5% or smaller probability that the difference is due to chance variation, we conclude that it was not caused by chance. But we can never be sure: there is always a possibility that the difference we find was due to chance even when we conclude that it was not. Conversely, we may find a difference and conclude that it is not significant (that it was due to random or chance variability in the scores) when in fact it was a 'real' difference. So there are two types of error we may make. These are referred to as type I and type II errors.

A type I error occurs when we reject a null hypothesis when it is true, i.e. we say there is a 'real' difference between the groups when in fact the difference is not 'real'. The probability that we shall make a type I error is given by the significance level we use. With an alpha or significance level of 5%, on 5% of occasions we are likely to make a type I error and say the groups differ when they do not.

We can reduce the probability of making a type I error by using a more stringent level of significance: 1%, say, rather than 5%. But as we reduce the chances of making a type I error, we increase the likelihood that we shall make a type II error, and say there is no difference between the groups when there is one.

2.6.4 Directional (one-tailed) and non-directional (two-tailed) hypotheses

Referring back to Table 2.3, the aim of the study was to test the hypothesis that there is a difference between the scores of the two groups of respondents. (The null hypothesis is that there is no difference between the scores of the two groups.)

Note that the hypothesis is that there is a difference. It does *not* say employer group 3 will score higher or lower than group 2, merely that group 3 and group 2 will differ. This is a non-directional or two-tailed hypothesis: group 3 could score less than group 2 or group 3 could score more than group 2.

If we had stated the hypothesis that group 2 will score less than group 3 (i.e. if we predict the direction of the difference between the groups), then we would have had a directional or one-tail hypothesis. Similarly, if our hypothesis were that group 2 would score more than group 3, this would also be a directional hypothesis since we would still be predicting the direction of the difference between the groups.

The distinction between directional and non-directional hypotheses is important when applying significance tests. Most SPSS printouts show the non-directional (two-tailed) probability of the calculated statistic. If you have stated a directional hypothesis before examining the data, you can use the one-tailed probabilities, which are the two-tailed probabilities divided by 2.

2.7 Interpreting the outcome of a significance test

Understanding what a significance test tells you is the most important part of statistical analysis: doing all the proper tests and getting the correct answers is no good if you then misunderstand what the outcome means! Unfortunately, in the drive to do the computations, some investigators forget that the interpretation is the rationale for the whole procedure. So try to remember some basic principles:

1   If the test tells you the difference between groups is not significant, you must conclude there is no difference, even though the mean scores are not identical.
2   If the difference between groups is statistically significant, this does *not* necessarily mean that it is practically meaningful or significant in the everyday sense. For example, in a study of people's ability to remember car licence plates, one group's score remained the same on two test occasions so the increase was 0, whereas another group's score increased from 3.22 to 3.42, an increase of 0.20; the difference was statistically significant. But it is a subjective judgement, not a statistical one, as to whether the increase of 0.20 for the second group has any practical importance.
3   If you are analysing the results of an experiment, remember that the assumption behind the experimental method is that one can conclude that significant changes in the dependent variable are caused by the changes in the independent variable. But the validity of this assumption depends on one's having used a properly designed and controlled experiment: finding a significant difference between group A and group B does *not* mean you can necessarily conclude the difference was due to the changes in the independent variable. If the experiment was confounded, and the different groups differed systematically on another variable in addition to the independent variable, no clear explanation of the differences in the dependent variable can be given. The statistical significance of the result does not by itself give grounds for concluding that the independent variable brought about the changes in the dependent variable.
4   Avoid the temptation to take the level of significance as an index of the magnitude of the experimental effect. By convention one usually uses the 5% significance level, but one can use a more stringent one, and find that a difference between groups is significant not only at 5% but also at 1% or 0.1%. Even eminent researchers have been known to argue that a difference significant at 1% is somehow more 'real' than

one significant at 5%. This is *not* a valid interpretation. If the result of your analysis is significant at the level you are using (usually 5%), just accept that and do not give in to the temptation to conclude that a difference significant at 1% is 'better'.

2.8 Parametric and non-parametric tests

Parametric significance tests rest upon assumptions that the data has certain characteristics. The assumptions for using parametric tests are as follows.

1 Observations are drawn from a population with a normal distribution. (Note that the population is normally distributed, not necessarily the sample of scores taken from it.)
2 The sets of data being compared have approximately equal variances. (This is referred to as homogeneity of variance.) If the groups are of equal size ($n_1 = n_2$), then this assumption is not so important. If the groups being compared have an n of 10 or less, it is acceptable for the variance of one group to be up to three times as large as that of another. With larger groups, you can still use the parametric tests if one group has a variance double that of another.
3 The data is measured on an interval or ratio scale.

If the data does not meet these assumptions, you can convert the data into a non-parametric form and then apply one of the non-parametric tests. The commonest way of converting data into a form for non-parametric analysis is to rank it.

2.9 Selecting the appropriate test

When analysing data it is vital that you use the appropriate form of significance test. To decide which test is the appropriate one, you have to be able to answer a number of questions:

1 Does the data consist of frequency counts?
2 Are you looking for a difference between sets of scores or a relationship between sets of scores?
3 Are you using data from different sets of people or different data obtained from the same people?
4 How many sets of scores are you analysing?
5 Are the dependent variables measured on an ordinal scale or are they measured on an interval or ratio scale? (Is a non-parametric or a parametric test appropriate?)

When you have answers to all these questions, you can use Figure 2.3 to help you identify the analysis you need. But the questions are not always easy to answer! If you feel you need some help, try Exercise 2.1 which will give you some practice.

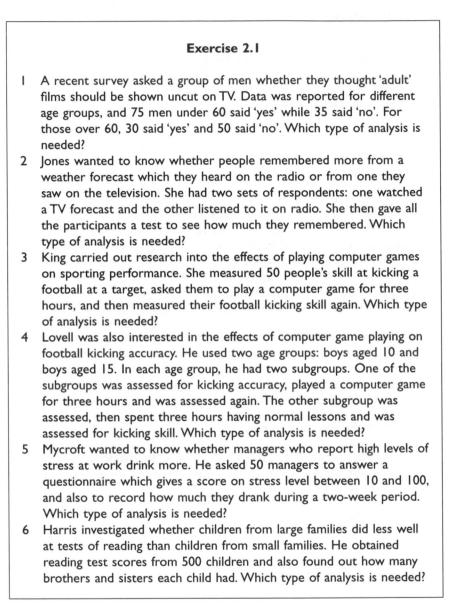

Exercise 2.1

1   A recent survey asked a group of men whether they thought 'adult' films should be shown uncut on TV. Data was reported for different age groups, and 75 men under 60 said 'yes' while 35 said 'no'. For those over 60, 30 said 'yes' and 50 said 'no'. Which type of analysis is needed?

2   Jones wanted to know whether people remembered more from a weather forecast which they heard on the radio or from one they saw on the television. She had two sets of respondents: one watched a TV forecast and the other listened to it on radio. She then gave all the participants a test to see how much they remembered. Which type of analysis is needed?

3   King carried out research into the effects of playing computer games on sporting performance. She measured 50 people's skill at kicking a football at a target, asked them to play a computer game for three hours, and then measured their football kicking skill again. Which type of analysis is needed?

4   Lovell was also interested in the effects of computer game playing on football kicking accuracy. He used two age groups: boys aged 10 and boys aged 15. In each age group, he had two subgroups. One of the subgroups was assessed for kicking accuracy, played a computer game for three hours and was assessed again. The other subgroup was assessed, then spent three hours having normal lessons and was assessed for kicking skill. Which type of analysis is needed?

5   Mycroft wanted to know whether managers who report high levels of stress at work drink more. He asked 50 managers to answer a questionnaire which gives a score on stress level between 10 and 100, and also to record how much they drank during a two-week period. Which type of analysis is needed?

6   Harris investigated whether children from large families did less well at tests of reading than children from small families. He obtained reading test scores from 500 children and also found out how many brothers and sisters each child had. Which type of analysis is needed?

Answers to Exercise 2.1

1 The two-sample chi-square test is used with nominal (frequency) data where subjects are assigned to categories on two variables, so is the appropriate one here. It is concerned with answering the question: is there a relationship between the two categorical variables (age and response 'yes' or 'no' in the example)?

2 Jones has data from two groups of respondents, and the data (scores on a memory test) are measured on an ordinal or possibly an interval scale. So she needs a test to compare two sets of scores and would use the independent t-test or the Mann–Whitney test.

3 King has two sets of scores and a variable measured on an interval scale. The two sets of scores were obtained from the same people, so a within-subjects t-test would be the first choice. Note that this study as described uses a very weak experimental design, and even if the two sets of scores were found to be significantly different, this would not show that the computer game affected football kicking performance. There needs to be a control group to see whether football performance alters even when people do not play a computer game.

4 Lovell's study is an improvement on that of King because a control group was used. The table of data would look like this:

Age group	Condition	Performance measured at	
		Pretest	Post-test
10	computer game		
10	no computer game		
15	computer game		
15	no computer game		

There are two between-subjects factors – age and whether or not a computer game was played – and one within-subjects variable: test condition, which has two levels (pretest and post-test). So this requires an analysis of variance.

5 Mycroft's study was concerned with establishing whether there is an association between stress and drinking. He would calculate the correlation between the two sets of scores.

6 Harris' study demonstrates the way in which alternative methods of analysis can be appropriate for answering a research question. He could see whether there is an association between number of siblings and reading attainment by correlating these two variables. Alternatively, he might set the data out in a table like this:

Number of siblings	Mean reading performance
0	
1	
2	
3	
4 or more	

There are five means to compare, so a one-way analysis of variance would then be appropriate.

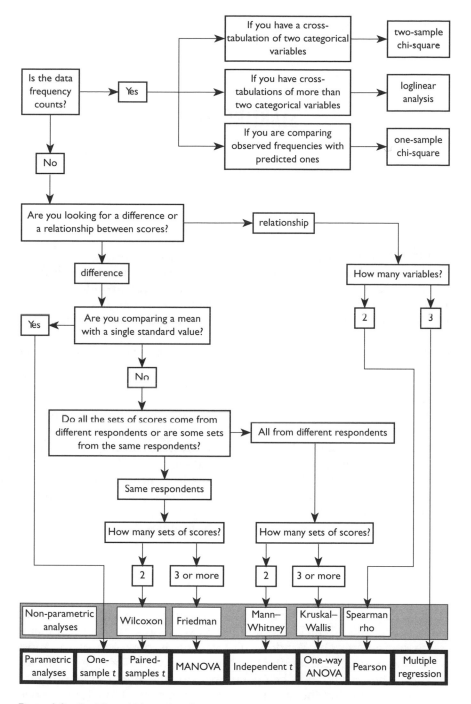

Figure 2.3 *Deciding which statistical test to use*

3

STARTING OUT

Summary

- SPSS data is stored in a file with the filename extension .sav.
- Tell SPSS which analysis you want done by selecting commands from the Window menus and pasting them into a syntax window.
- The syntax file is saved with the filename extension .sps.
- Tell SPSS to print each procedure or command it is following in the output file.
- The results from one case (respondent) form one line in the data file.
- A variable is whatever aspect of the respondent you have measured.
- Levels of a variable are the alternative values of the scores on the variable.
- The system-missing value is automatically inserted when a number is expected but none is provided by the data.
- When a respondent has failed to provide a measure on one of the variables, record a no-response by entering a particular number to represent 'missing value'.
- The package provides a range of Help facilities.

3.1 What is SPSS?

SPSS is a suite of computer programs, which has been developed over many years. The original SPSS and SPSSx were only available on mainframe computers. The Windows PC version is now one of the most widely-used programs of its type in the world. There are various versions, the current one being number 10; the underlying program remains the same but the menu organization does tend to alter from one version to another, and each version has some additional facilities. This book deals with versions 8 to 10, which operate under the Windows 95 or 98 environment.

All users will have the Base system of whichever version of SPSS they have available. In addition, one can purchase extra modules which provide additional analytic procedures, and some of the more commonly used ones are described in this book.

Even the Base system consists of a large set of programs, but the user does not need to know much about the actual SPSS programs; the important thing is learning to drive rather than learning how the car works! It is, however, important to understand the general characteristics of the structure of the package and the files that are used and created by it.

Like earlier versions, SPSS for Windows consists of a number of components. First, there are the programs making up the package itself; these read the data, carry out the analysis and produce a file of the results. The normal user needs to know little about these programs, just as a driver needs to know little about the structure of the internal combustion engine or the physical characteristics of a differential. Second, there are the numbers that the user wants analysed, and these have to be entered into a data window and saved as a data file. Third, there are the commands which tell the package which analyses the user wants performed on the data. Fourth, there are the results of the analysis.

Entering the data, providing the instructions on which analyses to perform, and examining the output can all be carried out on screen, with the data, commands and results being available in separate windows at the same time.

Figure 3.1 indicates the way in which the files are organized. (In this book it is assumed the data and command files are stored on a floppy disk, and that one of the output files, the .spo file is also sent to the floppy disk.) Essentially, SPSS itself sits on the hard disk. In order to use it you must provide it with data to be analysed, which is entered into a table presented on the screen and is then stored in a data file which has the filename extension .sav. When you want the data to be analysed, you have to tell SPSS which analysis you want done by issuing commands. The commands can be entered by selecting from the Window menus, and they can be pasted into a syntax window and stored in a syntax file. It is not essential to save one's commands in a file, but I strongly urge you to do so.

When SPSS for Windows runs, it either reacts to the commands selected from the menus directly and applies them to the data in the table or it reads the commands from the syntax window and responds to them by applying them to the data.

When it is running, SPSS for Windows creates two output files. One holds the results of the analysis it has performed and is put into a window on the screen initially entitled Output1. You will almost always want to save this file, and it will be saved with the filename extension .spo or .rtf, depending on whether you use the Output Viewer or Draft Output. For most purposes, the Output Viewer is to be recommended.

The other output file is named SPSS.jnl. It records a list of the commands which SPSS carries out and is stored in the windows/temp directory on the hard disk. Every time you use SPSS for Windows, the record of the commands you use is added to the end of the .jnl file, so over a series of sessions it can become very lengthy. You can turn off the process of recording the journal file, or you can ask the system to record only the .jnl file for the current session, overwriting any previous version. You can also have the .jnl file stored on the floppy disk rather than the hard disk. To do any of these, you use Edit /Options: the way to achieve these alterations to the way the .jnl file is saved will be clear once you have experience of using SPSS for Windows.

3.2 Naming files

SPSS will automatically give data files the extension .sav, output files the extension .spo, syntax files the extension .sps. When you are doing a number of analyses on a set of data it is very easy to lose track of all the files you create on the way. I have found it helpful to save the files created in each SPSS session using names which indicate the date when they were created. So, for example, if you are working on September 15th, save the syntax file with the name sep15.sps, the output file with the name sep15.spo. Then when you come back later and have to find a particular file on a crowded disk, at least you know that the syntax stored in sep15.sps produced the output stored in sep15.spo. In addition, you will know that the files named sep15.sps and sep15.spo are a pair and different from those named sep20.sps and sep20.spo. Another worthwhile tip is to be sure to keep all the files referring to one set of data in one directory, separate from the files referring to another set of data.

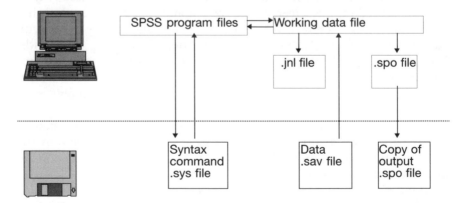

Figure 3.1   *Diagram of the structure of SPSS for Windows files*

One note of warning: do ensure that you keep the correct filename extensions for the type of file you are saving. So all syntax files must have the extension .sps, all data files the extension .sav and all output files the extension .spo. If you fail to do this you will have a chaotic situation, have great difficulties finding the files you want and may well lose vital files altogether.

3.3 Essential terminology for all SPSS users

You need to appreciate some of the terminology that is used when explaining how the package operates.

THE CASE When you approach SPSS, you have some data to be analysed, and this is in the form of responses or scores from a number of different respondents. A respondent may be a person or an organization such as a hospital ward or a school. (You might be dealing with the records of number of patients treated over a given period or the exam successes of each of 200 schools, for example.) Each respondent is known as a *case*, and the results from one case (respondent) form one line in the data file. In SPSS for Windows, the data from one case forms one row in a table.

VARIABLES AND LEVELS You will have a number of items of data from each case, such as the respondent's age, sex, income, score on an intelligence test, number of heart attacks, etc. Each of these is a score on a *variable* (age, sex, income, etc.). Each variable has to have a name, which cannot be more than eight characters long and must not contain a space. (So you could name a variable intell, but not intelligence since the full word has more than eight letters. And you cannot call a variable score 1, as that contains a space; you would have to use score1 or score_1 as the name.) In SPSS for Windows variables are automatically named var00001, var00002, etc. until you rename them (which you should always do).

When you tell SPSS to analyse the data from the data file, you have to tell it which variables to analyse by indicating their names. So if you have a variable which indicates the respondent's gender, you might name this variable sex. Then when you want to analyse the responses on this variable (for example, to find out how many respondents were male and how many female), you have to tell SPSS to analyse the variable sex, i.e. you use the name that has been given to that variable.

It is important to be clear about the difference between variables and levels of a variable. The variable is whatever aspect of the respondent you have measured: age, sex, number of times admitted to hospital, intention to vote for a particular party, etc. The levels are the number of alternative values that the score on the variable can take. For example there are two levels of the variable sex: male and female. Age can have many levels; if you record the age in years, it can vary from 0 to about

105, so there would be 106 levels. Usually, age is put into categories such as 0–20, 21–40, 41–60, over 60 and in this particular case this gives four levels of the age variable. (It is quite simple to enter the actual ages into SPSS and then have the program code the values into a smaller number of categories, using the Recode procedure described in chapter 12.)

SYSTEM MISSING AND USER-DEFINED MISSING VALUES You need to appreciate the concept of the system-missing value, and how it differs from a user-defined missing value. When you enter data into the Data Editor table, if you leave empty one of the cells in a column or a row that contains data, the empty cell will be filled with a full-stop (period). This cell will be detected as containing no data, and SPSS for Windows will give it the 'system missing' value. So the system-missing value is automatically inserted when a number is expected but none is provided by the data.

But when some respondents have not answered all the questions asked, or have failed to provide a measure on one of the variables, it is sensible (for reasons that will become clear later) to record a no-response by entering a particular number. So one might record male as 1, female as 2 and then use 3 to indicate that the person failed to indicate their sex. The value of 3 on the variable sex would then be a user-defined 'missing value'. Of course one has to tell SPSS that this value does represent 'no response': how to do this is explained in section 5.6.

When choosing a number to represent 'data missing', it is essential to use a number that cannot be a genuine value for that variable. If one wanted to define a missing value for age, for example, one would use a number that could not possibly be genuine, such as −1 or 150.

IDENTIFICATION NUMBERS AND CASE NUMBERS When entering data from a set of respondents, it is always worth inserting a variable, which you might call ID, that represents the identification number of the respondent. You can then readily find the data for any respondent you need, and check the entries against the original record of the responses. This identification number has to be entered as a 'score' on the variable ID, just like any other.

But SPSS also assigns its own identification number to each case, numbering each case sequentially as it reads the data file. This is the $casenum variable, which you may see listed when you ask for information about the variables in the data file. The first case in the data file, which may have any user-defined identification number you wish, will have the $casenum of 1, the next one will have $casenum 2 and so on. Do not rely on $casenum for identifying cases in the data file, as it can change if you put the cases into a different order. Use an ID variable as well!

PROCEDURES When SPSS analyses data, it applies a *procedure*: for example, that part of SPSS which calculates a correlation coefficient is one procedure, the part which reports the average score on a variable is another. Most of this book is concerned with explaining how you decide which procedure you want in order to achieve a particular type of analysis, and how you run that procedure on your data.

3.4 What you need to run SPSS for Windows

Assuming SPSS for Windows is installed on your hard disk, there are seven things you need to know in order to use it:

1   how to get to the SPSS programs;
2   how to create and save a file of data to be analysed;
3   which analyses you want done;
4   how to obtain the commands (procedures) which do those analyses;
5   how to get SPSS to apply the commands to the data file;
6   how to save the contents of the output (.spo) file on the floppy disk;
7   how to save the commands in a syntax file.

These requirements are covered in the following chapters. To begin, how do you get into SPSS for Windows (and how do you get out of it)?

3.5 Getting to SPSS for Windows

From the windows desktop, double-click on the SPSS icon. If you are presented with a window asking you 'What would you like to do?', click on the cancel button in the window. If you are using version 9, you will be presented with the screen shown in Figure 3.2 or something very like it: the exact details vary according to the version of SPSS you are using. If you are using version 10, the Data Editor is very similar, and is shown in Figure 3.4. The table shown in Figure 3.4 is a tabbed page labelled Data View. There is another tabbed page available, labelled Variable View. The facilities provided by this Variable View are described in section 3.9. The next subsections of this chapter describe the use of windows and dialogue boxes; if you are familiar with using these, go straight to section 3.9.

3.6 The components of a window

The *title bar* of a window is at the top and includes the window's title. At the left edge there is a control-menu box, and clicking on this will open the control menu which can also be opened using Alt followed by Spacebar on the keyboard. The control-menu entries allow you to restore

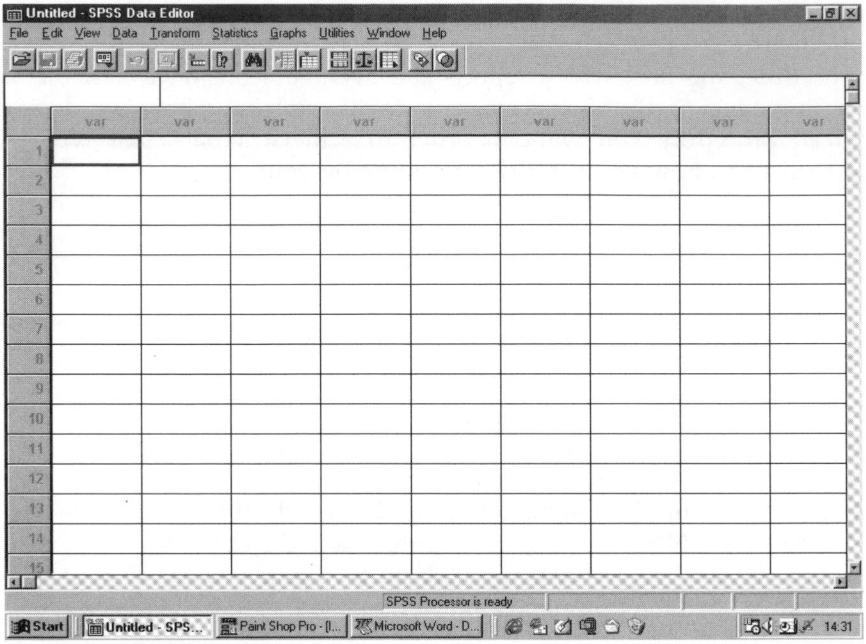

Figure 3.2   *The screen when SPSS for Windows version 8 is started*

a window to its previous size, move it via the keyboard, alter its size, reduce it to an icon, enlarge it to its maximum size or close the application.

At the right edge of the title bar there are the minimize, maximize and close buttons which allow you to reduce the window to an icon or enlarge it to its largest possible size. You can alter the size of a window more precisely by placing the mouse pointer in the bottom right corner and use the click/drag technique to reduce or increase the size of the window. The position of a window on the screen can be altered by click/dragging the title bar.

The *menu bar*, below the title bar, includes a number of menu headings (such as File, Edit). Each menu can be opened by moving the mouse cursor over it and clicking the left mouse button, or by using the keyboard: while holding down the Alt key press the letter key corresponding to the underlined letter in the menu's title. To select one of the entries in the selected menu, put the mouse cursor over it and click the mouse, or type in the underlined letter of the entry name which is underlined (you do not press Alt for submenu entries). A menu is closed by moving the pointer so it is outside it and clicking the mouse button.

Some windows in SPSS for Windows have a tool bar which contains command buttons with an icon rather than a verbal label to indicate their function.

The *scroll bars* are used to reveal information that is outside the limits of the window. You can scroll the information by clicking on the scroll arrows at the end of the scroll bar, click on the space between the scroll box (which shows which part of the file is being shown in the window) and the arrows, point at the scroll arrow and hold the mouse button down, or by click/dragging the scroll box to position the window where you want it to be in the file.

3.7 The components of a dialogue box

Examples of dialogue boxes are illustrated in Figure 3.3. *Dialogue boxes* are presented when you have to enter information about the task to be performed. They have a number of components. Right-clicking the mouse while the cursor is over one of the components provides brief explanations of its purpose.

Scroll bars are provided down the side and (when needed) along the bottom when a window or a drop-down list box cannot show all the information available.

Text boxes are areas where you type in text from the keyboard. Move the pointer into the text box, and an insertion point (flashing vertical bar) appears. Anchor the insertion point by clicking the mouse, and then type in material.

List boxes display a list of options; if there are more options than can be shown, the box has scroll bars which you use to scroll the list. To select one of the options, click on it: it will be highlighted. To select a number of adjacent items, use the click/drag technique to highlight the set of options you want. To select a number of non-adjacent items, hold down Ctrl while you click on each one you wish to select.

Drop-down list boxes show a selected option, but if you click on the down-pointing arrow, a list of alternatives will be revealed. You can select one of these by clicking on it.

Check boxes are small squares adjacent to a label indicating their function. By clicking on them, you either delete or insert a tick into the box. If there is a tick, the option is in force; if the box has no tick, it is not.

Command buttons are labelled rectangular areas which you click on to initiate an action or to reveal another dialogue box. Those buttons not available at the present time are dimmed.

Dialogue boxes in SPSS for Windows contain a Help button; clicking on this will open a window showing information about the topic with which the dialogue box is concerned.

Option buttons (sometimes known as radio buttons, these are circular) are organized in sets. The members of a set are exclusive: if you click on one of them, any other previously selected one will be deselected, since only one of the set can be operative at any one time.

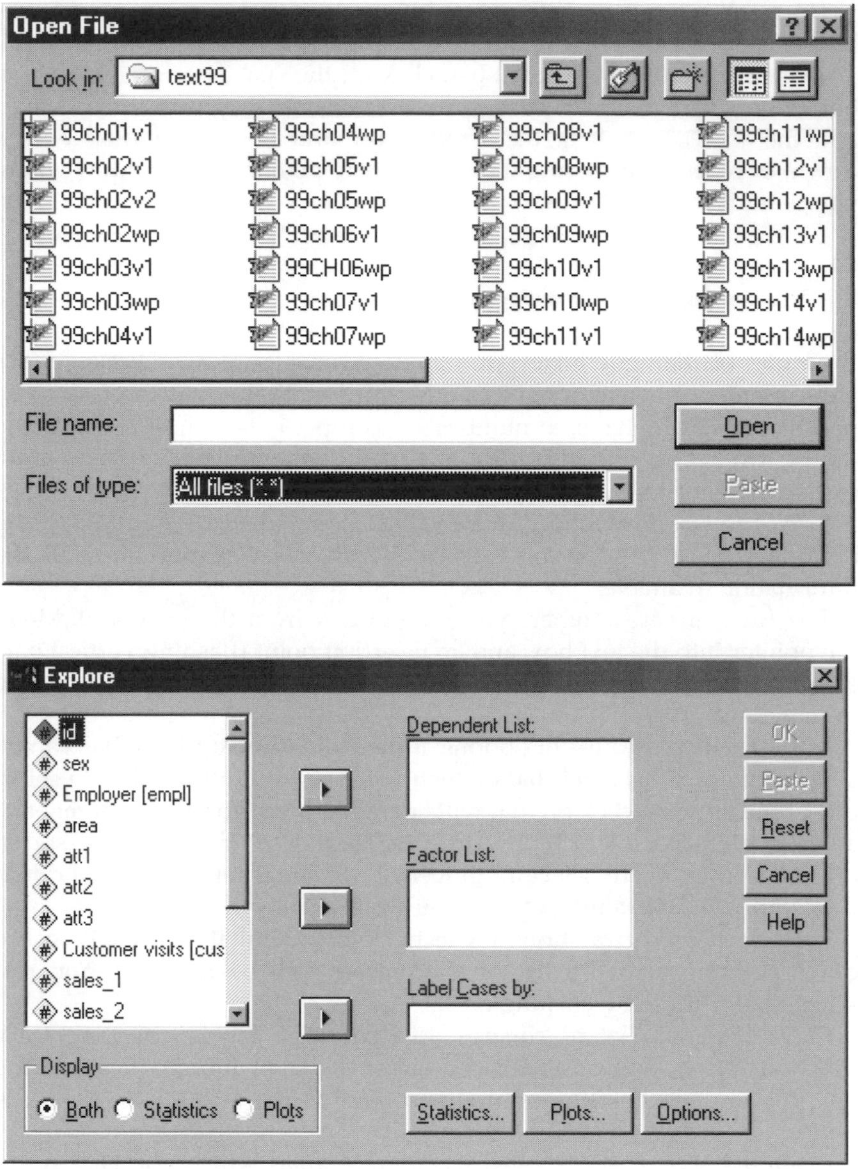

Figure 3.3 *Examples of dialogue boxes*

3.8 Using the keyboard if there is no mouse

IN THE WINDOWS

- To move to the menu bar, press Alt or the F10 key.
- To move along the menu bar, use the left or right arrow keys.
- To open and to move down a menu, use the down arrow key.

- To select an item in the menu, have the cursor over it and press the ↵ key on the keyboard.
- To cancel a selection, press Esc.
- To open Help Topics, press F1.

IN THE DIALOGUE BOXES

- Move between items with Tab (to move forward) or Shift+Tab (to move backward).
- To move up or down a list, use the down arrow and up arrow keys.
- To press a button, use Alt + the underlined letter in the button name.
- To select a highlighted item, press the ↵ key on the keyboard.
- To activate the OK or Continue buttons, use the Tab keys to highlight them and press the ↵ key on the keyboard.
- To cancel and close the dialogue box, press Esc.
- To open Help Topics, press F1.

3.9 The SPSS for Windows screens

When SPSS for Windows version 8 or 9 first starts, it presents the screen shown in Figure 3.2, the Data Editor. If you are using version 10, the Data Editor shown in Figure 3.4 is presented. The bottom left shows that there are two tabbed pages, Data View and Variable View, with the Data View being the one shown initially. The alternative views are selected by clicking on the appropriate tab or you can invoke Variable View from the Data View by double-clicking a variable name in a column heading. (In Variable View, each row of the table displays information on one of the variables, showing the variable name, type, width, value labels, etc. These values can be changed by clicking in the relevant cell, which calls up the dialogue box which would be obtained if you used the Data /Define Variable menu.) Data is entered into the Data Editor either by typing it in or by opening a file of data that has previously been saved on a disk.

The Help menu provides access to information which can assist you use SPSS for Windows; further information on Help is given in section 3.11 later in this chapter.

The bottom line of the window, the Information area, presents messages indicating what the package is doing. When first started, it reads 'SPSS Processor is ready'.

The icon button bar below the menu bar allows many operations to be carried out by pressing the appropriate icon button. The buttons differ according to the type of window. To see what each button does, put the mouse cursor over it; a description of the button's function is presented

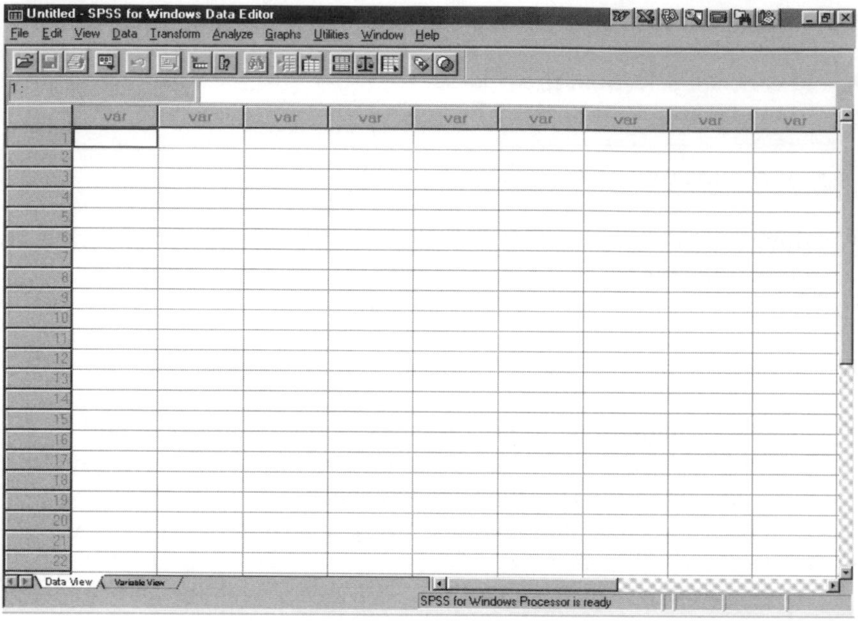

Figure 3.4   *The Data Editor of SPSS version 10*

and also appears in the information area at the bottom of the screen. The meaning of many of these buttons will only become clear when you have had some experience with the package.

The Data Editor window is a table with columns headed var and rows labelled 1, 2, etc. When needed, scroll bars are provided down the right side and along the bottom, so one can move the contents of the file within the window to reveal parts of it not otherwise visible.

THE OUTPUT WINDOW   When SPSS performs some action, the Data Editor is replaced by an output window, which will initially be entitled Output1 – SPSS Viewer or Draft1 – SPSS Draft Viewer, depending on which type of output the system is set up to generate. The Output Viewer provides much neater formatting than the Draft Viewer, and the examples shown in this book use it rather than the Draft Viewer. The Output Viewer window is shown in Figure 3.5, which shows that it consists of two panels. The one on the right is where output is placed, while the one on the left is an outline view on the contents of the right-hand pane. The width of the outline panel can be altered by using the click/drag technique on the bar separating the two panels. To go to a particular part of the output, click on its entry in the outline. You can move the contents of the output by moving the corresponding item in the outline.

It is simple to open more clean output windows, by using File /New. This is often useful so that you have separate output windows for each analysis that you carry out.

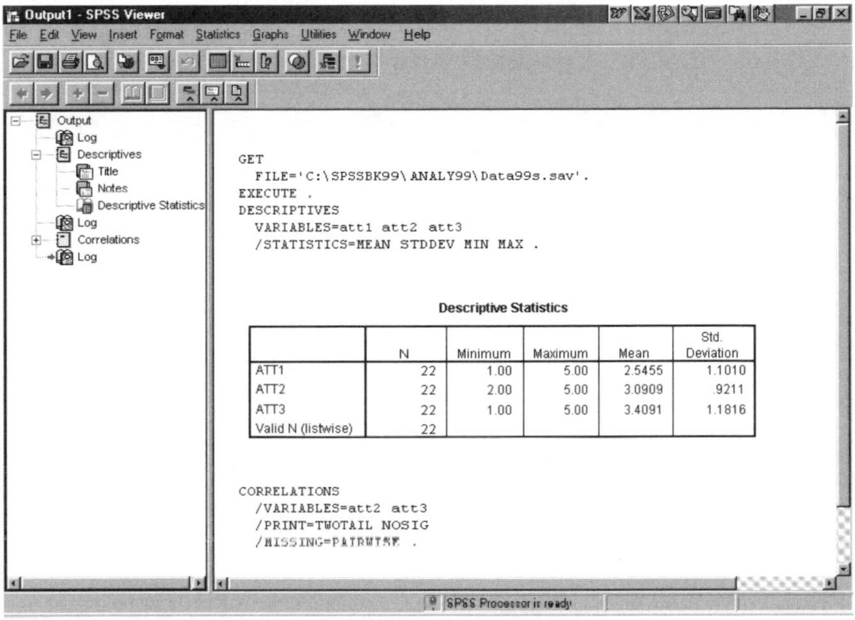

	N	Minimum	Maximum	Mean	Std. Deviation
ATT1	22	1.00	5.00	2.5455	1.1010
ATT2	22	2.00	5.00	3.0909	.9211
ATT3	22	1.00	5.00	3.4091	1.1816
Valid N (listwise)	22				

Figure 3.5 *Example of the Output Viewer*

THE SYNTAX WINDOW If you paste syntax (commands telling the package the analysis you want it to perform), as I shall recommend you to do, it will be pasted into a syntax window; an example is shown in Figure 3.6. The most important button to locate is Run, the one with the right-pointing arrow. It runs the command in which the cursor is located at the time the button is pressed.

ACTIVE AND DESIGNATED WINDOWS When using SPSS for Windows, you can have a number of output windows and a number of syntax windows on the screen simultaneously. (No syntax window is shown when the package first begins, but they are used for recording the commands you use in analysing the data.) For the moment, assume you have two output windows open. One of these is the one that will receive the results of the analysis you are performing, and this is known as the *designated* window. It is identified by having a ! in the information area on the bottom line.

The *active* window is the one that is currently on view. This may or may not be the designated window: if there is no exclamation mark in the information area, the window is not designated. You can make the window currently on the screen the designated one by clicking the red exclamation mark in the icon bar. The exclamation mark will then appear in the information area at the bottom of the window to show this is the designated window.

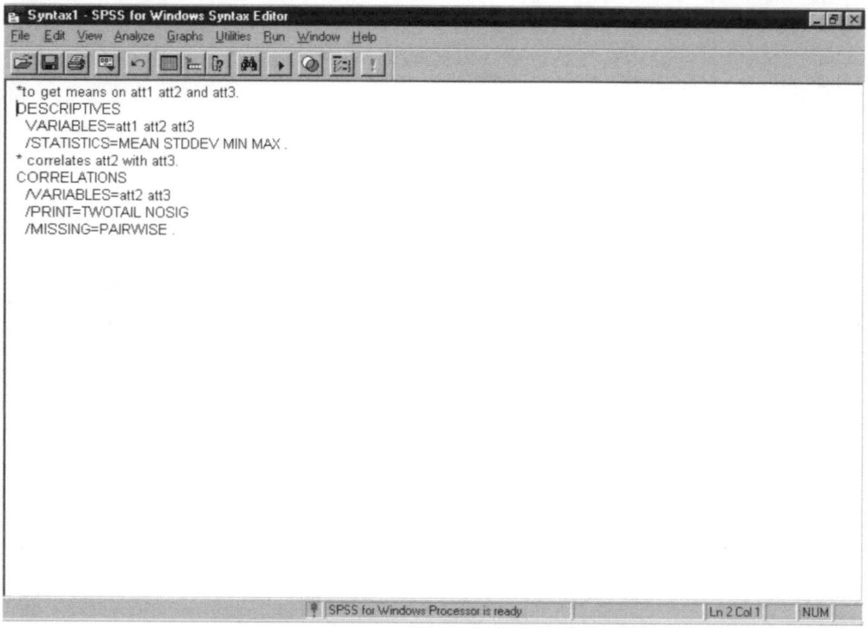

Figure 3.6   *Example of a syntax window*

As different windows are viewed, the other windows are closed and form a set of buttons in the taskbar along the bottom of the screen. To see any window, click on its button or open the Window entry in the menu bar and click on the name of the window you want.

3.10 Leaving SPSS for Windows

To leave the package, have the Data Editor on the screen, and either double click on the control box at the left edge of the window title bar, or select

```
File
      Exit
```

In either case you will be asked whether you wish to save the files that are at present in use: the data file, output files, and any syntax files.

3.11 On-screen help for SPSS for Windows

In addition to the Help system described here, right-clicking the mouse can provide brief explanations of the components of a dialogue box or a table in the Output Viewer. You will also find that a right-click can open menus in the Data Editor when the cursor is over the column or row headings. It is worth investigating the effects of right-clicking; you may find it provides a useful short-cut for some facilities that you frequently use.

Selecting Help from the menu bar provides access to a number of types of help. Help /Topics presents a display with a number of tabbed pages (Contents, Index, Find, Ask me). The Contents gives a series of chapters on major topics such as saving files, and also allows you to run the on-screen tutorials which can also be requested from the Help menu directly. If you want an explanation of a particular word, select Index; this invites you to enter a word, and will show a list of relevant topics, assuming there are some. You can select a topic and press the Display button to see the help information. Since the person asking a question often does not know where to find the answer, the Ask Me facility is probably going to be one of the most used alternatives. It also has its own entry in the Help menu.

The Help /Statistics Coach is designed to help you decide what type of analysis you need for any particular problem.

The Help /Syntax Guide gives you the details of the SPSS language commands' syntax. The syntax is really meaningful only when you are familiar with the way SPSS commands are structured. To a beginner, it is likely to be baffling; but if you follow the advice given in this book and always paste syntax into a syntax window, you will begin to see how the syntax is structured and then be able to make some sense of the help on the syntax.

All the dialogue boxes have a Help button; clicking it opens a Help window, in which information about the operation of SPSS is displayed. The information presented will be relevant to that part of the package you were in when you requested help. So clicking on the Help button in the Frequencies dialogue box will present information about the Frequencies command. The syntax information mentioned in the previous paragraph can also be accessed from the Help button of the Dialogue boxes, which provides a window with a Syntax button.

3.12 Copying parts of Help

The Help window has a menu bar which includes Print and Options entries. Under the Options you are offered the facility to Annotate, Copy, Print topic. The Copy option allows you to copy the Help window's contents and they can then be pasted into a word processor file.

3.13 Seeing a list of all the files on your floppy disk

Select File /Open, navigate up the directory structure until the Look In textbox contains drive a:, open the drop-down list for Files of Type and select the option All Files (*.*). All the files on the floppy will be shown in the file list, and you can scroll down it using the scroll bar.

4

CRUCIAL PRELIMINARIES

Summary

- Decide before you get to the computer what you want to find out, which statistical analyses you wish to apply.
- The data described in section 4.3 is used to explain how SPSS operates.
- It is usually more convenient to use numerical coding of all variables rather than have string variables.

4.1 Know what you want to find out

SPSS provides the opportunity to carry out a wide range of statistical procedures very rapidly and with little effort. The danger is that because it offers such power, the researcher is tempted to comb the data: 'Let's do a factor analysis/multiple regression/100 *t*-tests . . . and see what happens'.

It must be emphasized that there are real dangers in this approach. First, there is the statistical problem of interpreting significance levels when one has done a series of significance tests after the data has been given a preliminary examination. Practically, there is a risk that you obtain masses of output which overwhelm your ability to interpret and understand them: faced with a 4-inch pile of listing paper, many researchers, after the first flush of enthusiasm, have regretted their unrestrained proliferation of analyses!

SPSS offers the facility for obtaining plots and test statistics which may be unfamiliar to you. Do be very wary of obtaining analyses which you do not understand. If you have never heard of Lilliefors, you will only confuse yourself by being presented with it. Decide before you get to the computer what you want to find out, which statistical analyses you wish to apply. The power of the program is not a substitute for clear thinking. Without a definite idea of what you are looking for and how to find it you are likely to generate confusion rather than understanding. Section 2.9 is intended to help you decide which analyses you need, and therefore which SPSS procedures you require, in order to obtain the results you want from your data.

4.2 How to find answers to questions you are asking

HOW MANY RESPONDENTS GAVE THAT RESPONSE? In many types of investigation, the investigator wants to know *how many* respondents gave a particular answer or response. For example, how many cases in the data file were female, how many were female and under 40 years of age? Answers to this kind of question are provided if you use the Descriptive Statistics /Frequencies procedure (chapter 14).

You may want to obtain a table showing the number of cases that had certain scores on one variable, subdivided according to their scores on another variable. For example, suppose you want a table showing the number of males and females coming from the North and the South. This type of table is provided by Descriptive Statistics /Crosstabs (section 14.4) and by the Tables procedure (chapter 21).

Having produced a table showing the number of people of each sex coming from each part of the country, you might ask whether there is a significant relationship between these two factors: do proportionally more men than women come from the North? To see whether this type of relationship exists with frequency data, you need the chi-square test, which can be obtained within the Descriptive Statistics /Crosstabs procedure (section 14.5).

HOW ARE THE SCORES DISTRIBUTED? WHAT ARE THE PERCENTILE SCORES? If you want to see how the scores are distributed (perhaps to see whether they form a normal distribution) or discover the percentile scores, use Descriptive Statistics /Explore (chapter 9).

AVERAGES: WHAT ARE THE MEANS AND MEDIANS? You may want to know what was the average score on a certain variable: what, for example, was the average age of all the cases in the data file? This data can be found by using Descriptive Statistics /Descriptives (chapter 15). Note carefully that if you want the means of subgroups of respondents, such as the average age of males and then of females, you need the Descriptive Statistics /Means procedure (section 15.3). Tables showing these statistics can also be obtained using the Tables procedure (chapter 21).

AVERAGES: WHAT ARE THE MEANS FOR SUBGROUPS OF RESPONDENTS? If you want the average score of subgroups of respondents, such as the average age of men and of women, or the average income of people aged below 40 and the average income of people aged over 40, then you need the Descriptive Statistics /Means procedure (section 15.3) or the Tables procedure (chapter 21).

IS THERE A SIGNIFICANT DIFFERENCE BETWEEN SCORES? A large part of statistical analysis is involved with evaluating the differences between sets of scores, and determining whether they are statistically significant. The concept of statistical significance is summarized in Chapter 2, and identifying the particular test for a specific question is explained in section 2.9. Chapter 16 covers the *t*-test and analysis of variance for comparing means of sets of scores.

IS THERE A SIGNIFICANT DIFFERENCE BETWEEN NON-PARAMETRIC SCORES? If you need to use non-parametric analysis, the Nonparametric Tests procedure (chapter 18) offers a number of tests including the Kruskal–Wallis, Mann–Whitney and others.

ARE TWO SETS OF SCORES CORRELATED? As scores on one variable increase, do scores on another variable increase or decrease? This type of question is asking whether there is a correlation between the scores on the two variables, and is answered by using the Correlation procedure (chapter 17). Rank correlations are also obtained from Correlation. If you have to rank the data, you use Transform /Rank Cases (chapter 11).

HOW WELL CAN I PREDICT ONE SCORE FROM RESPONDENTS' OTHER SCORES? You may want to investigate whether responses on test1 and scores on test2 predict scores on test3, and this is a problem in multiple regression, which is dealt with using the Regression procedure (chapter 17).

HOW DO I ANALYSE SUBGROUPS OF RESPONDENTS SEPARATELY? You will frequently want to analyse the data for just some of the respondents: perhaps compare the scores on test1 and test2 only for people aged over 40, for example. To do this, you have to tell SPSS which subgroups you want to select, and then which analysis you wish to be carried out. You can use Data /Select If or Data /Split File (chapter 13).

HOW CAN I CALCULATE 'NEW' SCORES, SUCH AS EACH RESPONDENT'S AVERAGE ON A NUMBER OF VARIABLES? You will often find that you want to obtain a 'new' score from the data provided by your respondents. Suppose, for example, that you have scores on test1 and test2; you might want to find the average of these two scores for each respondent. To do this, use the Transform /Compute procedure (chapter 12).

HOW DO I PUT THE SCORES INTO A PARTICULAR ORDER? This is achieved using the Data /Sort Cases procedure (chapter 11).

CAN I CHANGE THE WAY DATA IS ENCODED? Suppose you have asked your respondents to indicate their age in years, and you find that their ages vary from 16 to 85. To make the data more manageable, you might decide that you would like the respondents grouped into different age groups of 16–35 years, 36–55 years, 56 and above. This can be achieved using the Transform /Recode procedure (chapter 12).

To transform scores into ranks, use Transform /Rank Cases (chapter 11).

HOW DO I OBTAIN GRAPHS?   The graphing facilities for SPSS for Windows versions 9 and 10 are considerably more sophisticated than for previous versions, and allow you to create barcharts, histograms, box plots, line graphs, area charts and pie charts, using the Graphs procedure (chapter 10).

HOW DO I GET A NEAT TABLE OF THE RESULTS?   The output which appears in the Output Viewer is neatly formatted as tables, so long as you are using the Viewer and not the Draft Viewer. You can also transfer your output to a word-processor and edit it there (section 7.8), although this is not so easy as it was with earlier versions of SPSS.

I HAVE DATA IN DIFFERENT FILES — HOW DO I MERGE THEM INTO ONE? The procedures needed are covered in chapter 6.

4.3 The data used in this book

The data file is simply the stored record of the numbers (data) which are to be analysed. The way you create a file of your data is described in chapter 5. In explaining how to create, store and use a file of data, it is helpful to have an example to refer to, and I shall be using the data described here.

Imagine that we have carried out a piece of research in which we gave a questionnaire to each of a group of 22 salespeople. They were employed by three different employers, and the respondents were asked their sex, the name of their employer, the area of the country they work in (either North or South), and then three questions intended to reveal their attitude towards their job. Each of these questions (numbers 5–7 in Figure 4.1) invited a response on a scale from 1 to 5. The questionnaire also asked the number of customers each salesperson had visited during the previous month, the total sales for the previous month, the sales for the current month, and the date the respondents started working for their company. Figure 4.1 shows an example of a completed questionnaire from one respondent, and in all there are 22 questionnaires like this.

When encoding these responses for SPSS, all the responses were encoded as numbers. Although the respondents indicated whether they are male or female, the answers were expressed as a number, with 1 representing male and 2 representing female. Similarly, each employer

<u>Sales Personnel Questionnaire</u>

Where there are alternative answers, please underline the one relevant to you. For the other questions, please fill in your answer.

                                          Respondent number: 01

```
1  What is your name?                    K Smith
2  Are you male or female?               M    F
3  What is the name of your employer?    (1) Jones and Sons
                                         (2) Smith and Company
                                         (3) Tomkins
```

4 In which area of the country do you work?   <u>North</u>   South

Please indicate your response to the following three questions by underlining one of the numbers, using the following scale:
     1 means that you strongly agree with the statement;
     2 that you agree with it;
     3 that you are uncertain;
     4 that you disagree;
     5 that you strongly disagree with the statement.

```
5 In general I enjoy my job              1   2   3   4   5
6 In my company, hard work gets rewards  1   2   3   4   5
7 I often wish I was doing a different job 1  2   3   4   5
```

```
8 How many customers did you visit last month?      43
9 What was your total sales value last month?       3450.60
10 What was your total sales value this month?      4628.90
11 Enter the date you started working for your present employer: 01 day 06 month 88 yr
```

Figure 4.1   *Completed sales personnel questionnaire*

was given a number and the respondent's employer was recorded as 1, 2 or 3; the value 1 was used to represent Jones and Sons, etc. The area of work was also coded numerically with 1 for North and 2 for South. (It is straightforward to have the verbal meanings of the numbers displayed in the printout or on the screen.)

Although this type of investigation may not be of any interest to you, the kind of responses obtained are similar to those yielded by many kinds of research. Essentially, we have series of numbers. Here they are used to represent sex, employer, area of country, attitude expressed on each of three questions, three performance measures (customers visited, last month sales, current month sales), and the date when the person started with the company. We could have data on socio-economic status, number of children, or a thousand other things which can be represented as numbers.

4.4 Numeric and string (alphanumeric) variables

SPSS does accept alphanumeric (known as string) data, in which the data is coded in the data file not as a number but as a series of letters (or letters and numbers). If the data contains any letters, it is a string variable.

There are some drawbacks to using string variables. First, typing in strings takes longer than typing in numbers. Second, there are limitations on what SPSS can do with string variables: one cannot use them in most statistical procedures. Consequently, it is usually more convenient to use numerical coding of all variables. For example, when recording a respondent's sex you might code male as 1 and female as 2. (It is simple to have the printout or the screen show that a score of 1 on sex means male and a score of 2 means female. In the Data Editor use the Value Labels icon button or select View /Value Labels to switch from the numerical code to their assigned labels.)

Bear in mind when using numbers instead of a string label, such as coding male as 1 rather than 'm' and female as 2 rather then 'f', that the numbers are merely labels and form a nominal scale.

In version 9, if you are using a string variable in your data file you have to tell SPSS that the variable is a string by using the Define Variable dialogue box, as described in section 5.5.

A string variable can be converted into a numeric one using the Automatic Recode procedure described in section 12.7 or by using Compute If, covered in section 12.3.

4.5 Scientific notation

In some cases, with very large or very small numbers, the output may be expressed in scientific notation such as 5E+5 or 2.7E−4. Remember that the exponential number (+5, −4 in these examples) tells you how many places to move the decimal place to obtain the number in the usual form. If the exponent is positive, the decimal point is moved to the right, and if it is negative it is moved to the left. So 5E+5 means that you start with 5.00 and move the decimal point five places to the right so the number is 500000.00. The scientific notation 2.7E−4 means you start with 2.7 and move the decimal place four places to the left so the number is 0.00027.

5

THE DATA FILE

Summary

This chapter explains how to:

- enter data into the Data Editor
- insert rows or columns anywhere in the table
- save the file on the floppy disk using Save As
- assign variable names and variable labels to the data
- assign value labels when appropriate (e.g. to show 1 represents 'male')
- use missing values
- use templates for defining a number of variables
- see information about the variables on screen or in the output
- retrieve a data (.sav) file
- import data from text files
- import data from Excel
- print the data file.

In SPSS for Windows, data is entered into the table which is automatically presented in the Data Editor window. When putting data into the Data Editor, each row of the table should contain the results from one respondent; SPSS refers to each line as a case.

Each column contains the results on one variable; for example the second column, var00002, might contain the data indicating the respondent's sex. The cell entries are values, usually numbers. (If you wish to use letters, refer to section 4.4)

If you do not want the grid lines separating the cells in the Data Editor window, turn them off by selecting View from the menu: the drop-down menu includes a Grid Lines option, and selecting it turns the lines off or on.

5.1 Entering data into SPSS

To enter data, have the Data Editor window visible and the cursor in the top left cell. (If necessary, press the Ctrl+Home key combination to move the cell selector to this cell.)

Type in the first set of numbers for the first case of your data set: I advise you always to have an identification number as the first 'score' for each respondent.

Press the right arrow key or the down arrow key or ↵ on the keyboard. If you press the right arrow key, the cell selector moves to the next cell on the right of the one you have just been addressing. It is usually more convenient and less prone to error to enter the data for each respondent (row) rather than each variable (column), so pressing the right arrow key is normally the easiest procedure. If you press Enter or down arrow, the cell selector will move down to the cell below the one you have just been addressing.

The first cell will now contain the figures you typed in, and the column will now be headed var00001. Type in the figures for the second cell, press the right arrow key and continue until all the figures have been entered in the appropriate row and column positions. Each time you put a number into a column for the first time, the column will be given a label: column 2 is labelled var00002, column 3 is var00003 and so on.

Exercise 5.1: Entering a set of data into the Data Editor

The data I shall use to explain how SPSS for Windows operates has been described in chapter 4 and will be referred to as salesq (for Sales Questionnaire). The table of data is shown in Table 5.1, and your first task is to enter it into the Data Editor. Put the first number (1, the id for the first respondent) into the top left cell of the table, the number 2 (representing the sex of respondent number 1) into the top cell of the second column. Then continue entering numbers until all the data has been put into the table. The complete number for sales_1 (3450.60 for the first case) goes into one cell in column 9 of the table. The three sets of numbers representing the date started go into separate columns, so you will have 13 columns of numbers altogether.

The variables (with their names shown in brackets) are, reading from left to right: id, sex, employer (empl), area, response to question 5 (att1), response to question 6 (att2), response to question 7 (att3), customer visits (cust), sales for last month (sales_1), sales for the current month (sales_2), day of date started (dstd), month of date started (dstm) and year started (dsty). The abbreviated variable names are shown in the table. (Remember that variable names cannot exceed eight characters in length.)

Table 5.1   *Data from the sales questionnaire study*

id	Sex	Empl	Area	Att1	Att2	Att3	Cust	Sales_1	Sales_2	Dstd	Dstm	Dsty
1	2	1	1	4	5	1	43	3450.60	4628.90	1	6	88
2	1	2	2	4	4	3	46	4984.42	5136.78	8	6	90
3	1	1	2	2	3	5	48	10432.82	10589.54	9	6	90
4	1	3	1	2	3	4	83	8235.21	9621.21	1	6	90
5	3	2	2	2	2	4	71	6441.38	6388.32	8	6	90
6	2	3	2	3	3	3	72	6497.05	4400.50	9	6	90
7	2	1	2	3	2	5	42	3835.26	2209.76	1	6	90
8	1	2	2	4	5	3	28	3819.00	4238.50	8	6	90
9	1	1	1	2	3	4	41	5723.52	5508.90	9	6	90
10	1	3	2	1	2	5	76	7937.45	8120.54	8	6	90
11	2	2	1	2	3	3	39	4582.44	5709.00	9	6	90
12	1	1	1	2	3	4	30	2005.30	3215.35	1	6	90
13	1	3	2	2	2	4	68	8914.50	9156.45	3	6	91
14	2	2	2	1	2	4	33	3124.20	2200.59	5	6	91
15	2	2	2	5	4	1	36	4222.45	3300.50	3	6	91
16	2	3	1	2	2	4	79	8881.28	10120.00	31	5	91
17	1	1	2	3	4	3	38	3449.35	4120.54	5	6	91
18	2	1	1	2	3	4	48	7882.60	8007.50	31	5	91
19	2	3	1	4	3	1	58	8779.00	8508.60	3	6	91
20	2	2	2	1	3	4	60	5822.68	4305.40	31	5	91
21	1	2	2	3	4	3	39	4004.80	4407.54	3	6	91
22	2	1	1	2	3	3	40	5886.40	7200.48	5	6	90

If some data were missing, you would just leave that cell empty. There are no empty cells in the salesq data, but if respondent number 5 had failed to indicate their sex, for example, you could just skip over that cell when entering the data. It would contain a full-stop, which is the 'system-missing' value. This is the value that SPSS inserts into any empty cell in a column that contains data. It allows the programme to keep track of the occupied cells – even those into which no data has been entered have some content. (The notions of the system-missing value and user-defined missing values are explained in section 5.6.)

5.2 Editing data

If you need to make corrections to any of the cell entries, simply move the cursor to that cell (most easily done by clicking on it), type in the correct numbers and press ↵ or an arrow movement key.

If you want to alter one number in a long numerical entry, click on the relevant cell. The cell contents are reproduced in the line below the icon bar of the window; click at an appropriate position in this cell editor line, and you can edit the entry. To insert it in the table, press ↵ or use the mouse to select another cell in the table.

INSERTING ROWS OR COLUMNS IN THE TABLE   Rows can be inserted into a table by selecting a cell in the row below the one where you want a row inserted and then using from the menu bar

```
Data
     Insert Case
```

A column is inserted by selecting a cell in the column to the right of where you want one inserted, and then choosing from the menu bar

```
Data
     Insert Variable
```

COPYING OR MOVING DATA IN THE TABLE   To copy or move cells, select them using the click/drag technique, and while they are highlighted, select Edit from the menu bar of the Data Editor window. If you are copying the cells (so they are repeated elsewhere), click on Copy. If you are moving the cells from one place to another, click on Cut. Then move the cursor to the point where you want the cells to be repeated or inserted, click to select that cell and select from the menu bar

```
Edit
     Paste
```

You can paste the copied or cut cells to an area outside the current table, but any empty cells that result will be filled with the system-missing value, the full stop.

   To move a complete column or row, insert an empty column or row as described above. Highlight the column or row you want to move by clicking in the area showing the variable name or the row number, select

```
Edit
     Cut
```

and then click in the empty column or row you obtained when you inserted a variable or case. Select

```
Edit
     Paste
```

and the column or row you cut earlier will be inserted.

DELETING ROWS (CASES) OR COLUMNS (VARIABLES)   Click on the case number on the left side of the row, or on the variable name at the top of the column and from the menu bar choose

```
Edit
      Clear
```

5.3 Moving around in the data table

With a large table, you will want to be able to move around it rapidly. The Home key takes you to the first cell in a row, End to the last cell in a row, Ctrl+up arrow to the first row of a column, Ctrl+down arrow to the last row of a column. Page Up and Page Down scroll up or down one window-height, and Ctrl+Page Up or Ctrl+Page Down scroll one window left or right.

TO GO TO A PARTICULAR VARIABLE   Select Utilities /Variables from the menu bar, highlight the variable in the list presented in the box then revealed, and click on the Go To button.

TO GO TO A PARTICULAR ROW   Select the Go to Case icon button from the icon bar, or from the menu select

```
Data
      Go To Case
```

Enter the case (row) number in the text box, and click on OK. Note that the case number is the number of the row, $casenum, not any identification number that you may have entered as a variable. If you want to find the row of data for a particular respondent, use the procedure described in the next paragraph.

TO GO TO A PARTICULAR SCORE OR TO A PARTICULAR RESPONDENT   Select a cell in the column containing scores on the variable, and select from the menu bar

```
Edit
      Find
```

You can then enter the value to be searched for in the text box of the Search for Data dialogue box, and click on the Search Forward or Search Backward buttons. (Clicking on Close will remove the dialogue box after the search has been made.) This technique can be used to find a particular respondent, so long as you have given each a unique identification number (id), as I recommend you always do. Put the cursor at the top of the column containing the id numbers and then select Edit /Find. If you put the id number of the respondent you want in the Search text box and click on Select Forward, the row for that respondent will be found in the Data Editor.

5.4 Saving the data file

SAVING THE DATA FILE FOR THE FIRST TIME   Once you have entered the
data, the first thing to do is to save it so that if anything goes wrong later
you have a copy you can use. In most cases you will want to save the file
on a floppy disk, so make sure your formatted disk is inserted into drive
a:. To save the file on the floppy disk, follow these steps:

● While viewing the Data Editor, from the menu bar, select

```
File
     Save As
```

  You will be presented with the Save Data As dialogue box which is
  shown in Figure 5.1 as it appears when the drop-down list of the Save
  In options has been opened.
● Type in the filename which you want the file to be called (for
  example, salesq). Remember that the name cannot exceed 8 characters and must not contain any spaces, full-stops or commas.
● Open the drop-down list for the Save In alternatives and click on the
  icon for drive a: so it appears in the Save In text area. This means the
  file will be stored on the floppy disk.
● Unless you have a reason for doing otherwise, save the file in the
  format for the version of SPSS you are using. To save in a different
  format, open the drop-down menu for Save File as Type, which lists a
  number of alternative file formats. Select the one you want.
● Click on the Save button. The data file will then be stored on your
  floppy disk, with the name salesq.sav (If you used the filename
  mydat, the file will be mydat.sav.) The name will now appear in the
  Title bar of the Data Editor window.

If you think you made a mistake, just repeat the steps given above,
checking that you are making the right selections at each point.

SAVING THE DATA FILE FOR THE SECOND TIME   When you are working
on a data file and have saved it once, or are working on a file that you
have retrieved from disk, you can save the file under the same name as it
already has by simply selecting

```
File
     Save
```

from the Data Editor window menu bar. The version you are now saving
will overwrite the previous one. If you want to keep the old version and
the current one, use File /Save As (as described above), and type in a
different name from the current one. For example, suppose you have

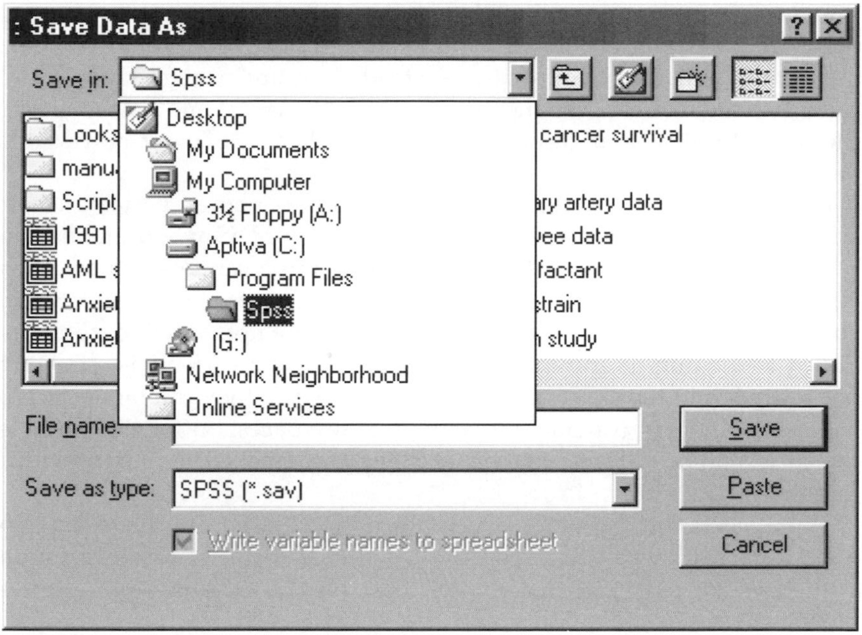

Figure 5.1   *The Save Data As dialogue box*

made some changes to salesq.sav and want to keep both the original and the altered versions; you would save the current version under a new name by typing in a name such as salesq2, and the file will then be saved as salesq2.sav.

Exercise 5.2: Save the data

Save the file as salesq.sav, following the procedure described above.

5.5 Assigning names and labels to variables and values

VARIABLE NAMES   Variable names are used by SPSS to refer to the variables (columns) when it is processing the data. Left to itself, SPSS names the variables (columns) as var00001, var00002 and so on, which is not at all informative when you are looking at the table. So you need to insert meaningful names into the column headings.

When deciding on a variable name, it is sensible to use one that reminds you of what the variable actually is. So you would call sex 'sex', and age 'age'. But variable names cannot be longer than 8 characters, cannot contain a blank space between characters, must not end in a full stop (although one can be enclosed by characters), and must not use punctuation characters such as ! or *. Also, the name can only be used once. We have two sets of sales figures in the data file used in this book, but cannot call them both sales; instead they are named sales_1 and sales_2. Note that case is ignored, so SALARY, salary and Salary are all the same to SPSS and cannot be used together in one set of variable names.

It is important to distinguish between variable names, variable labels and value labels. The variable name is used by SPSS when identifying which variables it is to analyse, and as explained cannot be more than eight characters long, cannot contain a space, etc. So sales_1 is an acceptable variable name but sales*1 or sales 1 are not. Variable labels are added to the output and serve to explain what the variable is. They are not restricted in the way variable names are, since they can be up to 120 characters and can contain any characters or spaces. So for the variable which is named sales_1 you could have the label 'Sales for previous month'.

Value labels, on the other hand, are added to the output to explain what a particular value or score on a variable denotes; so the printout will show, for example, that a score of 1 on the variable sex indicates 'male'.

ASSIGNING VARIABLE NAMES AND VARIABLE LABELS IN VERSIONS 8 OR 9 OF SPSS   To name the variable and/or assign a variable label, click on one of the cells in the column containing the data on that variable, and from the menu bar of the Data Editor window select

```
Data
     Define Variable
```

Clicking on this entry yields a dialogue box (Figure 5.2), with the cursor already positioned in the text box marked Variable Name. Type in the new name of the variable.

To change the name of a variable, repeat the process of naming the variable by opening the Define Variable dialogue box and typing the new name into the Variable Name text box.

To assign a variable label, click on the Labels button in the Define Variable dialogue box. This will reveal another dialogue box, headed Define Labels (Figure 5.3). Type the label into the text box to the right of Variable Label:, and click on the Continue button. This will return you to the Define Variable box, and the label will be shown on the relevant line of the centre part of the box, the area marked as Variable Description. Click on OK, and the name and label will be assigned. The column containing the data on that variable will now be headed with the variable name you assigned.

ASSIGNING VALUE LABELS   To give labels to each value (score) on a variable, you use the Define Labels box (Figure 5.3), obtained from the Define

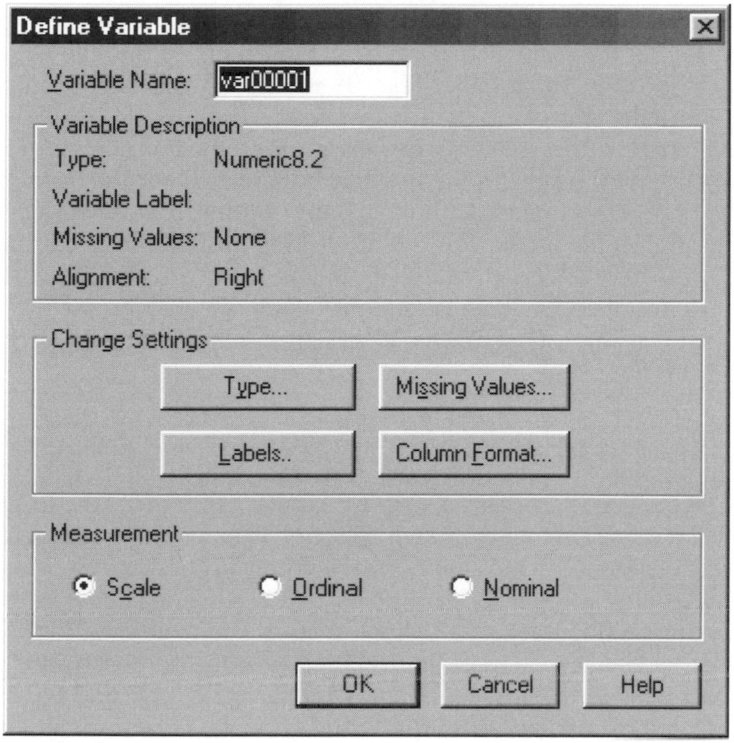

Figure 5.2   *The Define Variable dialogue box*

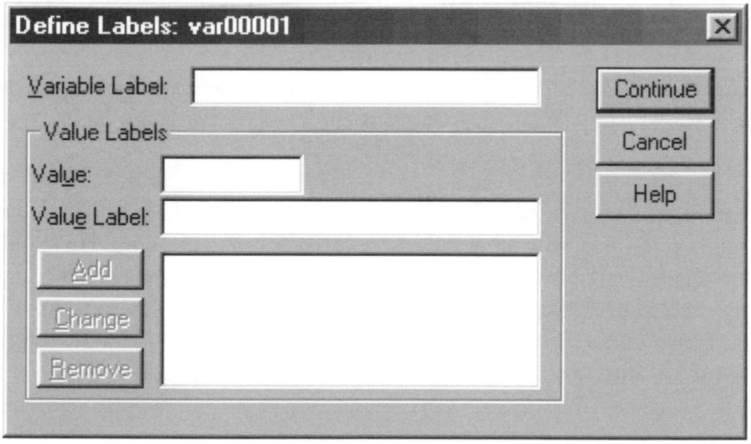

Figure 5.3   *The Define Labels dialogue box*

Variable box by clicking on the Labels button as explained above. Move
the pointer so it is in the Value text window, click the mouse to anchor
the cursor, and type in the value. Then type the label into the Value Label

text box and click on the Add button. For example, to insert the value label 'male' for the score of 1 on sex, you would type 1 into the Value box and male into the Value Label box, then click on the Add button. The result, 1='male' appears in the list box to the right of the Add button.

If you need to change one of the labels, get to the box shown in Figure 5.3 and click on the label in the list that is shown. Enter the new label in the Value Label box and click on the Change button. You delete a label by clicking on it in the list box and then clicking on the Remove button.

Once you have assigned value labels you can readily switch between seeing the numbers or their label equivalents by clicking on the Value Labels icon in the Data Editor's icon bar or by selecting View /Value Labels from the menus.

ASSIGNING VARIABLE NAMES AND VARIABLE LABELS IN VERSION 10 OF SPSS In version 10, while viewing the Data Editor select the Variable View tabbed page to obtain a display similar to Figure 5.4. To enter a variable label, type it into the Label column. To enter value labels, click in the Values column for the row corresponding to the variable for which you are defining value labels. A button will become available in the cell, and clicking on it will reveal a Value Labels dialogue box which is shown as the Value Labels section of Figure 5.3. Move the pointer so it is in the Value text window, click the mouse to anchor the cursor, and type in the value. Then type the label into the Value Label text box and click on the Add button. For example, to insert the value label 'male' for the score of 1 on sex, you would type 1 into the Value box and male into the Value Label box, then click on the Add button. The result, 1='male' appears in the list box to the right of the Add button.

Exercise 5.3

Assign names to each of the variables in salesq, using the names shown just above the first row of numbers in Table 5.1: id, sex, empl, att1 and so on. Assign variable labels: 'Employer' to empl, 'Customer visits' to cust, 'Start day' to dstd, 'Start month' to dstm and 'Start year' to dsty. Assign value labels to sex: 1 represents 'male' and 2 represents 'female'. Finally, assign value labels to area: 1 represents 'North', 2 represents 'South'.

5.6 When data is missing: missing values

When a respondent fails to provide a response on a variable it is important to encode the fact that there is no response, using a separate number which is defined as indicating 'missing value'. In versions 8 and

	name	type	width	decimals	label	values	missing	columns	
1	ID	Numeric	8	2		None	None	8	ric
2	SEX	Numeric	8	2		{1.00, male}...	3.00	8	ric
3	EMPL	Numeric	8	2	Employer	{1.00, Jones an	None	8	ric
4	AREA	Numeric	8	2		{1.00, North}...	None	8	ric
5	ATT1	Numeric	8	2		None	None	8	ric
6	ATT2	Numeric	8	2		None	None	8	ric
7	ATT3	Numeric	8	2		None	None	8	ric
8	CUST	Numeric	8	2	Customer visits	None	None	8	ric
9	SALES_1	Numeric	8	2		None	None	8	ric
10	SALES_2	Numeric	8	2		None	None	8	ric
11	DSTD	Numeric	8	2	Start day	None	None	8	ric
12	DSTM	Numeric	8	2	Start month	None	None	8	ric
13	DSTY	Numeric	8	2	Start year	None	None	8	ric

Figure 5.4 *The Variable View of the Data Editor in SPSS version 10*

9 of SPSS, you inform the program of the missing value for a variable by selecting Data /Define Variable from the Data Editor menu bar which exposes the Define Variable box (Figure 5.2). When presented with the Define Variable dialogue box, click on the Missing Values button. This exposes the Define Missing Values box shown in Figure 5.5. In SPSS version 10, select the Variable View tabbed page of the Data Editor, to obtain a display similar to Figure 5.4; click in the Missing column for the row corresponding to the variable you are defining. A button will become available, and clicking it will open a Missing Values dialogue box similar to that shown in Figure 5.5.

When presented with Figure 5.5, you can enter up to three different values each of which will be classed as missing (i.e. not a genuine data value). Having a number of different missing values can be useful: you may have one number to represent 'no response given', another to represent 'response was "Don't Know"', another to represent 'response was "Undecided"'. You will, of course, have had to encode these responses with the relevant numbers when you enter the data in the data editor. As suggested by the contents of Figure 5.5, you can also have a range of numbers defined as missing values or a range plus a single discrete value.

To define a particular number as a missing value, type it into one of the Discrete missing values boxes and click on Continue.

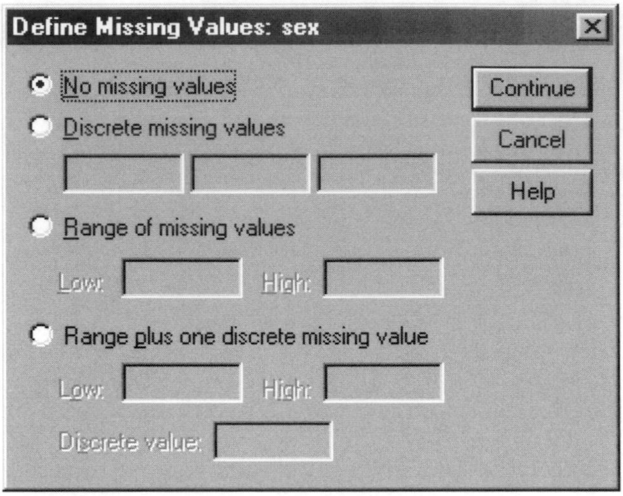

Figure 5.5   *The Define Missing Values dialogue box*

Exercise 5.4

Using the technique described above, tell SPSS that a score of 3 on sex is a missing value (i.e. signifies that the respondent's sex is unknown).

5.7 Setting the column width of a variable and aligning entries in a column

In SPSS versions 8 and 9, selecting Data /Define Variable from the menu reveals the Define Variable dialogue box (Figure 5.2). The Variable Description area of this display provides further information about the variable. Type shows whether it is a numeric variable (i.e. numbers only), a date variable, a string variable (meaning it includes letters rather than just numbers), or one of a range of other types. It also indicates the width of the variable as it is displayed in the table.

In Figure 5.2 the variable is of Numeric type and has a width of 8.2: this means the numbers displayed in this column can be up to 8 characters wide, including the decimal point, and there are 2 decimal places allowed. So the largest number which could be shown in this variable column is 99999.99. The settings are altered by ensuring the cursor is in the appropriate column in the Data Editor and then selecting from the menu Data /Define Variable and clicking on the Type button.

The width settings only control the width as displayed on the screen, and not the way the variable is stored in the program, where numeric variables are 40 characters wide with up to 16 decimal places. So although you may type in a number like 44.444, the table may only show 44.44; but in carrying out calculations the program uses the full number, with (in this example) three decimal places.

The Alignment entry in the Variable Description area of the Define Variable box tells you how the entries in the column will be aligned; for numeric variables, the conventional setting is right aligned. It can be changed to left aligned or centred by selecting the Column Format button from the Define Variable box shown in Figure 5.2 and clicking the relevant radio button in the Define Column Format dialogue box.

In SPSS version 10, the column width of a variable and its type, number of decimals shown, alignment, etc. can be set if you select the Variable View tabbed page of the Data Editor (Figure 5.4). Click in the appropriate column (type, width, decimals, align) of the row for the variable you are defining, and a control will become available allowing you to change the default setting. For example, to alter the number of decimals you click in that column and then use the up or down arrows to increase or decrease the number of decimal places.

5.8 Using templates to assign value labels etc. to a number of variables

You may have a large number of variables for which you wish to assign the same value labels, missing values, column width, alignment specification or some combination of these features. It is tedious to go through the process of defining these attributes for each one, and in versions 8 and 9 you can use a template to do it for you. (In version 10 you can copy and paste variable definition attributes to multiple variables from the Variable View tabbed page of the Data Editor.) You create a template from

```
Data
      Templates
```

in the Data Editor menu bar, which exposes a Template dialogue box. Clicking on the Define button allows you to access Define Template buttons, and from them you can enter the settings you want. You can then save the template by clicking on the Add button. In the Template dialogue box you can give your specification a particular name or have it as the default template.

Having specified a template, you will want to apply it to a number of variables. When in the Data Editor, select the variables to which the template is to be applied by dragging along the row so that entries in the appropriate variables are highlighted. Then click on Data /Templates . . . and select which attributes of the template you wish to apply by clicking on the relevant items from the list provided in the Apply area of the box.

You can apply any combination of Type, Value Labels, Missing Values, Column Format specifications. Then click on the OK button, and the highlighted variables in the Data Editor will have the designated template attributes applied to them.

Exercise 5.5

Make any adjustments you wish to the variable names, column widths, value labels features of the data in the file salesq and then save it again.

5.9 Seeing information about the variables in the data file

You may sometimes forget what the features of a variable are and want information about the variables displayed. In SPSS versions 8 and 9, select

```
Utilities
      Variables
```

which opens a window in which the variables are listed and information about the selected one is shown. If you want a printout of a description of all the variables in the data file, select

```
Utilities
      File Info
```

and a listing will be sent to the output viewer.

If you have version 10, information about the variables is obtained simply by selecting the Variable View tabbed page of the Data Editor, which gives a display like that shown in Figure 5.4. You can also use Utilities /Variables to obtain a window in which the variables are listed and information about the selected one is shown and Utilities /File Info to have a description of all the variables sent to the Output Viewer.

5.10 Retrieving data files

RETRIEVING A .SAV DATA FILE   To retrieve a data file from your floppy disk, select from the Data Editor menu bar

```
File
      Open
            Data
```

You will be presented with the Open File dialogue box shown in Figure 5.6. Assuming the data file you want is on the floppy disk and has been saved previously by SPSS, open the Look In drop-down list and click on the icon for drive a:. All the files on drive a:, the floppy disk, ending with the .sav extension will be listed in the files list. Click on the name of the file you want to retrieve, and it will appear in the File Name box. Click on the Open button on the right hand side of the dialogue box. The file will then be put into the Data Editor window. If it is not immediately visible, select the Window menu and click on the name of the data file.

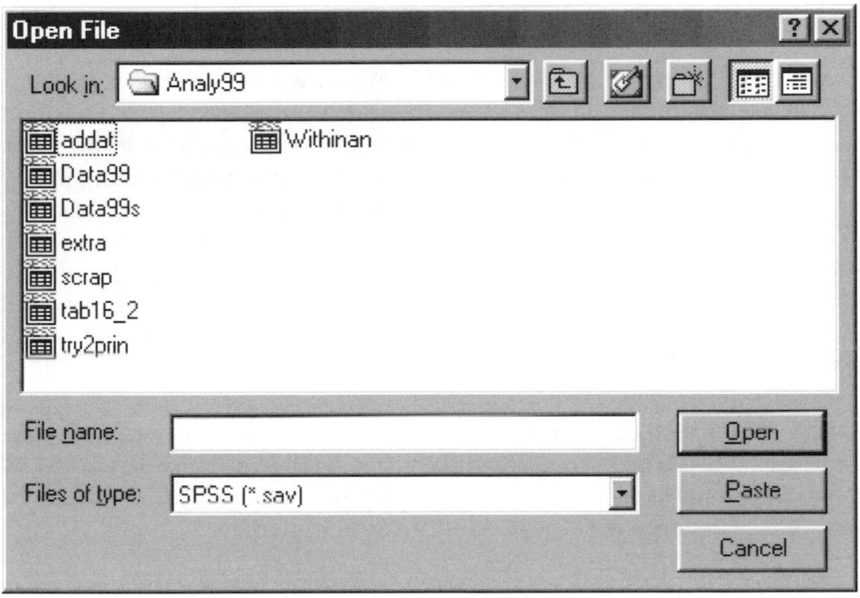

Figure 5.6   *The Open File dialogue box*

RETRIEVING A DATA FILE WITH A FILENAME EXTENSION OTHER THAN .SAV
Select from the Application window menu bar

```
File
     Open
          Data
```

You will be presented with the Open File dialogue box shown in Figure 5.6. If the data file has a filename extension other than .sav, you need to open the drop-down list and select the appropriate file type. The final entry in the list is All Files (*.*), which allows you to see all the files in the subdirectory. Selecting this option means that all the files will be listed and you can click on the one you want. If the file is on a floppy, open the Look In drop-down list and click on the icon for drive a:. All the files on the floppy disk will be shown in the file list, and you can use the scroll bars to scroll down the list. When the name of the file you want is visible, click on it and it will appear in the File Name text box. Then click on the Open button.

When you open the File of Type drop-down list of the Open File dialogue box, you will see that you can import files from other packages, such as Excel and dBase. How to import Excel files is described in section 5.12 below.

5.11 Importing data prepared in a word processor

Data can be prepared outside SPSS for Windows. If possible, it is better to prepare the data in a spreadsheet rather than a word processor and then import it into SPSS. You can then use the spreadsheet to do some tasks such as graph drawing, and the data in a spreadsheet will already be organized into columns and rows. Importing from a spreadsheet is explained in section 5.12 below. But you can use a word processor to prepare the data and then import it into SPSS. When writing the data in a word processor, use a Tab between each of the variables if possible and use the first row for the variable labels; this makes it simpler to import it into SPSS.

IMPORTING A TAB-DELIMITED FILE INTO SPSS VERSIONS **8** OR **9**   If data is prepared in a word processor with scores on the variables separated by tabs and the file saved in Text Only format, the data files can be imported into SPSS version 8 or 9 by selecting from the menus

```
File
    Open
```

Open the Files of Type drop-down menu. From the list of file types, choose Tab-delimited and the names of files with the .txt filename extension will be shown in the list of files. Click on the appropriate one, then on the Open button. You will be presented with a File Open Options dialogue box. If you have prepared the text file so that the first row contains the variable names, check the option Read Variable Names. These names will become the names of the variables (columns) in the SPSS file. If the file is on a floppy disk, open the Look In drop-down list and click on the icon for drive a:. Select the file to be imported from the list of file names or type the name in so that it appears in the File Name text box. Click on Open.

IMPORTING A TEXT FILE WITHOUT TABS INTO SPSS VERSIONS **8** OR **9**   If you are preparing the data in a word processor but not using Tabs to separate the different variables, use a fixed-width font and ensure the data is lined up in columns in a consistent way. For example, make sure that for all respondents id is in columns 1 to 3, age is in columns 5 and 6 and so on, and also make sure the data is right-aligned. This means that if id numbers run from 1 to 100, the number 1 is put in column 3, the number 10 is put in columns 2 and 3 and the number 100 is in columns 1, 2 and 3. This is easier to do if you make all the data for any one variable the same length so that id 1 would be typed as 001, 10 as 010.

The text file of the data can be imported into SPSS for Windows by selecting

```
File
      Read ASCII Data
            Fixed Columns
```

If the file is on a floppy disk, click the Browse button of the Define Fixed Variables dialogue box, open the Look In drop-down list and click on the icon for drive a:. Select the file to be imported from the list of file names or type the name in so that it appears in the File Name text box and click on the Open button which returns you to the Define Fixed Variables dialogue box. Here you have to specify the name of the variables. If the data for each case extends over more than one line you must indicate which line of the case has the variable you are defining by entering the line number in the box marked Record. You must also indicate the columns in the ASCII file which each variable occupies. (In salesq for example, id is in columns 1–2, sex in column 4 and so on.) The type of data must be specified in Data Type. (For the beginner, the default Numeric as is will be appropriate but other types are available in the drop-down list). Then click on the Add button, and the information you have provided will appear in the Defined Variables list.

When you have entered the specifications for all the variables, click on OK. The file will be read and the data appear in the Data Editor window: before you do anything else, check that the data is as you expected!

IMPORTING A TEXT FILE INTO SPSS VERSION 10 To import a text file into version 10, select

```
File
      Read Text Data
```

Select the file to be opened from the list of files presented, and this will then lead to the Text Import Wizard. This guides you through the process of importing the file.

5.12 Transferring data files to/from other packages such as Excel version 4

Data files can be saved in a number of formats so they can be read by other packages such as Excel or dBase. The options are offered when you select File /Save As for a data file and open the drop-down list Save File as Type. Similarly, data files from these other packages can be read into SPSS for Windows. This is extremely useful, since you can prepare the data in a program such as Excel and do not need a computer with SPSS installed.

If you are preparing the data in MSWorks or Excel, it is easiest if you save the spreadsheet file in the format for Excel 4 or lower, not Excel 5 or 7. This means that you only save one sheet of the Excel workbook; if you are using Excel 5 or higher and have a workbook with a number of tabbed sheets, it can be imported into SPSS but you need to read section 5.13 below.

When preparing the spreadsheet file of the data, you can put variable names into the first row of the sheet and these can then be imported and will form the column names in the SPSS file.

IMPORTING AN EXCEL 4 FILE INTO SPSS VERSIONS 8 OR 9   When you have an Excel 4 file to import, select

```
File
     Open
```

The usual dialogue box is presented. Open the drop-down list Files of Type and select Excel. If the file is on a floppy disk, open the Look In drop-down list and select the icon for drive a:. Enter the name of the Excel file into the File Name text box by selecting it from the file list. If the Excel file contains only the data with no variable names in the first row of the spreadsheet, clicking on Open will load the file into SPSS. If you have written the variable names into the first row of the Excel table, check the option Read Variable Names in the Opening Files Options dialogue box before clicking Open. The data will be imported into SPSS with the variable names already assigned.

Whenever importing data from another package, check the data carefully so that you can be sure the transfer has been accurate and complete.

5.13 Importing data files from Excel version 5 and above into SPSS versions 8 or 9

Although it is claimed to be possible to create a data file from a number of sheets in a multi-sheet workbook such as Excel 5 provides, it is not easy. (Which is a disguised way of saying that I could not make this feature work!) But importing data from one of the tabbed sheets of an Excel 5 file is possible. Use the first row of the spreadsheet to contain the variable names, so that the sheet looks like this:

var1	var2	var3
11	12	13
21	22	23

To import an Excel 5 or higher spreadsheet, select from the menu

```
File
      Database Capture
            New Query
```

This starts the Database Capture Wizard shown in Figure 5.7. Select the Excel Files option from the list which is offered and click on the Next button. This presents the Select Workbook dialogue box and you can navigate to the subdirectory containing the Excel file and then click on the particular .xls file from the list which is shown.

This opens the next screen of the Database Capture Wizard, shown in Figure 5.8. You can select which sheets of the .xls file to enter into SPSS by dragging and dropping from the left-hand list of Available Tables to the Retrieve Fields in This Order list. I advise you to select only one of the sheets. The fields will be shown in the Retrieve Fields in This Order list, and you can click on Finish. The data will be entered into SPSS's Data Editor, with the names of the variables being the names used in the first line of the spreadsheet. (So in the example above, the variable names will be var1, var2 and var3.) If you click on the Next buttons rather than Finish, further complicated options are offered; you might like to experiment with them to see how they function. But the facilities they offer (such as altering the variable names or selecting only cases which meet some criterion) can more easily be accomplished either while you are running the spreadsheet program or once the data has been entered into SPSS.

5.14 Importing data files from Excel version 5 and above into SPSS version 10

To import an Excel 5 spreadsheet, select from the menu

```
File
      Database Capture
            New Query
```

This starts the Database Capture Wizard shown in Figure 5.7. Select the Excel files option from the list which is offered and click on the Next

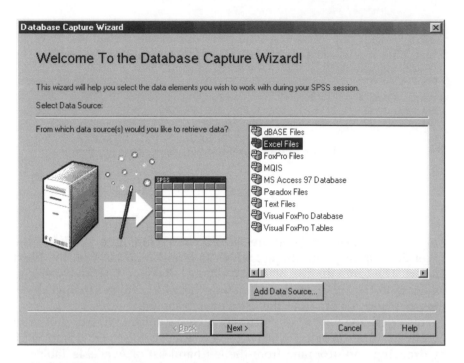

Figure 5.7   *The opening screen of the Database Capture Wizard*

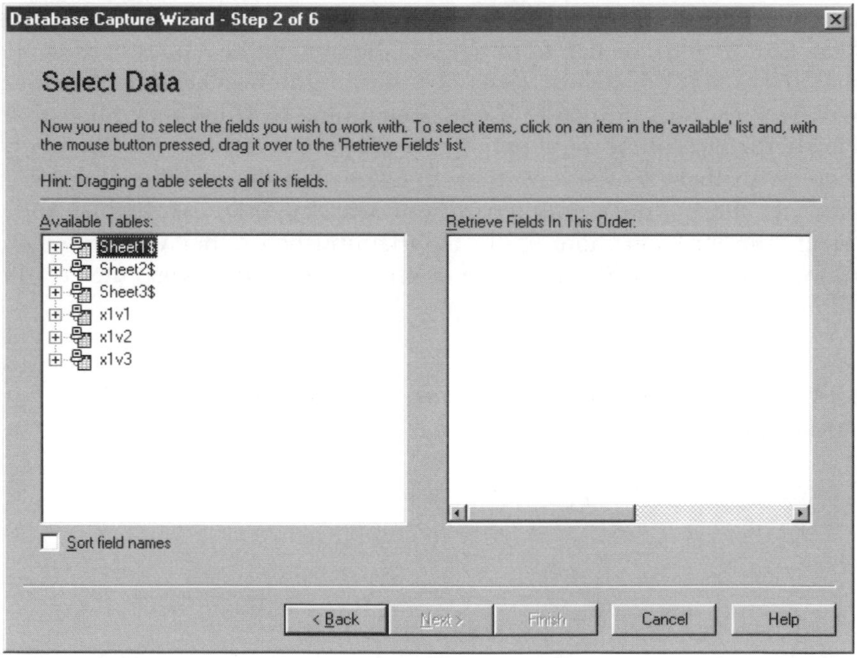

Figure 5.8   *The second screen of the Database Capture Wizard*

button. This presents the Select Workbook dialogue box and you can navigate to the subdirectory containing the Excel file and then click on the particular .xls file from the list which is shown.

This opens the next screen of the Database Capture Wizard, shown in Figure 5.8. You can select which sheets of the .xls file to enter into SPSS by dragging and dropping from the left-hand list of Available Tables to the Retrieve Fields in This Order list. I advise you to select only one of the sheets. The fields will be shown in the Retrieve Fields in This Order list, and you can click on Finish. The data will be entered into SPSS's Data Editor, with the names of the variables being the names used in the first line of the spreadsheet. (So in the example above, the variable names will be var1, var2 and var3.) If you click on the Next buttons rather than Finish, further complicated options are offered; you might like to experiment with them to see how they function. But the facilities they offer (such as altering the variable names or selecting only cases which meet some criterion) can more easily be accomplished either while you are running the spreadsheet program or once the data has been entered into SPSS.

5.15 Printing the data file

Check the data window is the active window and select

```
File
      Print
```

from the Data Editor menu bar. The Print dialogue box will appear. By default, one copy of the whole file will be printed. To print more than one copy, type in the number required in the Copies box. Click on OK. In SPSS version 10, the File menu has a Print Preview entry so you can see what will be printed before committing yourself.

If you do not want the grid lines printed, remove them from the data editor window before you select File /Print. While viewing the Data Editor, select View /Grid Lines from the menu and click on Grid Lines.

If you have assigned value labels to the data so that, for example, a value of 1 in the variable sex has the label 'male' and value 2 has the label 'female', you can have these labels printed instead of the numbers when you print out the file. To do this, while viewing the Data Editor, select View and click on Value Labels or use the Labels icon button to have the labels shown instead of the numbers. Then print the file by selecting File /Print as explained above.

6

MERGING DATA FILES

Summary

This chapter explains how to:

- merge files which have sets of data from different respondents
- merge files which have additional data for the same respondents.

6.1 When do you need to merge data files?

You may find that you have two sets of data, in separate files, that you want to merge to form one file. There are two situations where this is likely to happen. First, you have collected data from a sample of respondents, and later obtain data from some more respondents which you want to add to your first set. The obvious way of doing this is to retrieve the original data file and simply add the new cases on the end, but this is not always feasible. (Perhaps you have the data from 1000 children in Mexico, and a colleague has data from 1000 children in Poland. Both of you have written a file containing the data you have collected, neither of you wants to type in another 1000 cases!) You can merge the two data files using Add Cases as described below.

The second situation where you want to merge data is when you have data from a set of respondents, and then obtain another series of responses from the same respondents. For example, imagine we surveyed 500 adults on their alcohol drinking behaviour six months ago and yesterday. We want to add the data we collected yesterday to the file of their responses of six months ago, so we can look at changes in drinking behaviour over the six month period. We are not adding new cases to our data file, only adding new data to existing cases. We could go back and add the new data to our data file, but it may be that we have the two data sets in separate files and want to merge them. For this type of situation, use Add Variables (section 6.3).

6.2 Adding cases

Suppose we have a file which contains data on additional respondents to
be added to salesq and this additional data, shown in Table 6.1, has been
saved in a file called extra.sav, with the same names for the variables as
were used in salesq.

Table 6.1   *Additional data from three respondents to be added to the data file*

23	1	1	1	3	2	3	055	03800.50	010691
24	2	2	2	4	2	4	060	04780.60	030690
25	2	1	2	3	2	5	078	06782.00	040690

To add these cases to salesq, retrieve salesq so it is in an active Data
Editor window. From the menus, select

```
Data
     Merge Files
          Add Cases
```

This opens a dialogue box entitled Add Cases: Read File. Click on the
name of the file to be added (extra.sav in this example) so it appears in
the File Name text box, and click on the Open button.

This reveals another dialogue box (Add Cases From), and variables in
the two data files which match are listed in the text box headed Variables
in New Working Data File. So if both data files have a variable called sex,
this will be listed in this box. The dialogue box also has a list of variables
in a text box headed Unpaired Variables. Those variables followed by a *
are present in the current, open data file and those variables followed by
a + are present in the external file (extra.sav in this example). These are
variables which do not have the same name in the two files. You can
make a pair of them, so a variable called sex in the current file can be
matched with a variable called gender in the external file, by clicking on
the first of these two names and then do a Ctrl + click on the second
name. If necessary, variables in the Unpaired Variable list can be
renamed by selecting them and clicking on the Rename button.

If you want the merged file to include a variable that only exists in one
of the files being merged, select its name and click on the right arrow
button to add it to the list of Variables in New Working Data File.

When the definition is complete, Paste the command into a syntax
window and run it. A file called Untitled will appear in the Data Editor.
Save this file, but before carrying out any analysis check it carefully to
see that the new cases have been added accurately.

6.3 Adding scores to existing cases: Add Variables

This procedure merges two data files that contain different data on the same respondents. Imagine we have additional data for the respondents recorded in salesq: perhaps we now have their date of birth as a six-digit number like this: 050870, representing 5th August, 1970. This data has been assigned to three variables: dobd (day), dobm (month) and doby (year), and is stored in a data file (addat.sav). An example of the data for the first two respondents is:

```
01 120870
02 221070
```

We want to add this additional data on each respondent to the salesq file. First, the data in both files must have been sorted into the same order on the key variable which will be used to ensure the data is assigned to the correct case: this is one reason for having identification numbers (id) in data files such as salesq. Having sorted both salesq and addat.sav by id, ensure one of the files is in the active Data Editor. (Assume for this explanation that salesq is the active file.) From the menu select

```
Data
     Merge Files
          Add Variables
```

Select the name of the other file (addat.sav in this example) from the list in the Add Variables: Read File dialogue box. Then click on Open.

Any variables which appear in either of the data files are shown in the New Working Data File list of the dialogue box entitled Add Variables From. Those variables followed by a * are present in the current, open data file and those variables followed by a + are present in the external file (addat.sav in this example). Any variables which appear in both of the data files are shown in the Excluded Variables list, since one does not want them to appear twice in the merged file.

If the second file (addat.sav) has data on every case in the current file (salesq), you can click on Paste and run the syntax. The two sets of data will be merged and seen in the Data Editor window. Save the data file and check it carefully for accuracy before analysing it.

If the external file (addat.sav) does not have data for every one of the cases in the current file (salesq), see the next section.

6.4 Add Variables with incomplete data

Suppose we have a set of additional data, the marital status of some of the respondents in salesq. The variable is named as marst, and 1 means unmarried, 2 is married. The data is shown in Table 6.2, the first two digits being the respondent's id (identification number). This data has been saved in a data file called marry.sav.

Table 6.2 *Additional data on the respondents to be added to the data file*

06	1
03	2
05	2
18	1
11	2

Marry.sav has scores on marst for 5 respondents. (Note that in marry-.sav the respondents are not in the same order as in the original data file; this is so you see how to cope with this situation.)

When one merges the data from the two files, it is obviously essential that the data from marry.sav is added to the appropriate persons in salesq. There must be some way of identifying which lines from salesq match which lines from marry.sav, and in this example the variable id, referred to as a key variable, lets us do that because id is included in both the data files.

The key variable must have the same name in both files, but you can if necessary use the Rename facility to bring this situation about by clicking on the variable name in the list of variables and then on the Rename button in the Add Variables From dialogue box. Then ensure that both data files have the cases sorted on the key variable (id, in this example); if necessary, retrieve each file, sort the data and then save the file.

Once the files have been sorted on the key variable, the procedure for matching salesq and marry.sav is to select from the menu

```
Data
     Merge Files
          Add Variables
```

When faced with the Add Variables From dialogue box, click on the key variable name (id in our example) in the Excluded Variables list, check the box entitled Match Cases on Key Variables in Sorted Files and then enter the key variable into the Key Variables text box by clicking on the right arrow button. Then click on Paste.

When the syntax is run, the files will be merged and the new merged set of data will appear in the Data Editor window where you can inspect it to ensure the data has been matched correctly. Then save the new file.

7

RUNNING A SIMPLE ANALYSIS AND OBTAINING THE OUTPUT

Summary

This chapter explains how to:

- set the output page length and page width
- obtain analyses from the Statistics menu in the Data Editor window
- modify the source list of variables in dialogue boxes
- open new output windows
- ensure an output window is the designated window which receives the output
- save and retrieve output files
- edit the output
- print the output
- transfer the output to a word processor or web browser
- obtain on-screen help on statistical terms.

7.1 Setting output page length, page width and inserting commands in output

The output is shown in either the Output Viewer or the Draft Viewer, depending in which you select to be the default and which you select when you open a new output window. The Draft Viewer gives a rather crude appearance with its simple text output and you are likely to use the Output Viewer most of the time.

SPSS is set up so that it assumes that you are using a non-A4 page and it is sensible to alter the settings to the paper size you are actually using, which will usually be A4. SPSS is very prolific with paper, and will waste a huge amount by inserting page breaks at very frequent intervals. While you are carrying out analyses you can save a few trees by turning off this wasteful feature.

It is extremely useful, when you are trying to follow a series of complicated tables and statistics, to have the output contain the commands used to obtain it. To have the commands inserted in the output, use Edit /Options as described below.

Select from the menu

```
Edit
     Options
```

This presents the dialogue box shown in Figure 7.1. (In version 10 there are some slight differences, but the general appearance is the same.) Select the Viewer tab and the window shown in Figure 7.2 will be revealed.

To have the syntax commands printed in the output viewer immediately before the output which the syntax produces, ensure that in Figure 7.2 there is a tick in the box alongside the wording Display Commands in the Log. If there is no tick, just click in the box.

To stop SPSS inserting page breaks in the output, set the page length to 'Infinite' by selecting that option in the Length area of the part of the display headed Text Output. If you want to set the page length to A4 paper, click on the Custom option in Length and type 70 into the text box beside it. To alter the page width from the default value, select the Custom option and type in a figure for the width of the page. The width is measured in characters, and a normal full width is 80. As can be seen in Figure 7.2, you can also set the fonts and typesizes for the title and for the text output. (To change the page size for the Draft Viewer, use the Draft Viewer tab of the window shown in Figure 7.1.)

7.2 Using the menus to analyse the data

Once you have a data file open (an active Data Editor window containing data) and have decided which analyses you require, you are ready to run SPSS. Most of the analyses can be obtained by selecting from the menus in the Data Editor window.

Clicking on the Application window Analyze or Statistics menu reveals the drop-down menu shown in Figure 7.3 with some or all of these options:

```
Reports
Descriptive Statistics
Custom Tables
Compare Means
Geneal Linear Model
```

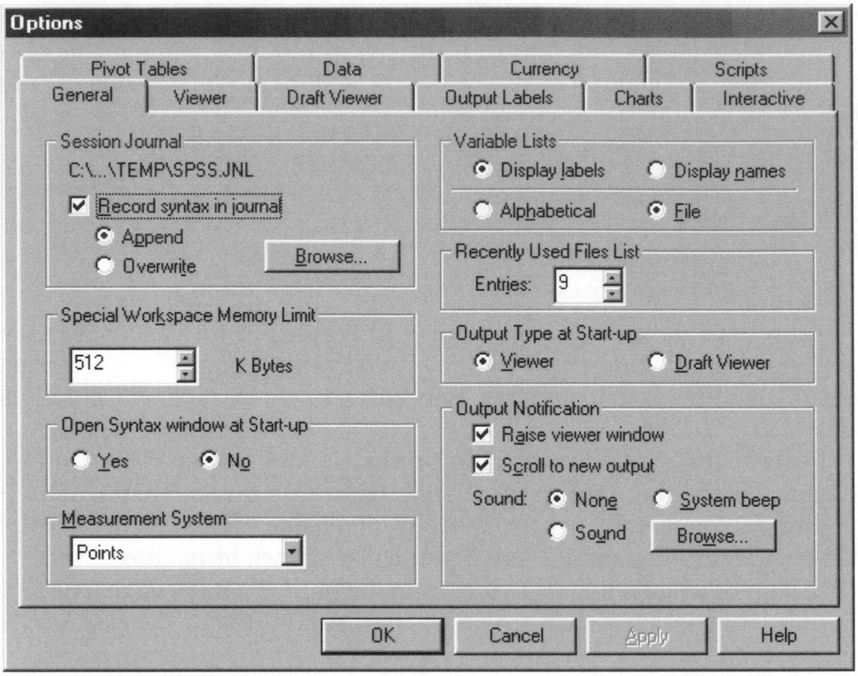

Figure 7.1   The Edit Options dialogue box

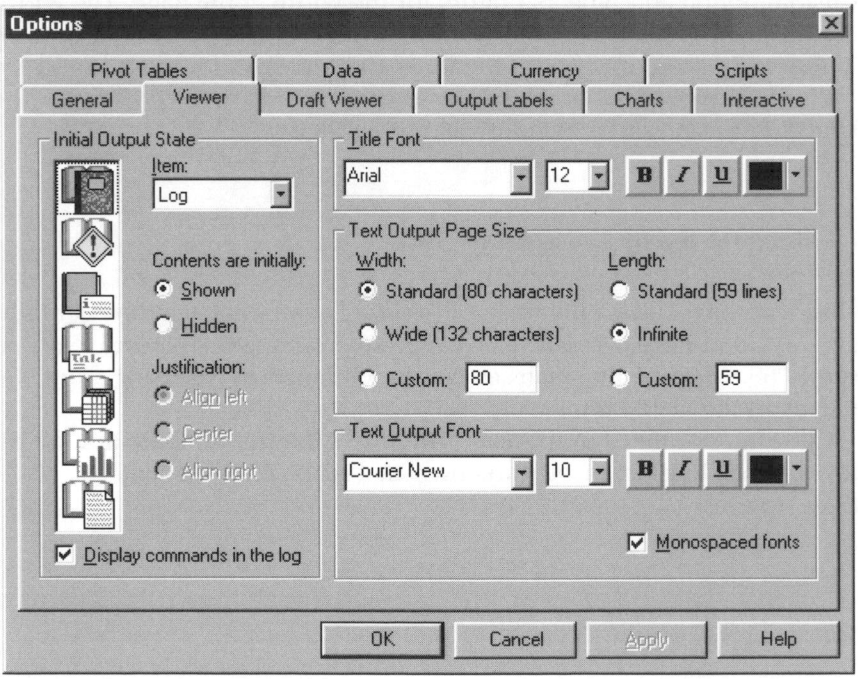

Figure 7.2   The Edit Options window for setting the format of the Output Viewer

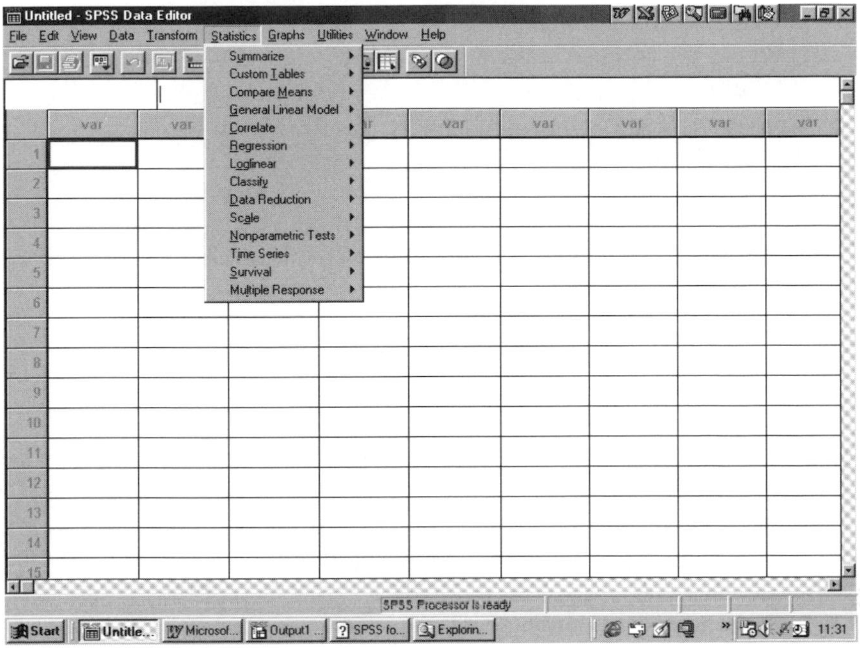

Figure 7.3 *The Statistics drop-down menu*

```
Correlate
Regression
Loglinear
Classify
Data Reduction
Scale
Nonparametric Tests
Time Series
Survival
Multiple Response
```

(Version 8 users will find that Reports and Descriptive Statistics are replaced by the single entry Summarize.) Each entry has an arrowhead to show that there is another menu which can be obtained by clicking on the entry or by pressing the key of the underlined letter.

The Descriptive Statistics entry, for example, has a submenu containing these entries:

```
Frequencies...
Descriptives...
Explore...
Crosstabs...
```

The submenu for Reports contains

```
OLAP Cubes
Case Summaries...
Report Summaries in Rows...
Report Summaries in Columns...
```

The ... indicates that if you select that entry, a dialogue box will be revealed in which you enter more details about the analysis you want.

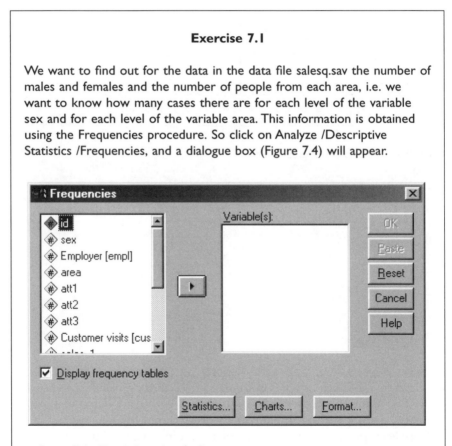

Exercise 7.1

We want to find out for the data in the data file salesq.sav the number of males and females and the number of people from each area, i.e. we want to know how many cases there are for each level of the variable sex and for each level of the variable area. This information is obtained using the Frequencies procedure. So click on Analyze /Descriptive Statistics /Frequencies, and a dialogue box (Figure 7.4) will appear.

Figure 7.4   *The dialogue box for Frequencies*

Dialogue boxes for the statistical procedures have a common format. In the left-hand box, which has no title but is known as the source variable list, there is a list of the variables in the Data File; the variable names are those which are given at the top of the columns in the Data

Editor, so will be var00001, var00002, etc. unless you have assigned variable names as explained in section 5.5.

You have to tell SPSS which variables you want analysed. To do this, select each variable by clicking on its name, which will then be highlighted. Then click in the button marked with a right-pointing arrow, and the variable will appear in the right-hand box, the one headed Variable(s). Select whichever variables you want to analyse in this way. If you want to select a number of variables, you can use the drag method of selecting a set in one movement; pressing on the arrow button will transfer the names of all the variables in the set to the Variable(s) box.

If you make a mistake, and have selected a variable you do not want to analyse, you remove it from the Variable(s) box by clicking on it; the arrow in the arrow button will become a left-pointing one, and clicking on that will remove the highlighted variable from the list and return it to the left-hand box.

In our example, click on sex in the left-hand box and then on the right-pointing arrow; then click on area in the left-hand box and on the right-pointing arrow again. The variable names sex and area will appear in the Variables(s) box.

Now click on the OK button at the top right of the dialogue box. (For the moment ignore the other buttons down the right hand side and along the bottom of the dialogue box.) The Frequencies procedure will run, and the results will appear in the output window, Output1. It is as simple as that!

The result of running this example is shown in Figure 7.5. The first few lines, which may not appear in your output, show the syntax for the analysis. Syntax is explained in chapter 8. The first table headed Statistics shows the number of valid and missing cases for each of the two variables. The missing case under Sex is because one of the cases in the data file has a sex value of 3, which has been designated a missing value indicating that the sex of that person is unknown. The table headed Sex shows the frequency of males, females and sex unknown (missing), corresponding to values 1, 2 and 3 on the variable sex. The Area table shows the frequency of each level (North corresponding to 1 and South corresponding to 2) on the variable area. (Further explanation of the output from Frequencies is provided in section 14.1.)

When you are looking at the output on screen, the outline is shown in the left-hand panel. You can select the part of the output to look at by clicking on its entry in the outline, and can also move parts of the output. You will see that there is an item entitled Notes, which may not be shown in the Output Viewer itself. (This depends on the settings in the Edit /Options /Viewer.) To see the Notes, double click on its icon; the Notes information tells you the file and syntax used but is rarely of much use.

```
FREQUENCIES
  VARIABLES=sex area
  /ORDER  ANALYSIS .
```

Frequencies

Statistics

		SEX	AREA
N	Valid	21	22
	Missing	1	0

Frequency Table

SEX

		Frequency	Percent	Valid Percent	Cumulative Percent
Valid	male	10	45.5	47.6	47.6
	female	11	50.0	52.4	100.0
	Total	21	95.5	100.0	
Missing	3.00	1	4.5		
Total		22	100.0		

AREA

		Frequency	Percent	Valid Percent	Cumulative Percent
Valid	North	9	40.9	40.9	40.9
	South	13	59.1	59.1	100.0
	Total	22	100.0	100.0	

Figure 7.5 *Output from running Frequencies for sex and area on the data in salesq.sav*

Exercise 7.2

Now try a second example, to obtain the mean and standard deviation of the number of customer visits (the variable is labelled cust) for the data in salesq. Means can also be obtained via the Frequencies procedure, so select from the Application window

```
Analyze
        Descriptive Statistics
                Frequencies
```

The dialogue box may still have sex and area listed in the Variable(s) box. Remove them by clicking on them and pressing the left-pointing arrow button. Select cust from the source variable list, and click on the right-pointing area so that cust appears in the Variable(s) box.

To obtain the means using Frequencies, you need to request them by clicking on the button labelled Statistics... in the dialogue box which reveals another dialogue box illustrated in Figure 7.6. This is where you indicate the statistics you want: click on the word Mean in the area labelled Central Tendency, and on Std. deviation in the area labelled Dispersion. As you click on these, the small squares next to the words will have a tick put into them to show they have been selected. If you click on the wrong thing, just click on the wrongly-selected item and the cross will be removed from its indicator square to show it is not selected. (Clicking the Cancel button will cancel all the selections you have made and take you back up one level, to the Frequencies dialogue box.) Now click on Continue in the upper right of the dialogue box, and you will be returned to the Frequencies dialogue box; click on the OK button. The Frequencies procedure will run, the results again appearing in the Output1 window. The output is illustrated in Figure 7.7; the mean and standard deviation of the data on the cust variable are shown in the table headed Statistics.

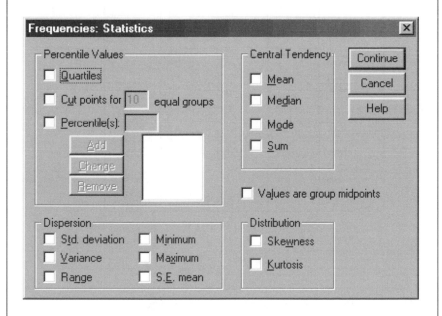

Figure 7.6   *The dialogue box for indicating the statistics required under Frequencies*

```
FREQUENCIES
  VARIABLES=cust
  /STATISTICS=STDDEV MEAN
  /ORDER  ANALYSIS .
```

Frequencies

Statistics

Customer visits

N	Valid	22
	Missing	0
Mean		50.8182
Std. Deviation		17.0116

Customer visits

		Frequency	Percent	Valid Percent	Cumulative Percent
Valid	28.00	1	4.5	4.5	4.5
	30.00	1	4.5	4.5	9.1
	33.00	1	4.5	4.5	13.6
	36.00	1	4.5	4.5	18.2
	38.00	1	4.5	4.5	22.7
	39.00	2	9.1	9.1	31.8
	40.00	1	4.5	4.5	36.4
	41.00	1	4.5	4.5	40.9
	42.00	1	4.5	4.5	45.5
	43.00	1	4.5	4.5	50.0
	46.00	1	4.5	4.5	54.5
	48.00	2	9.1	9.1	63.6
	58.00	1	4.5	4.5	68.2
	60.00	1	4.5	4.5	72.7
	68.00	1	4.5	4.5	77.3
	71.00	1	4.5	4.5	81.8
	72.00	1	4.5	4.5	86.4
	76.00	1	4.5	4.5	90.9
	79.00	1	4.5	4.5	95.5
	83.00	1	4.5	4.5	100.0
	Total	22	100.0	100.0	

Figure 7.7 *Output from running Frequencies for cust on the data in salesq.sav with mean and standard deviation requested*

7.3 Modifying the source list of variables in dialogue boxes

It is possible to modify the variables shown in the source lists of the dialogue boxes, and the order in which they are listed. The variables are shown in the source list of the dialogue boxes in alphabetical order or in the order in which they occur in the data file. To select which order you want, use Edit /Options and select the General tab. There is an area headed Variable Lists and buttons for Alphabetical or File orders.

When you have a very lengthy set of variables in the data file, it can be convenient to restrict those which are presented in the source list in the dialogue boxes. This can be done using Utilities / Define Sets from the menu bar. Give the set a name, specify the variables to be included in a set, and then click the Add Set button to create it. To have this newly created set used in the dialogue boxes, select Utilities / Use Sets, enter the name of the new set in the Sets in Use list and remove from the list the ALLVARIABLES entry.

You can change the order in which variables are listed in the target lists by clicking on the name of the variable to be moved and then clicking on the control box in the top left of the dialogue box title bar: options to Move Selection Up and Move Selection Down are offered.

7.4 Sending the output to a different output window

When SPSS for Windows starts, it always creates an output window entitled Output1, and the results of any analysis will be put in that window. You can open another output window, by selecting

```
File
     New
          Output
```

A number of output windows can be open simultaneously, but only one of them, known as the designated window, can receive output. Any fresh output that you generate will be appended to the bottom of the currently-designated output window.

When a new output window is opened it is automatically made the designated window. You know which is the designated window because it has an exclamation mark in the message bar at the bottom of the window. Any output window can be made the designated one by clicking its ! icon button in the icon bar.

7.5 Saving an output file

SAVING THE OUTPUT FILE FOR THE FIRST TIME   As you have seen, the output is displayed in an output window. By default, this will be saved on the hard disk when you leave SPSS with the name Output1.spo. It is almost always more convenient to save it on a floppy. While viewing the output window, select from the menu bar

```
File
     Save As ...
```

The dialogue box you will see is similar to that for saving the data file shown in Figure 5.1. Enter the name of the file into the File Name box.

Open the Save In drop-down list, click on the icon for drive a: and then click on the Save button.

SAVING A PREVIOUSLY SAVED OUTPUT FILE AFTER EDITING IT Any changes you make to an output file you have retrieved from disk will be lost unless you save the file. While viewing the window, select from the menu bar

```
File
```

To save the current version of the file, overwriting previous ones, select

```
Save
```

The new version will be saved on the same drive from which it was retrieved.
    To save the current version while keeping the previous one, select

```
Save As . . .
```

which will present the Save As dialogue box. Type in a new name for the output file in the File Name text box; remember it must not contain a blank space or full stop. To save the file on the floppy disk, open the Save In drop-down list, click on the icon for drive a: and click on the Save button.

7.6 Retrieving an output file from the floppy disk

To retrieve a saved .spo file, it has to be opened in an output window by selecting from the window menu bar

```
File
    Open
        Output
```

The Open File dialogue box will be presented. If the file you want is on your floppy disk, open the Look In drop-down list and click on the icon for drive a:. If Files of Type shows something other than Viewer Document (*.spo), open the drop-down list and scroll down until you get to Viewer Document (*.spo) and click on this entry. When the Files of Type shows Viewer Document (*.spo), all files with the .spo filename extension will be listed in the file list on the left hand side. If necessary, you can scroll down the list. Click on the name of the file you want, so that its name appears in the File Name text box, and then on the Open button. The file you have retrieved will be displayed in an output window.

To open a Draft Viewer file, the procedure is the same except that the Files of Type is Draft Viewer Document (*.rtf), so this should be used instead of *.spo.

7.7 Editing the contents of the output viewer

In the Output Viewer, some of the material is text but most consists of tables. In the examples used in this book, the commands which are shown before the results of a procedure are text material.

ADDING TEXT TO THE OUTPUT VIEWER   If you want to insert extra text into the output, the Insert /New Text will insert a box into which you can type the new material. The box can be moved within the output by dragging it with the mouse.

EDITING TEXT MATERIAL   Text, not tables, can be edited if you click on that part of the output so that it becomes surrounded by a sizing frame and has a red arrow pointing to it. To edit the contents of the frame, double-click in it or select

```
Edit
     SPSS Rtf Document Object
```

when you can then choose either Edit or Open. If you choose Open, a new window will be opened with the selected text material in it. You can edit the text and apply formatting such as bold face, changing the typeface and so on. When you have finished the editing, close the window with

```
File
     Exit and Return to Output
```

or in version 10 just click outside the area being edited. If you choose Edit rather than Open, you edit the text material within the Output Viewer. To change the formatting, the Format menu allows you to apply bold face, italic and underlining; from this menu you can select Font, which allows you to change the typesize as well as the typeface.

EDITING TABLES   To edit a table of the Output Viewer, either double-click in it or select it and then from the menu bar choose

```
Edit
     SPSS Pivot Table Object
```

This offers the alternatives of Edit or Open.

If you choose the Open option, a fresh window will open with the table in it. From the menu of the window, you use Edit /Select to select the part of the table you want to edit. If you click on the row or column headings in the table, you will be able to select Data Cells or Data and Label Cells as well as Table or Table Body. With the appropriate selections, you can modify the format of the table by, for example, using the Format drop-down menu. To add a caption, title or footnote use the Insert drop-down menu. The range of possibilities is too vast to describe in detail; the best procedure is to experiment with the various alternatives. It may be worth taking notes as you go, so you have a record of just how you achieved any particular effect in case you want to use it again! To close the window in which the pivot table is edited, use File /Close from the Pivot Table editing window.

You may find that after editing, you return to the Output Viewer and the table is shaded. This happens if you fail to use the File /Close sequence to leave the editing window; the situation can be restored if you select the table again with Edit /SPSS Pivot Table Object /Open and then do a File /Close.

The alternative to using a separate window for editing the pivot table is to select from the drop-down menu

```
Edit
      SPSS Pivot Table Object
                  Edit
```

You can then edit the table within the Output Viewer window. Use Edit /Select to select the part or aspect of the table to be edited. Click in a row or column heading to permit the selection of Data Cells or Data Cells and Labels as well as Table or Table Body. When the appropriate aspect of the table has been selected, the Insert and Format drop-down menus allow access to a wide range of formatting alternatives. Try the Format /Table Properties and Format /TableLooks to see what a wide set of alternatives are available.

To stop the editing, just click on some other part of the output in the Output Viewer.

EDITING THE DRAFT OUTPUT VIEWER   The Draft Output Viewer contains only text, and the formatting possibilities are rather limited. You can select text and apply bold face, italic and underlining or change the typeface and size from the Format drop-down menu. The Edit menu offers a find/replace facility.

7.8 Changing fonts and type style in output

The facility for altering output fonts is available by selecting

```
Edit
      Options
```

and the Viewer tab.

7.9 Adding or removing a title before each procedure

When SPSS runs a procedure such as Frequencies, it can put the title of the procedure before the table of results. This can be turned on or off from Edit /Options: select the Viewer tab and in the list under Initial Output State click on the titles entry. You can select either Shown or Hidden radio buttons.

7.10 Rounding numbers in the output

The output may show more decimal places than you want. You can modify the output display by selecting the table for editing, and then using the click/drag procedure to highlight the cells to be modified. Right-click or from the menu bar choose Format. In either case, selecting /Cell Properties will present the dialogue box shown in Figure 7.8. Click on the first entry in the Format list, and the Decimals control shown in Figure 7.8 will be added to the dialogue box. Change the number shown in the Decimals text box using the up and down arrow keys to its side, and then press the Apply button.

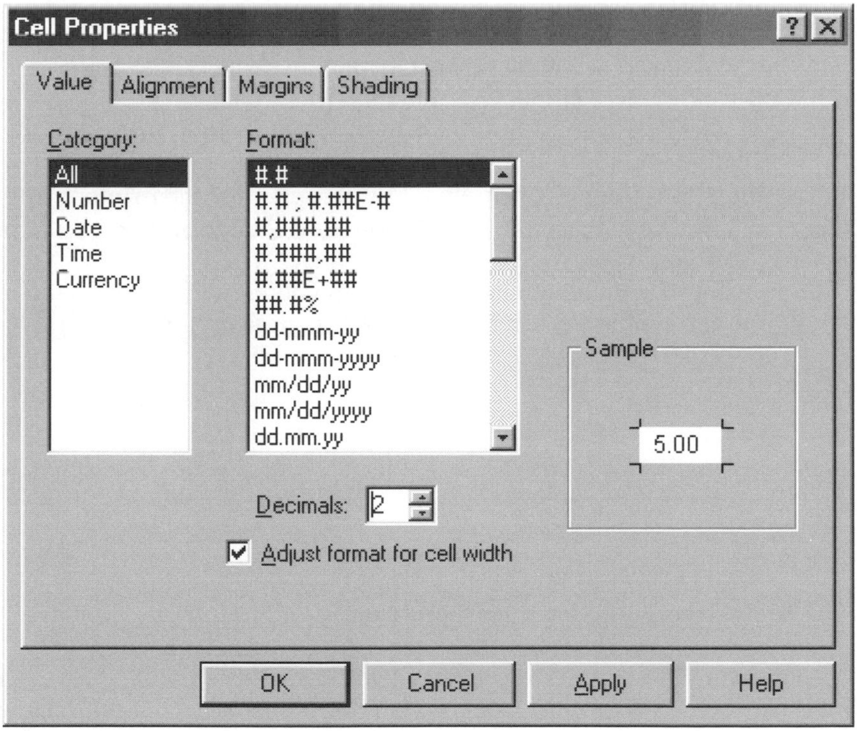

Figure 7.8   *The dialogue box for altering the number of decimals shown in an Output Viewer table*

7.11 Printing output files from SPSS

PRINTING THE WHOLE FILE While viewing the output window to be printed, from the window menu bar select

```
Edit
      Select All
```

and then

```
File
      Print...
```

The Print dialogue box will appear. To print more than one copy, type in the number required in the Copies box. Click on OK

PRINTING PART OF THE FILE To print just one part of the output, such as one table, click on it and then from the menu bar select

```
File
      Print...
```

The Print dialogue box will be presented; ensure the Selection alternative in the Print range area is checked and then press OK.

To print some parts of the output, select each of them in turn using the Ctrl + Click method of selecting a number of different items and then choose File /Print from the menu bar. You can preview the printout from File /Print Preview to confirm that you have made the selection of material that you want.

If you want to print all the tables (or all the notes, all the titles, etc.) in the output and nothing else, you can select them from the menu:

```
Edit
      Select
```

When you have selected the type of material you want to print, go to File /Print.

7.12 Transferring output to a word processor

Output from the Output Viewer can be imported into a word processor but it is necessary to use the Copy /Paste facility. Most of the material in the Output Viewer is tables, and to put them into a word processor such as Word97 you need to click on the table in SPSS and then select Edit /Copy. To make an exact copy of the SPSS table, open the word processor and use Edit /Paste Special. (Remember to use Edit /Paste Special, not Edit /Paste.) A window is shown, and it is important to select the Picture option. The table will then be pasted into Word and will look just as it did in the SPSS Output Viewer. It can be resized and moved around the window by using the handles.

If you want to put the table into the word processor so that you can edit it, paste it into the word processor with Edit /Paste. It will not look the same as it did in SPSS, but in Word97 it is in the table editor so you can alter the column widths and generally alter its appearance until it is how you want it.

If you have some straight text to import to a word processor, such as the commands printed before the tables of output, select it in the Output Viewer by clicking it and then select Edit /Copy. Open the word processor, and use Edit /Paste to put the text into the word processor file.

Output files from the Draft Viewer are simple rich text format files, saved with the filename extension .rtf. They can be loaded into a word processor directly. For example, if you are using Microsoft Word, you use the normal File /Open procedure and tell Word to list All Files (*.*) from the Files of Type drop-down list. Files with the suffix .rtf will then be shown in the set of file names and can be selected for opening.

7.13 Exporting output files to a web browser

In the output viewer, the menu entry File /Export allows the file to be exported either as a text file or in the .htm format for viewing in a web browser and editing. Charts can be exported in a number of formats including .bmp, .tif, .eps, .jpg and .cgm.

7.14 On-screen help on statistical terms

You may come across statistical terms in the output of your analyses which you do not understand or have temporarily forgotten. You can obtain an explanation of them by using the various Help systems. The main ones are obtained from the Help drop-down menu. The Statistics Coach is intended to help you decide which statistical procedure you need for a particular type of question. The Help /Topics gives access to a help file which explains statistical terms and SPSS's own terminology. Use the Index or Ask Me sections to find information you need.

You can obtain a short explanation of the terms in a dialogue box if you put the cursor over it and right click.

When you are viewing a table in the Output, it can be activated with a double click. Then a right-click on any terms in the table will open a menu and selecting the What's this? entry will show an explanation.

8

SYNTAX FILES

Summary

This chapter explains how to:

- use the Paste button to paste commands into a syntax window
- run commands from a syntax window by selecting them with the click/drag procedure and clicking on the Run current button or by using the Run drop-down menu
- save the syntax window as a syntax file
- add comments to the syntax by typing them in
- make a syntax window the designated window by clicking the ! button. Any fresh pastings of syntax will be appended to the bottom of the currently-designated window.

If you have followed the exercises in chapter 7, you carried out a simple analysis by selecting commands from the menu and clicking on OK. But I strongly urge you not to do that again! It is far better to store the commands in a syntax window and run them from there.

8.1 What is a syntax file?

A syntax file is a file containing the commands for the analyses you have requested expressed in SPSS's language. There are a number of reasons for always creating a syntax file of the commands you have selected. First, if you need to run an analysis again you do not have to go through the menus a second time; you can run the commands from the syntax window. Secondly, by saving the syntax window as a separate file you have a permanent copy to use again whenever you like. Thirdly, when you know the SPSS language for the analyses you want you can write the SPSS commands using a normal word processor, save them in text file form, import them into a syntax window and run them: so one can do the preparatory work even on a machine that does not have SPSS installed.

If you carried out the simple analyses contained in the previous chapter, you may have noticed that the dialogue box for the Frequencies procedure has a button labelled Paste. All the dialogue boxes which are used for selecting an analysis have a Paste button, and you are most strongly urged to use them every time you use SPSS. Pressing the Paste button pastes the SPSS language command for the procedure you have selected into a separate window, the syntax window. When you first start a session with SPSS there may not be a syntax window, but the first time you press Paste one is opened and the command you have created from your menu selections is pasted into it. As you make further menu selections and press Paste, the commands are added to the bottom of the set that already exists in the syntax window. Get in the habit of pressing Paste rather than OK!

8.2 Entering commands in a syntax window using Paste

When you have selected items from the on-screen menus, paste the commands into a syntax window by using the Paste button in the dialogue box for the procedure you have selected. If no syntax window is open the first time you use Paste, one is automatically opened to receive the commands you are pasting. Subsequent uses of Paste add the current commands to the syntax window, appending them to the existing contents. If you want to start pasting into a second syntax window, you need to open a new one, which you can do by selecting File /New /Syntax from the menu bar. Ensure it is the designated syntax window with a ! in the information bar on the bottom line. If necessary, make it the designated window by pressing the ! button in the icon bar. The syntax window can be saved as a file and edited.

Exercise 8.1

Repeat exercise 7.1 from chapter 7 but instead of pressing OK in the dialogue box, press Paste. The SPSS language for the Frequencies procedure will be pasted into a syntax window, shown in Figure 8.1.

Try running the command. Make sure the cursor is in the line containing the word FREQUENCIES and click the Run icon button in the application window icon bar; it has a right-pointing arrow in the lower right corner. SPSS will carry out the command and produce the output shown in Figure 7.5 in chapter 7.

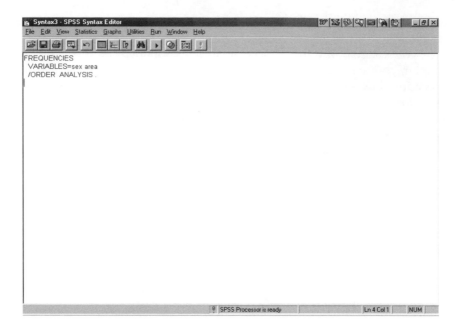

Figure 8.1   *The syntax window*

8.3 Structure of procedure commands

All commands must start on a new line, and must end in a full-stop
(period). So in Figure 8.1, the command starts with the word FRE-
QUENCIES and continues as far as the full stop. Although there are three
lines of text, this is one command. Subcommands are used to specify
how the procedure (FREQUENCIES in Figure 8.1) should operate. For
example, VARIABLES = sex area is a subcommand which indicates that
the procedure should be applied to the variables sex and area in the data
set. Subcommands are separated (usually) by the / character.

8.4 Running the commands from a syntax window

The benefit of a syntax file is that you can run all or some of the
commands it contains directly, without having to go through the process
of making menu selections again. An example of a syntax window
containing a series of commands is shown in Figure 8.2. To identify the
commands to run, select them with the click/drag procedure (or from
the keyboard by holding down shift and using the up/down arrow
keys), so they are highlighted, and then click on the Run button. If you
want to run all or some of the commands, use the syntax window's
menu bar Run entry and then click on All, Selection, Current or To End.
To run just one command, put the cursor anywhere in the line containing
the command and click on the Run icon button.

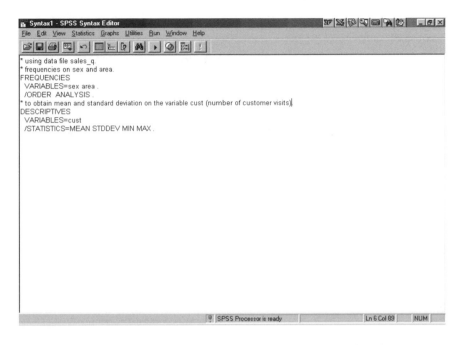

```
* using data file sales_q.
* frequencies on sex and area.
FREQUENCIES
 VARIABLES=sex area .
 /ORDER  ANALYSIS .
* to obtain mean and standard deviation on the variable cust (number of customer visits)
DESCRIPTIVES
 VARIABLES=cust
 /STATISTICS=MEAN STDDEV MIN MAX .
```

Figure 8.2 *Example of a syntax window containing a series of commands and comment lines*

8.5 Saving the syntax window as a syntax file

SAVING THE SYNTAX FILE FOR THE FIRST TIME   To save the contents of the syntax window as a file on a floppy, check that the window is active and select from the Application window menu bar

```
File
      Save As ...
```

The dialogue box presented is the same as that for saving data or output files. Type the name of the file into the File Name box. Open the Save In drop-down list and click on the icon for the a: drive. Click on the Save button. The file is saved with the filename extension .sps.

SAVING A PREVIOUSLY SAVED SYNTAX FILE AFTER EDITING IT   Any changes you make to a syntax file will be lost unless you save the file. Ensure the window is active and select from the menu bar

```
File
```

To save the current version of the file, overwriting previous ones, select

```
Save
```

The new version will be saved on the same drive from which it was retrieved.

To save the current version while keeping the previous one, select

```
Save As ...
```

which will present the Save As dialogue box. Type in a new name for the file; remember it must not contain a blank space. Check that the Save as Type shows the file will have the .sps extension, or open the drop-down list and select that alternative. Open the Drives drop-down list and click on the icon for the a: drive. Click on the Save button.

8.6 Retrieving a saved syntax file from disk

In versions 8 or 9, to retrieve an existing syntax file, select

```
File
     Open
```

If you are using SPSS version 10, select

```
File
     Open
          Syntax
```

A dialogue box will appear. Check that Files of Type shows syntax (.sps): if it does not, open the drop-down list and select this option. If the file is on a floppy disk, open the Drives drop-down list and click on the icon for the a: drive. The files on the floppy which have the filename extension .sps will appear in the list of files. Click on the name of the file you want to open, check that its name appears in the File Name text box, and click on the Open button.

8.7 Opening another syntax window

The first time you use a Paste button, a syntax window is opened automatically. But you can open a new (empty) one by selecting from the window menu

```
File
     New
          Syntax
```

You can have more than one syntax window open at one time, but as with output files only one can be the 'designated' window to which commands are pasted, and from which commands can be run. You know which is the designated window because it has an exclamation mark in the bottom line, the information area. To make a syntax window the designated window, while viewing it click on the ! icon button in the icon bar. Any fresh pastings of syntax will be appended to the bottom of the currently-designated window.

8.8 Transferring syntax files to a word processor

Syntax files are simple text files. So a syntax .sps file prepared in SPSS can be loaded into a word processor and reformatted and printed from there.

8.9 Loading a text file into a syntax window

You can type SPSS syntax using a word processor, and save the file in text format. The text file can be copied and pasted into a syntax window, so that if you are familiar with the exact syntax you can prepare your syntax file's contents on a machine that does not have SPSS installed. When using a word processor, each line of data or commands must be ended with a carriage-return. It should be saved in the word processor as a text file, preferably with the filename extension .sps. It can then be opened within SPSS as a syntax file.

Assume you have written a text file of SPSS syntax and stored it on a floppy disk with the filename syn.sps. To load it into SPSS, select from the Application window menu bar

```
File
    Open
```

When the dialogue box appears, open the Look In drop-down list and click on the icon for the a: drive. The File of Type box needs to show Syntax (.sps); if it shows something else, open the drop-down list and select the Syntax option. The list of .sps files on the disk will then be shown and you can click on the name of the file you want. Then click on Open and the file will then appear in a syntax window.

8.10 Entering commands in a syntax window by typing

You can edit the contents of a syntax window just like any other text file, and type straight into it. This is beneficial to those who are familiar with the command language of SPSS, but if you are not experienced with SPSS be careful when trying to create commands directly. The syntax of commands is not simple, and there are a number of rules you must follow. For example, all command lines must start on a new line, and must end in a full-stop (period). Subcommands are separated (usually) by /.

To enter the names of variables in the commands in the syntax window, you can readily type them in. Or you can use the Variables dialogue box which is obtained from the Utilities / Variables menu of the syntax window. This displays a dialogue box and you can select a variable from the list in the left-hand side of the box. Information about the variable appears in the right-hand window. If the Paste button at the bottom of the window is clicked, the highlighted variable name is pasted into the syntax window at the point where the cursor was located. This is rather laborious and most users will probably find this method not worth the effort.

Exercise 8.2

Try editing the contents of the syntax window created in Exercise 8.1 so that you obtain a Frequencies analysis of the data on the variable att1. To do this, while viewing the syntax window move the cursor (using the mouse) so it is to the right of the words sex area and click the mouse to anchor the insertion point. Use the backspace Delete key to delete these words and type in att1 in their place. Then run the command by clicking the Run icon button. SPSS should then run the commands, and give you in the Output1 window the results of applying the frequencies procedure to the variable att1.

8.11 Typing comments into the syntax window

It is always worthwhile adding comments to the syntax so that later you will be reminded of what a particular procedure achieves. For example, you might want to add the explanatory comment that the command calculates the mean for a certain variable.

Add comments to the syntax by typing them in, but make sure that the line begins with an asterisk * and ends with a full stop. An acceptable comment line would be

```
* This calculates mean on cust.
```

If you omit either the * or the full stop, SPSS will not understand and will give you an error message when you try to run the syntax window's contents.

8.12 Help on syntax: the Syntax button in a syntax window

When you are using a syntax window, pressing the Syntax help icon in the icon bar will provide help information about the procedure on the current line of the syntax file. The help information can be highly complex, consisting of material from the SPSS technical manuals, and is likely to be meaningful only to those who have a thorough under-standing of SPSS commands. Nevertheless, you may find it valuable once you have developed some expertise with the package. So do try using the facility, but do not be depressed if the result is not very helpful.

8.13 Printing syntax files

To print the file, while viewing it select from the window menu bar

```
File
     Print
```

The Print dialogue box will appear. By default, one copy of the whole file will be printed. To print more than one copy, type in the number required in the Copies box. Click on OK.

PRINTING PART OF THE FILE Highlight the area to be printed using the click/drag technique, and then select File /Print from the menus. When the Print dialogue box appears, check that the Selection radio button is selected and click on OK.

As a syntax file is a simple text file it can be loaded into a word processor and printed from there.

8.14 Altering the page size for printing

To omit page breaks so you get just one continuous printing or to have the output fit A4 paper, change the page size from the dialogue box presented when you choose Edit /Options, as explained in section 7.1.

9

TAKING A PRELIMINARY LOOK AT THE DATA

Summary

This chapter explains how to:

- use Explore to obtain an overview of the data, to discover any possible errors in the data file
- use Explore to find the mean, median, standard error, variance, standard deviation, minimum, maximum, range, interquartile range (IQR), and indices of skew
- display the cases with the five largest and five smallest values on any variables
- obtain stem-leaf plot and boxplots
- investigate whether subgroups show homogeneity of variance and whether the scores are normally distributed
- use Case Summaries to obtain a listing of the data file.

9.1 Checking the data

Before proceeding with detailed statistical investigation, it is always worth having an overview of the data to reveal any peculiarities or possible errors in the data file. If you have coded sex as 1 for male, 2 for female, 3 for missing value (i.e. sex is unknown), then any respondent with a sex score of 8 has obviously been miscoded. It is crucial to make sure the data is correct before analysing it, and so the first step once the data file has been created is to search for possible coding errors. The SPSS procedures Explore and Case Summaries allow you to do this. The most useful is Explore.

9.2 Running the analyses

If you have completed the example exercises described in previous chapters, you will be familiar with the techniques used to get SPSS for Windows to carry out an analysis:

- Select the appropriate menu (e.g. Analyze) from the menu bar to reveal a drop-down menu;
- Select the appropriate entry (Descriptive Statistics, Compare Means, etc.) from the drop-down menu;
- Select the appropriate entry from the next submenu (e.g. Frequencies, Descriptives, etc.);
- When presented with a dialogue box for the procedure you are requesting, specify the variables to be analysed;
- Click on Paste to have the procedure commands you have selected pasted into a syntax window;
- Click on the Run icon button or use the Run drop-down menu.

The output appears in the Output window.

Once you have learned how to use the various dialogue box options, the procedure should be straightforward. To alter any of the choices you made in the dialogue box, you merely have to get back to it by working through the menu selection process, and then you can change the choices you made and paste the revised commands into the syntax window. Alternatively, you can edit the commands in the syntax file by typing directly into it, as described in chapter 8.

9.3 Exploring the averages and distributions of scores using Explore

Note: Although the Explore command is selected from the menu, it is named Examine in the syntax window.

The Explore procedure allows you to find the mean, median, and standard deviation of the scores on any or all of the variables. It provides you with measures of skewness in the distribution, gives box plots and shows the maximum and minimum scores so you can see if there are any aberrant values that might indicate a coding error when the data was keyed in.

The Explore procedure is obtained from

```
Analyze
    Descriptive Statistics
        Explore...
```

When presented with the dialogue box illustrated in Figure 9.1, specify the variables to be analysed by adding them to the Dependent List text area and Paste the command into a syntax window. Run the procedure by clicking the Run icon or using the Run drop-down menu, to obtain a printout as shown in Figure 9.2 which Explored the variable cust in the file salesq.

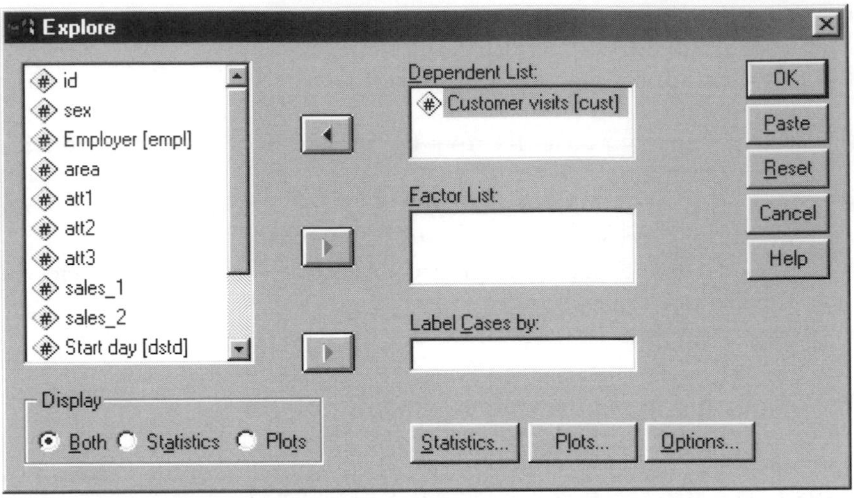

Figure 9.1   *The dialogue box for the Explore procedure*

Figure 9.2 shows two tables, the Case Processing summary which gives the number of cases and the number of missing cases, and then the Descriptives tables provide a range of statistics including the mean, median, standard error, variance, standard deviation, minimum, maximum, range, interquartile range, and indices of skew. The 5% Trimmed Mean figure is the mean of the scores when the most extreme 10% of the scores are omitted from the calculation: the highest 5% of scores and the lowest 5% of scores are both deleted before this mean is calculated. The trimmed mean can be a useful indicator of the 'average', less influenced by one or two extreme, outlying scores than the simple arithmetic mean.

The figure for skewness indicates how non-symmetric the distribution is. A positive value on kurtosis indicates that the distribution of the scores has heavier tails than a normal distribution curve. The values for both skewness and kurtosis will be close to zero if the distribution is normally distributed.

The stem-leaf plot is similar to a histogram but numbers indicate the actual values plotted. The first column, headed Frequency, shows the number of scores in the band indicated by the stem. For example, the first line of the stem-leaf part of Figure 9.2 shows there was one respondent who scored in the twenties on customers visited (the stem is 2). The actual score of this respondent was 28 (the leaf is 8, so the actual score is 2, the stem, and 8 the leaf).

The Explore dialogue box allows you to refine the analysis further. From the Display area of the box, you can ask for the output to show statistics, plots (stem-leaf plot) or both, which is the default option. To obtain a histogram, press the Plots button and select histogram.

```
EXAMINE
  VARIABLES=cust
  /PLOT BOXPLOT STEMLEAF
  /COMPARE GROUP
  /STATISTICS DESCRIPTIVES
  /CINTERVAL 95
  /MISSING LISTWISE
  /NOTOTAL.
```

Case Processing Summary

	Cases					
	Valid		Missing		Total	
	N	Percent	N	Percent	N	Percent
Customer visits	22	100.0%	0	.0%	22	100.0%

Descriptives

			Statistic	Std. Error
Customer visits	Mean		50.8182	3.6269
	95% Confidence Interval for Mean	Lower Bound	43.2757	
		Upper Bound	58.3607	
	5% Trimmed Mean		50.3081	
	Median		44.5000	
	Variance		289.394	
	Std. Deviation		17.0116	
	Minimum		28.00	
	Maximum		83.00	
	Range		55.00	
	Interquartile Range		30.0000	
	Skewness		.605	.491
	Kurtosis		-1.000	.953

```
Customer visits Stem-and-Leaf Plot

Frequency    Stem &  Leaf

     1.00      2 .  8
     6.00      3 .  036899
     7.00      4 .  0123688
     1.00      5 .  8
     2.00      6 .  08
     4.00      7 .  1269
     1.00      8 .  3

Stem width:     10.00
Each leaf:       1 case(s)
```

Continued on next page

It is possible to have Explore display the cases with the 5 largest and 5 smallest values on any variables, which is useful for identifying aberrant, possibly mis-keyed items of data. After pressing the Statistics button in the Explore dialogue box of Figure 9.1, select Outliers; an example of the output is shown in Figure 9.3. It shows the five smallest and five largest scores on the variable, together with the case number of those scores. The case number is the number assigned to each case by the system when it

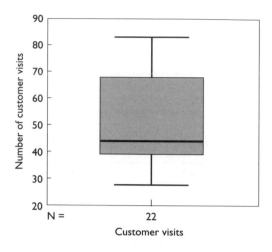

Figure 9.2   *Output from the command Explore/Variable cust*

reads the data file; the first case is row number 1 in the data table, the second is row number 2 and so on. The data file salesq includes ids (identification numbers), which are for this particular set of data the same as the case number, since they count up from 1 in regular sequence. But many data files do not do this: the ids may not be in sequence. Assuming you have a variable labeled id in the data file, you can tell Explore to print the entries on the variable id by inserting id into the Label Cases By box of the Explore dialogue box shown in Figure 9.1.

To obtain further statistics, click on the Statistics button of Figure 9.1. You can request maximum-likelihood estimators of location such as M-estimator which provide estimates of the central tendency when extreme values are given less weight than more central values. Percentiles are also available.

Explore will exclude from the analysis any case that has data missing on any of the variables to be explored. You can alter this by selecting the Options button of Figure 9.1; the box revealed lets you choose Exclude Cases Pairwise, which means that every case that has data for the variable being Explored will be included in the analysis of that variable. So the number of cases Explored for different variables will fluctuate: a case that has missing data on the variable sex will not be included in the analysis of sex, but if the same case does have data for the variable area then it will be included when that variable is Explored.

If you have cases where there is no data on the variables that make up the Factor List, these cases can be made into a separate category or group of respondents by selecting the Report Values option. Their scores on the variables being Explored will then be reported.

```
EXAMINE
  VARIABLES=cust
  /PLOT NONE
  /COMPARE GROUP
  /STATISTICS EXTREME
  /MISSING LISTWISE
  /NOTOTAL.
```

Case Processing Summary

	Cases					
	Valid		Missing		Total	
	N	Percent	N	Percent	N	Percent
Customer visits	22	100.0%	0	.0%	22	100.0%

Extreme Values

			Case Number	Value
Customer visits	Highest	1	4	83.00
		2	16	79.00
		3	10	76.00
		4	6	72.00
		5	5	71.00
	Lowest	1	8	28.00
		2	12	30.00
		3	14	33.00
		4	15	36.00
		5	17	38.00

Figure 9.3   *Using Explore to list outliers, the extreme scores on a variable*

You may wish the scores to be analysed separately for subgroups of cases, depending on their scores on one or more of the variables. For example, in salesq, suppose we want to Explore the scores on sales_1 for men and women. Here sex is a factor variable, and we would need to have this variable inserted into the Factor List text box in Figure 9.1. You can have a number of Factor variables; if sex and area are inserted into the Factor List, SPSS would Explore the scores of the variables listed in the Dependent List for each level of sex and then for each level of area. Figure 9.4 shows the output when the command was to Explore sales_1 by sex.

From menus, you cannot ask for separate analyses of subgroups defined by combining scores on separate Factor variables: so you cannot get an analysis broken down into men from one area, men from the second area, women from the first area and women from the second area. To achieve this, you have to paste the command into a syntax file, and then edit it so that it separates the factor variables with the word BY. If we wanted the scores on sales_1 to be analysed for each sex subdivided by area, the syntax file command would have to read:

```
EXAMINE VARIABLES=sales_1 BY sex BY area.
```

```
EXAMINE
  VARIABLES=sales_1 BY sex
  /PLOT BOXPLOT STEMLEAF
  /COMPARE GROUP
  /STATISTICS DESCRIPTIVES
  /CINTERVAL 95
  /MISSING LISTWISE
  /NOTOTAL.
```

Case Processing Summary

		Cases					
		Valid		Missing		Total	
SEX		N	Percent	N	Percent	N	Percent
SALES_1	male	10	100.0%	0	.0%	10	100.0%
	female	11	100.0%	0	.0%	11	100.0%

Descriptives

SEX				Statistic	Std. Error
SALES_1	male	Mean		5950.6370	876.7274
		95% Confidence Interval for Mean	Lower Bound	3967.3418	
			Upper Bound	7933.9322	
		5% Trimmed Mean		5920.8122	
		Median		5353.9700	
		Variance		7686509	
		Std. Deviation		2772.4555	
		Minimum		2005.30	
		Maximum		10432.82	
		Range		8427.52	
		Interquartile Range		4678.4450	
		Skewness		.266	.687
		Kurtosis		-1.233	1.334
	female	Mean		5723.9964	629.9147
		95% Confidence Interval for Mean	Lower Bound	4320.4591	
			Upper Bound	7127.5337	
		5% Trimmed Mean		5693.0248	
		Median		5822.6800	
		Variance		4364717	
		Std. Deviation		2089.1906	
		Minimum		3124.20	
		Maximum		8881.28	
		Range		5757.08	
		Interquartile Range		4047.3400	
		Skewness		.396	.661
		Kurtosis		-1.275	1.279

Continued on facing page

9.4 Boxplots of score distributions from Explore

Boxplots such as those shown in Figure 9.2 and 9.4 summarize the scores on a variable by displaying the median (as an asterisk), the 25th and 75th percentiles as the lower and upper edges of a box surrounding the median. The box length represents the interquartile range of the scores. Outliers are any cases which are between 1.5 and 3 boxlengths from the edge of the box, and Extremes are more than 3 boxlengths away. Lines are drawn from the edge of the box to the largest and smallest values which are not outliers.

```
SALES_1 Stem-and-Leaf Plot for
SEX= male

Frequency      Stem &  Leaf

    5.00         0 .  23344
    4.00         0 .  5788
    1.00         1 .  0

Stem width:   10000.00
Each leaf:        1 case(s)


SALES_1 Stem-and-Leaf Plot for
SEX= female

Frequency      Stem &  Leaf

    3.00         3 .  148
    2.00         4 .  25
    2.00         5 .  88
    1.00         6 .  4
    1.00         7 .  8
    2.00         8 .  78

Stem width:    1000.00
Each leaf:        1 case(s)
```

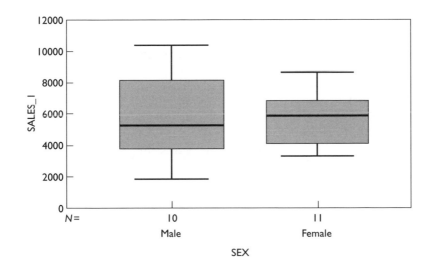

Figure 9.4 *Extract of output from the command Explore Variables sales_1 by sex*

A boxplot allows you to make a number of 'eyeball' judgments about the distribution of the scores. The median is the indicator of the central value, and the length of the box indicates the variability of the scores. If the median is not in the middle of the box, the distribution of scores is skewed.

Explore provides boxplots automatically, but pressing the Plots button of Figure 9.1 opens a dialogue box in which you can specify the characteristics of the boxplots or suppress them completely, and ask for a histogram. The box plot options are Factor Levels Together, which is used for comparing subgroups of respondents (see Figure 9.4 for an example), and Dependents Together which is used to compare the scores of one set of respondents on a number of variables. When plots are selected, the output is shown in the Viewer. Details on saving and printing charts are provided in chapter 10.

9.5 Do subgroups show homogeneity of variance?

If you select the Plots button from the Explore dialogue box (Figure 9.1), the section entitled Spread vs. Level with Levene Test allows you to request plots of the spread of scores against the level of the scores, and to test whether the subsets of scores show homogeneity of variance.

Imagine we wanted to know whether in the data file salesq the variability of the scores of men and women on sales_1 was equal: the Levene test is one method of investigating this. You obtain the test by having at least one Factor List variable and then selecting the Plot button from Explore's dialogue box, and choosing Untransformed. (If subgroups of respondents show unequal variances on the variables being compared, you may wish to apply a transformation to the raw data. There are options for applying various transformations to the data, or leaving it untransformed.) If the Levene test is significant, reject the null hypothesis that the groups have equal variances.

As well as the Levene test, this procedure gives a boxplot and a graph showing the spread of scores (interquartile range) in each group plotted against the level (median). An example of this type of plot is shown in Figure 9.5. It permits one to see how variability varies with average level.

9.6 Are the scores normally distributed?

If you select the Plots button from the Explore dialogue box (Figure 9.1), the Normality Plots with Tests button provides a graph of the data plotted in such a way that it would be a straight line if the data were normally distributed. This is described as a Normal Q–Q plot, and an example is shown in Figure 9.6. If the data is not normally distributed, the points will differ from the straight line, and the amount by which they differ is itself plotted as a detrended normal plot also shown in Figure 9.6. If the data were normally distributed, the detrended plot would be a horizontal line passing through 0. These plots allow you to judge visually whether the data is normally distributed.

```
EXAMINE
  VARIABLES=sales_1 BY sex
  /PLOT BOXPLOT STEMLEAF SPREADLEVEL(1)
  /COMPARE GROUP
  /STATISTICS DESCRIPTIVES
  /CINTERVAL 95
  /MISSING LISTWISE
  /NOTOTAL.
```

Test of Homogeneity of Variance

		Levene Statistic	df1	df2	Sig.
SALES_1	Based on Mean	1.552	1	19	.228
	Based on Median	1.114	1	19	.305
	Based on Median and with adjusted df	1.114	1	17.390	.306
	Based on trimmed mean	1.498	1	19	.236

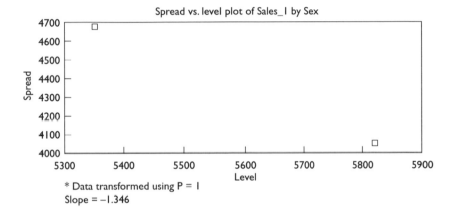

* Data transformed using P = 1
Slope = −1.346

Figure 9.5 *Example of output from Explore: Plot Spread vs. Level*

Tests of whether a set of data is normally distributed are the Kolmogorov–Smirnov test and the Shapiro–Wilks test (when the number of scores is less than 50), and these are calculated and the probability values shown when you ask for Normal plots with tests. A low significance value means that the scores are not normally distributed, but with large sets of data non-perfect normal distribution is almost certain to occur and so the interpretation of these tests should be treated cautiously: the visual displays indicate how non-normal the distribution is.

9.7 Obtaining a listing of the data using Case Summaries

A listing of the data merely reproduces the lines from the data file, and is probably less helpful than printing the data file itself. To obtain a simple listing of the data, select

```
EXAMINE
  VARIABLES=sales_1
  /PLOT  NPPLOT
  /STATISTICS DESCRIPTIVES
  /CINTERVAL 95
  /MISSING LISTWISE
  /NOTOTAL.
```

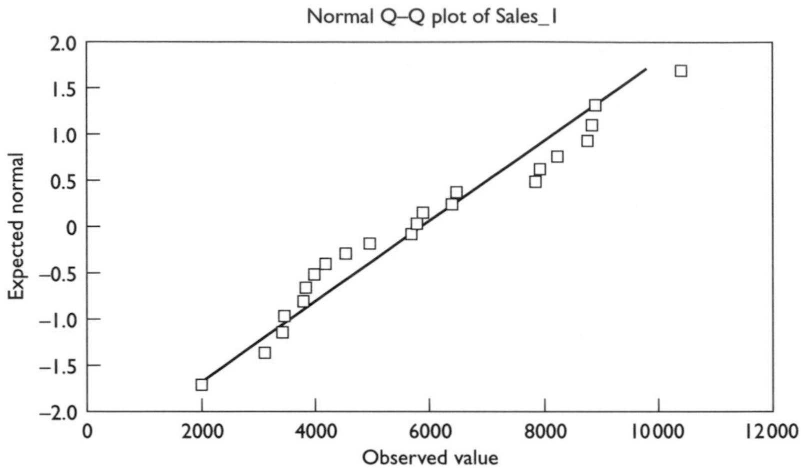

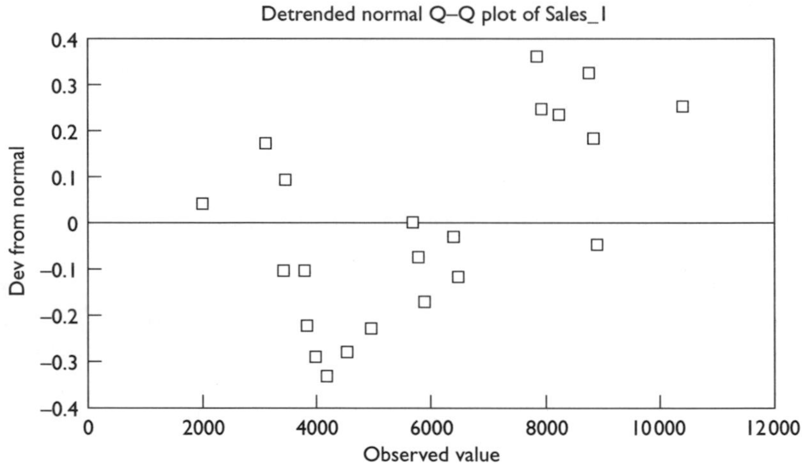

Normal Q–Q plot of Sales_1

Detrended normal Q–Q plot of Sales_1

Figure 9.6   *Example of normal plot output from Explore: Plot Npplot*

```
Analyze
     Reports
          Case Summaries
```

The dialogue box requires you to specify which variables should be listed. The box area entitled Limit Cases to First lets you indicate whether you want to limit the output to the first 100 cases. This can be changed by typing a number into the box. (If you ask for the first 20, these will be the first 20 rows of the data file.) You can have the case number included in the listing by checking Show Case Numbers from the bottom of the dialogue box; remember this is the number of the row in the Data Editor table, not any identification number which you may have added as a variable (such as id in the salesq data file).

Further details on this facility are given in section 21.3.

10

GRAPHS

Summary

This chapter explains how to:

- use Interactive Graphs to obtain various types of graph
- use Interactive Graphs to edit graphs
- obtain histograms, barcharts, stem-and-leaf plots and box plots using the Analyze /Descriptive Statistics /Frequencies or /Explore menus
- obtain scattergrams and other types of chart by using the Graphs menu
- edit charts in the Chart Editor
- suppress any missing values from being plotted
- save, retrieve, print charts and transfer them to other applications.

Version 8 of SPSS introduced a feature known as interactive graphs, which is available from the Graphs drop-down menu. It is intended to make it much easier to create graphs than using the Graphs menu itself. But note that although the Interactive Graphs facility produces visually impressive output comparatively easily, it does not always provide more complex graphs such as the clustered bar chart (Figure 10.10) or the multiple line graph (Figure 10.15). To achieve these more complex graphs, use the Graphs menu. The way interactive graphs operate will be described first, and then the more traditional ways of creating graphs in SPSS will be covered.

10.1 Creating graphs using Interactive Graphs

The Interactive Graphs facility is available from

```
Graphs
    Interactive
```

This offers a list of alternative types of graph. How to create bar graphs, line graphs, histograms, scatterplots and ribbon graphs will be described here. Once the basic idea of how to use Interactive Graphs has been grasped, you will be able to investigate the mass of facilities which are available.

When an interactive graph is being created as explained in the following sections, you make selection from tabbed pages like those shown in Figure 10.3. One of the tabs is headed Options and offers a list of alternative ChartLooks. These are pre-designed styles and you can select one of them to give an impressively professional appearance to your graph.

Note that when a graph has been created using Interactive Graphs, it can be edited by double-clicking on it. It will then be surrounded by an editing frame, illustrated in Figure 10.1. Moving the mouse cursor over the various icons will, after a few seconds delay, reveal an explanation of what each does. In addition, putting the cursor over an element of the graph and right-clicking will open a relevant drop-down menu which allows modification of that part of the display. There is yet another feature: an icon in the top icon bar of Figure 10.1 opens the Chart Manager, shown in Figure 10.2. The Chart Contents are listed, and when one of these is selected, the Edit button can be pressed to reveal further windows which allow editing of the element selected. So the alternatives are enormous; the only way to deal with all these possibilities is to experiment, keeping notes on what you did and which selections you made so you can repeat it if needed in the future!

10.2 Bar graphs from Interactive Graphs

From the menu select

```
Graphs
        Interactive
                Bar...
```

and the window shown in Figure 10.3 will be revealed. Move the variable to be plotted on the vertical axis from the variable list to the textbox on the vertical axis using the click/drag procedure, and do the same to allocate a variable to the horizontal axis. Only when you have done this will the Bars Represent feature appear in the window. If you open the drop-down list you will find that the bars can represent many different statistics apart from the mean.

To produce separate graphs for each level of a variable, enter the variable into the Panel Variables box. For example, if sex is entered as a panel variable, separate graphs for males and females are obtained.

As is indicated in Figure 10.3, there are tabbed pages which allow you to set the characteristics of the bars, add a title, etc.

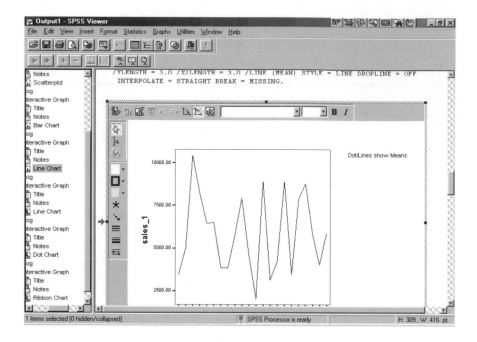

Figure 10.1 *An interactive graph prepared for editing*

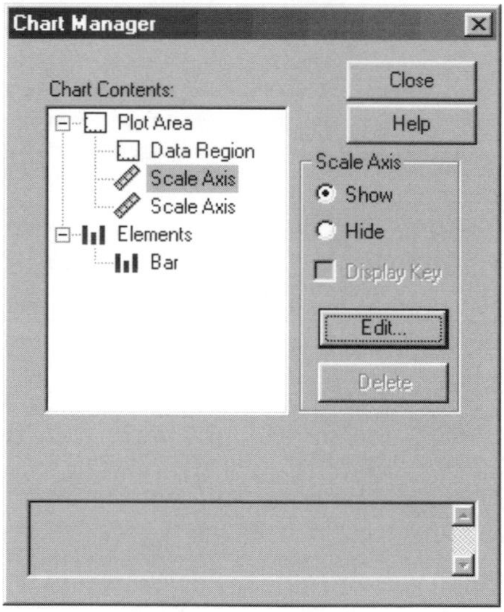

Figure 10.2 *The Chart Manager for editing an interactive graph*

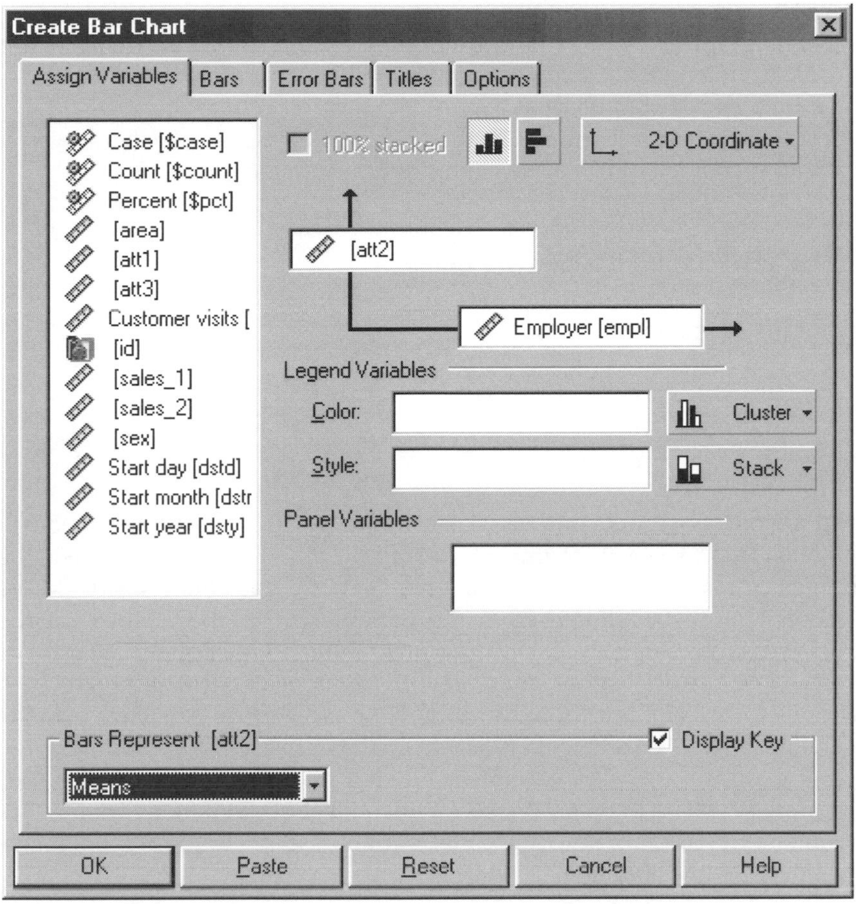

Figure 10.3 *The window for creating a bar chart using Graph Interactive*

10.3 Line graphs from Interactive Graphs

From the menu select

```
Graphs
      Interactive
            Line...
```

and a window similar to that shown in Figure 10.3 will be revealed but with the title Create Lines. Move the variable to be plotted on the vertical axis from the variable list to the textbox on the vertical axis using the click/drag procedure, and do the same to allocate a variable to the horizontal axis. Only when you have done this will the Lines and Dots Represent feature appear in the window. If you open the drop-down list you will find that the lines can represent many different statistics apart from the mean. If a variable is entered into the Panel Variables box, separate graphs will be produced for each level of the panel variable. For example, by entering sex as a panel variable, separate graphs for males and females are obtained.

As is indicated in Figure 10.3, there are tabbed pages which allow you to set the characteristics of the lines, add a title, etc.

10.4 Histograms from Interactive Graphs

From the menu select

```
Graphs
      Interactive
            Histogram...
```

and a window similar to that shown in Figure 10.3 will be revealed but with the title Create Histogram. A histogram plots on the vertical axis the frequency (as a number or as a percentage) of a variable's scores. Move the variable to be plotted from the variable list to the textbox on the horizontal axis using the click/drag procedure. To have the histogram of percentage values rather than actual frequencies, use click/drag to remove Count ($count) from the textbox on the vertical axis back into the variable list and take Percent ($pct) from the variable list and put it in the vertical axis textbox. If a variable is entered into the Panel variables box, separate graphs will be produced for each level of the panel variable. For example, by entering sex as a panel variable, separate graphs for males and females are obtained.

As is indicated in Figure 10.3, there are tabbed pages which allow you to set the characteristics of the histogram, add a title, etc. Three-dimensional effects and a superimposed normal curve are available from the Histogram tab.

10.5 Scatterplots from Interactive Graphs

From the menu select

```
Graphs
      Interactive
            Scatterplot...
```

and a window similar to that shown in Figure 10.3 will be revealed but with the title Create Scatterplot. Move the variable to be plotted on the vertical axis from the variable list to the textbox on the vertical axis using the click/drag procedure, and do the same to allocate a variable to the horizontal axis. If a variable is entered into the Panel Variables box, separate graphs will be produced for each level of the panel variable. For example, by entering sex as a panel variable, separate graphs for males and females are obtained.

As is indicated in Figure 10.3, there are tabbed pages which allow you to set the characteristics of the lines, add a title, etc. To have a regression line fitted to the data, use the Fit tab.

10.6 Ribbon graphs from Interactive Graphs

A simple example of a ribbon graph is shown in Figure 10.4. Although these can look impressive you are advised to use them, if at all, with care. They can detract from accurate communication, and may be more appropriate for a commercial presentation rather than a scientific report. If you decide to try them out, from the menu select

```
Graphs
     Interactive
          Ribbon...
```

and a window similar to that shown in Figure 10.3 will be revealed but with the title Create Ribbons. Move the variable to be plotted on the vertical axis from the variable list to the textbox on the vertical axis using the click/drag procedure, and do the same to allocate a variable to the horizontal axis. Only when you have done this will the Ribbons Represent feature appear in the window. If you open the drop-down list you will find that the lines can represent many different statistics apart from the mean. If a variable is entered into the Panel Variables box, separate graphs will be produced for each level of the panel variable. For example, by entering sex as a panel variable, separate graphs for males and females are obtained.

As is indicated in Figure 10.3, there are tabbed pages which allow you to set the characteristics of the ribbons, add a title, etc. When you have obtained a ribbon graph in the Output Viewer, double click on it to invoke the editing facilities. Among many other things, the ribbon graph can be rotated in both left-right and up-down dimensions, which is fun to do if not immediately of any great use.

10.7 Histograms, barcharts and piecharts from Frequencies

Histograms and barcharts, stem-and-leaf plots and box plots showing the distribution of scores on a variable are obtained from the Analyze /Descriptive Statistics /Frequencies menu. Scattergrams and all other types of chart, including more complex barcharts and histograms, are

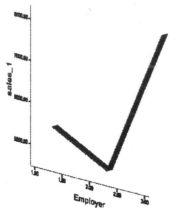

Figure 10.4   *Example of a ribbon graph*

obtained by using the Graphs menu, which is covered in later sections of this chapter.

Histograms and barcharts have a superficial similarity in that they both represent data as the length of a bar on a chart. A histogram such as that shown in Figure 10.5 is used to show a frequency distribution when the variable being plotted is continuous. With large sets of data, it may be necessary to group the scores into intervals before plotting a histogram. For example, if you have data on people's age you might group them into intervals of 0–20 years old, 21–40 years old, etc. as explained in section 12.6.

Barcharts are used to show a distribution of scores on a noncontinuous or categorical variable. For example, Figure 10.6 is a barchart of scores on the variable sex; the categories of sex are not continuous and the bars are separated rather than being adjacent to each other as they are in the histogram of Figure 10.5. In SPSS, a histogram shows an empty space for a value having no cases, whereas a barchart does not: any category having no entries will be omitted from the graph. Piecharts, such as Figure 10.7, are an alternative way of presenting the data.

Histograms, barcharts and piecharts of the distribution of the scores on variables in the data file can be obtained from

```
Analyze
      Descriptive Statistics
            Frequencies
```

Click on the Charts button of the dialogue box to reveal another. You can ask for histograms, barcharts or piecharts, ask for a normal curve to be superimposed on a histogram, for barcharts or piecharts to plot actual frequencies or percentages. Click on Continue, then on the Paste button in the Frequencies dialogue box and run the syntax to obtain the graph.

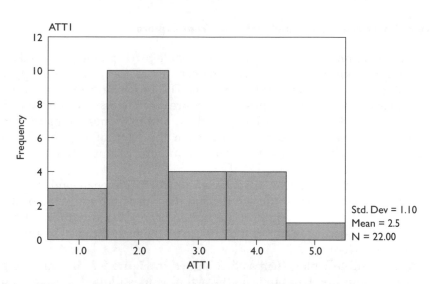

Figure 10.5   *Example of histogram showing distribution of scores on att I*

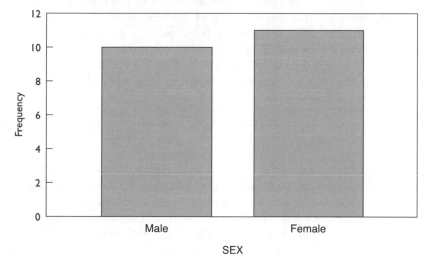

Figure 10.6   *Example of barchart showing frequency of scores on the variable sex*

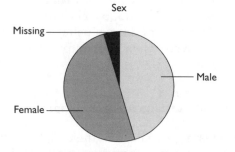

Figure 10.7   *Example of piechart showing frequency of scores on the variable sex*

10.8 Boxplots and stem-and-leaf plots from Explore

A boxplot summarizes the scores on a variable by displaying the median (as an asterisk), the 25th and 75th percentiles as the lower and upper edges of a box surrounding the median. The box length represents the interquartile range of the scores. Outliers are cases which are between 1.5 and 3 boxlengths from the edge of the box, and Extremes are more than 3 boxlengths away. Lines are drawn from the edge of the box to the largest and smallest values which are not outliers. Examples are given in Figures 9.2 and 9.4.

The boxplot allows you to make a number of 'eyeball' judgements about the distribution of the scores. The median is the indicator of the central value, and the length of the box indicates the variability of the scores. If the median is not in the middle of the box, the distribution of scores is skewed.

A stem-and-leaf plot, such as that shown in Figure 9.2, is similar to a histogram, but numbers indicate the actual values plotted. The column headed Frequency shows the number of scores in the band indicated by the stem. For example, the first line of the stem-leaf plot in Figure 9.2 shows there was one respondent who scored in the twenties on customers visited (the stem is 2). The actual score of this respondent was 28 (the leaf is 8, so the actual score is 2, the stem, and 8 the leaf).

Stem-and-leaf plots, histograms, boxplots and spread-by-level plots can be obtained from

```
Analyze
     Descriptive Statistics
          Explore
```

Identify the variable(s) to be plotted by entering them into the Dependent List. If data from subgroups of cases are to be plotted separately, enter the variable for separating the subgroups into the Factor List box. In Figure 9.4, scores on sales_1 are plotted for each sex separately, since sex was entered into the Factor List. Clicking the Plots button opens the dialogue box shown in Figure 10.8. Select Stem-and-leaf or Histogram or both and then click the Continue button, and Paste.

When the Explore /Plots procedure has run, the output is shown in the Viewer. If you want to edit it, double-click on it and it will be opened in a window titled SPSS Chart Editor which is described in section 10.15 below. The chart is saved when the output file (with the filename extension .spo) is saved.

10.9 Graphs, charts and scattergrams from Graphs

The basic steps in creating a chart from the Graphs menu are straightforward, but there are numerous alternatives in format. It would be tedious

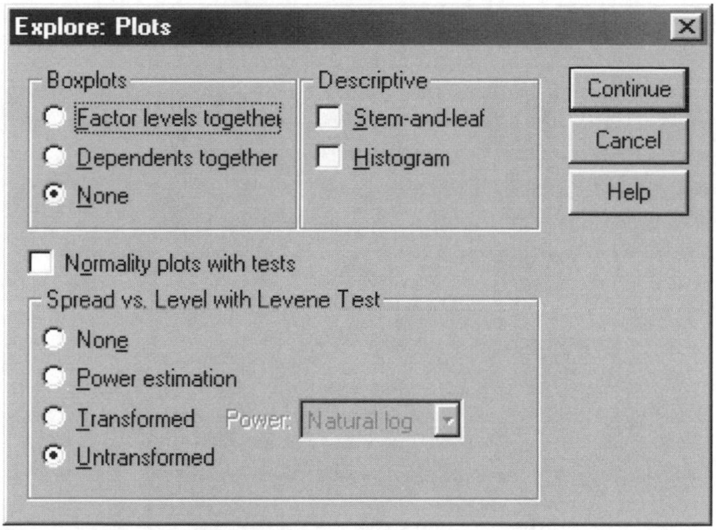

Figure 10.8   *The Explore Plots dialogue box*

and unnecessary to describe them all here. Once the user is familiar with the basic steps, there should be little difficulty in investigating the other features available.

To create a chart via the Graphs menu, you must have a data file open. Open the Graphs drop-down menu, and select the type of chart you want to create. Note that the first entry in the menu list, Gallery, shows the types of graph available and provides immediate access to help and instructions on creating charts. The menu offers a barchart, line graph, area chart, pie chart, boxplot, scattergram, histogram and others. The system will guide you through a series of dialogue boxes in which you can specify how you want the chart drawn, the titles and legends to be put on it, the scales for the axes, etc. The particular boxes presented to you depend on the choices you have made previously, so I shall only describe the general structure of the system here. Once you have understood the basic techniques, you will undoubtedly enjoy some hours investigating the many other options.

When you have indicated which type of chart you want, the first dialogue box has a Define button which takes you further into the system. (Figure 10.9 illustrates the dialogue box when a bar graph has been requested.) But it also has an area entitled 'Data in Chart Are', with three alternatives. The headings offered are rather unclear, and the following explanation may be helpful.

If you want a chart showing the average score of subgroups of your respondents on one of the variables you measured, or if you want to show how many people obtained each score on one or more of the variables, ask for 'Summaries for groups of cases'. This option can plot,

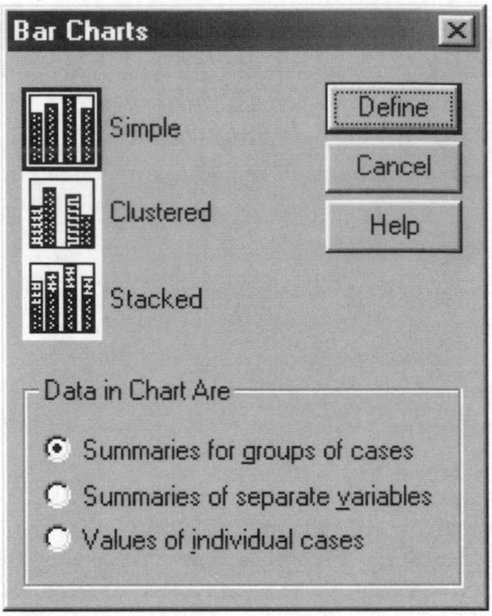

Figure 10.9   *Dialogue box from the Graphs Bar ... menu*

for example, a barchart showing the number of males and females in the data set, or the average on sales_2 of the respondents from different employers. This is the default option – the one that is active unless you select one of the others. Figure 10.10 provides an example of the output.

If you want to summarize more than one variable, such as the mean score on sales_1 and sales_2, select the 'Summaries of separate variables' option. The charts produced can be quite complex, as you can obtain summaries of a number of variables for subgroups of respondents. So you could have the average of sales_1 and of sales_2 for men and women from the data file salesq plotted on one chart, as in Figure 10.11.

The third option is 'Values of individual cases'. This means that the data on the selected variables are plotted for each case (row of data). Respondent (case) is plotted along the horizontal axis with this option. An example is shown in Figure 10.12, which displays the values on the att1 variable of salesq for each case. It is worth emphasizing that this type of display is rarely useful (although they are popular with many beginners).

If the Summaries for Groups of Cases option has been selected from the Define Chart dialogue box (Figure 10.9) and the Define button is pressed, you are presented with another dialogue box allowing you to specify what the lines/bars represent. The options vary according to the type of chart you have chosen. The box presented after selecting Graphs /Bar... and Summaries for Groups of Cases is shown in Figure 10.13. By default, the chart shows the number of cases having a particular value on

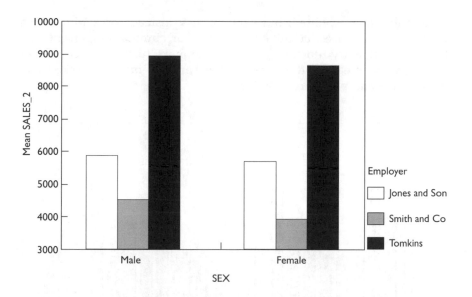

Figure 10.10   *Example of barchart showing mean on sales_2 subdivided by sex for each employer. Note: This graph was obtained with the Summaries for Groups of Cases option*

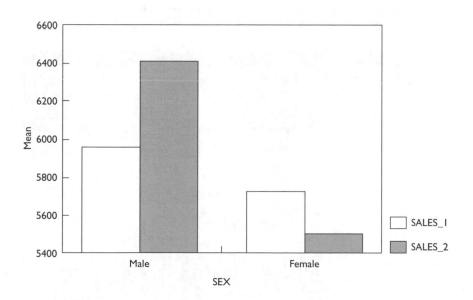

Figure 10.11   *Example of barchart of scores on sales_1 and sales_2 for each sex. Note: This graph was obtained by selecting the Summaries of Separate Variables option*

the variable being plotted, but you can ask instead for a plot which shows the % of cases, cumulative number or cumulative percentages. The Other summary function allows you to make further choices: Other is usually the mean of the data for the variable, but for stacked bar, stacked area and pie charts it is the sum.

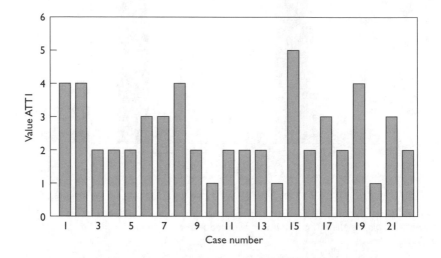

Figure 10.12   *Example of barchart of scores on att1 for each respondent. Note: This graph was obtained by selecting the Values of Individual Cases option*

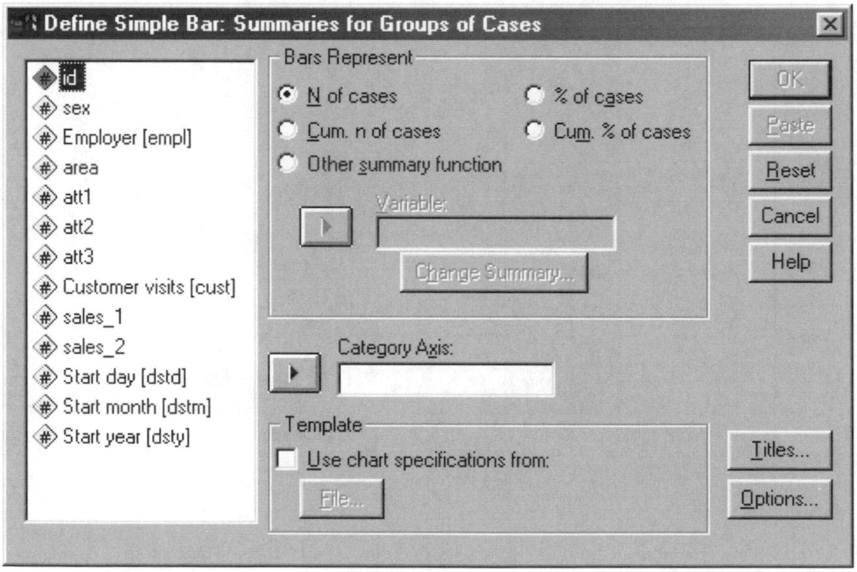

Figure 10.13   *The dialogue box for choosing which summary of data for groups of cases is required*

It is possible to have different Summary statistics, by selecting the variable and entering it in the Variable box of the Bars Represent section, then clicking on the Change Summary button. From the Summary Function dialogue box you can specify the summary statistics you want from the list of alternatives offered which includes median, mode, number of cases, standard deviation and others. You can also ask for a plot of the number or percentage falling above or below a particular value (which you enter into the Value text box), percentiles, even the percent or number of cases with values between and including a Low and High value which you enter into text boxes. The range of possibilities is enormous, and experimentation is the best way to discover what they all do!

10.10 Dealing with missing data when creating charts with Graphs

When you are charting data that has some data missing, SPSS will omit any case that has data missing on the variables being plotted. This cannot be altered when you are plotting data for individual cases, nor if you are plotting a histogram. But for other charts, you do have a choice. To over-ride the default setting, you must select the Options button from the Define Chart dialogue box such as that shown in Figure 10.13. 'Exclude cases listwise' means, although the name is rather confusing, that any row of data which has a missing data point for any of the variables selected for plotting will be omitted from the graph. This is the default condition. The alternative is 'Exclude cases variable by variable', which means that when a particular variable is plotted, any case with missing data is omitted, but when you analyse another variable the case is included if it has a score on that variable.

For some charts, missing values are plotted as a separate category. For example, in Figure 10.7 the piechart includes a sector for the case where the sex is unknown (sex had a value of 3 which was defined as a missing value). You may wish to suppress the plotting of these missing value cases. To do so, select the Options button from the Define Chart dialogue box and click on the button entitled 'Display groups defined by missing values', so the tick in the box is removed. Missing value cases will not then be plotted.

10.11 Creating a bar chart from Graphs

Suppose we want a barchart showing the means on sales_2 of respondents subdivided by sex and employer (Figure 10.10). To obtain this graph, select

```
Graphs
     Bar...
```

which opens the Bar Charts window. You can choose a Simple, Clustered or Stacked barchart by selecting the appropriate icon. A Simple barchart represents each value on the variable being plotted as a bar, and the bars are equally spaced along the axis. In Clustered charts, some bars are clustered together as in Figure 10.10. A stacked barchart shows two or more variables in each bar.

To create Figure 10.10, select the Clustered barchart option, check that Summaries for Groups of Cases is selected in the area headed Data in Chart Are, and click on Define. This reveals the Define Clustered Bar dialogue box.

You must identify the variables to be plotted: in this example it is sales_2. Click in the list on the left of the box the variable to be plotted, on the button marked Other summary function, and on the arrow button to insert the variable name in the text box headed Variable which will then contain MEAN(sales_2). Enter the variable sex into Category Axis and empl into Define Clusters by. Click on the Options button and deselect Display Groups Defined by Missing Values. Click Continue and then Paste. The syntax should read:

```
GRAPH /BAR(GROUPED)=MEAN(sales_2) BY sex BY empl.
```

Run the syntax; after a few seconds the chart will be presented in the Output Viewer.

10.12 Creating a scattergram from Graphs

To create a scattergram select

```
Graphs
     Scatter
```

Indicate whether you want a simple scatterplot, an overlay in which multiple scatterplots are put into the same frame, a scatterplot matrix or a 3-dimensional plot. Initially, the Simple option is likely to be most useful. An example is shown in Figure 17.1. You may wonder what a scatterplot matrix is. Suppose you selected three variables and asked for this option, then you would obtain scatterplots for variable1 versus variable2, variable2 v variable3, and variable1 v variable3 . . . and the same plots with the axes swapped so you also get variable2 versus variable1, variable3 v variable2 and variable3 v variable1!

Having selected the type of scatterplot required, click on Define and this will produce a window in which you specify the variables to be plotted on each axis by selecting them from the list on the left and clicking the right-pointing arrow for the Y (vertical) axis and then repeating the procedure for the X (horizontal) axis.

You can separate the plots for subgroups of respondents: for example, one could plot cust versus sales_1 for all the respondents in salesq, but have the data for females indicated by a different marker from those used to plot males' data. This is achieved by entering sex as the variable in the Set Markers By text box. Click on Paste, run the syntax and the graph will be presented on screen.

Individual points can be labelled if you enter a variable in Label Cases By in the dialogue box revealed when you select Graphs /Scatter.

Scatterplots in three dimensions require you to specify the three variables to be used as the axes. When the plot is presented you can enjoy playing with it by rotating it around various axes if you select from the menus

```
Edit
     Format
          Spin Mode
```

and click the 3-d rotation buttons in the icon bar.

10.13 Obtaining the regression line on a scattergram from Graphs

If you want the regression line to be shown in the scatterplot then, while the graph is shown, double click it so it is opened in the Chart Editor. Click on the Chart /Options menu to reveal the dialogue box shown in Figure 17.2. In the Fit Line area, make the selection to tell the program whether you want to fit a line for the Total data set or for subgroups separately. The Fit options button then becomes available, and clicking it reveals Figure 17.3. The linear regression line is the default, although quadratic and cubic can be selected instead. Click on Continue to return to the Scatterplot Options box, and then on OK. The regression line will be added to the plot.

10.14 Creating a line graph of means of subgroups from Graphs

It is often helpful when trying to interpret the results of an analysis to plot the means of subgroups of respondents. This is particularly true if analysis of variance with more than one independent variable has been performed, as it demonstrates the effects of any interaction between the variables. Although a line graph is not the most appropriate way of plotting means when the subgroups are divided on a non-continuous scale, it can be a useful aid to understanding the pattern of results. Relevant line graphs of estimated marginal means can readily be obtained from the dialogue boxes used when you request an analysis of variance, as is explained in chapter 16.

Suppose we wished to plot the means of the data on the variable sales_ 2 for males and females from each of the two areas North and South as in Figure 10.14. Select Graphs /Line from the menu, to reveal a dialogue box in which you select the Multiple option icon and the Summarize for Groups of Cases alternative. Click on Define to open another dialogue box; click on sales_2 then on Other summary function and finally on the right-pointing arrow button next to the Variable text box. MEAN(sales_2) will appear in the text box. Insert the variable area as the Category axis and insert sex as Define Lines by. Use the Options button to allow access to the method for suppressing the displaying of missing value cases. Click on Continue and then on Paste. The syntax should read:

```
GRAPH
    /LINE(MULTIPLE)MEAN(sales_2) BY area BY sex.
```

When the syntax is run and the chart made visible on the screen by pressing the Chart icon in the output window, the graph should look like Figure 10.14.

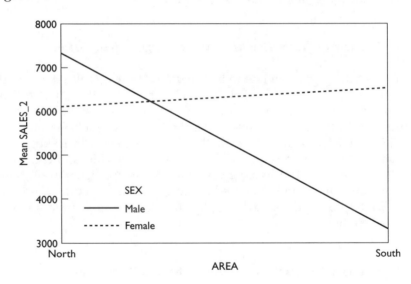

Figure 10.14   *Line graph of means of sales_2 for each area for each sex*

10.15 Editing the chart created from Graphs

When the chart is first created, it is displayed in the Output Viewer. For editing, it needs to be placed in the Chart Editor shown in Figure 10.15. This is done by double clicking the chart or by selecting it and then choosing Edit /SPSS Chart Object /Open. The facilities for editing charts are so numerous that it is best to learn by experimentation: once the basics are understood, the user will learn most, and most enjoyably, by experimenting with the host of alternatives, so only some of the alternatives will be described here.

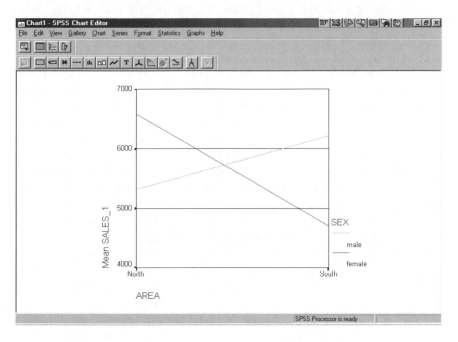

Figure 10.15   *The Chart Editor window*

With the Chart Editor window open, the menu bar contains these entries which allow you to make numerous alterations to the chart:

```
File Edit View Gallery Chart Series Format Statistics
Graphs Help
```

The icon bar of the Chart Editor duplicates the commands available from the Format menu. By clicking on the icons, you can, among other things, set the pattern for filling enclosed areas, set the colours, specify the marker used to plot a point, set the thickness and style of lines, specify whether bars have a shadow or 3-d appearance, determine whether bars are labelled, decide how interpolated lines are drawn, vary the font and size of text used in the chart, apply 3-d rotation for a 3-d plot, swap axes, explode the slice of a pie chart, spin a 3-d plot.

The File menu allows you to save Chart Templates and Export the chart in various file formats. To alter the typeface used in the charts and to have grid lines displayed, use Edit /Options from the menu bar.

You can replace the current chart with another of a different type, using the same data, by selecting Gallery. Line graphs, area charts, pie charts can be requested at the first stage of creating a chart. But more complex charts such as mixed bars and lines, exploded pie charts, or dropped line charts are available once you have created a chart, by putting it into the Chart Editor, and selecting Gallery from the menu bar. Experimenting with the possibilities is perhaps the best way to learn how to control these displays. As usual, the system provides appropriate dialogue boxes at every point.

To use the editing facilities, you need to appreciate that a chart contains two kinds of object. 'Series objects' are the bars, lines and markers that represent the data. 'Chart objects' are the layout and labelling features. To modify an object, you either use the Chart or Series menus of the Chart Editor window, or you can double-click on the object you wish to modify. With either procedure, an appropriate dialogue box is then presented allowing you to specify the attributes of the object. For example, to change the way the bar in a barchart is filled with a pattern, double click on one of the bars. To change the label for the vertical axis, double click on the existing label.

To alter the title of the chart, select Chart /Title from the menus, and type text into the Title 1 and/or Title 2 text boxes; then click on OK.

To alter the title or labels of the horizontal axis, double click on the existing ones. This reveals the Category Axis box, and you can enter a different title. To alter the labels of the categories, click on the Labels button. In the Category Axis: Labels dialogue box you can set the number of decimal places, change the orientation of the labels and make other adjustments. When the label settings have been altered, a click on the Continue button returns you to the Category Axis box and you click on OK.

To alter the title, scale or labels of the vertical axis, double click on the existing vertical axis title, and the Scale Axis box is exposed. It functions in a similar way to the Category Axis box used to modify the horizontal axis described above.

That part of the chart which indicates which variables are shown is known as the legend. Double clicking on the existing legend will reveal a Legend box allowing you to add a title to the legend, alter the labels of the legend, vary its position or suppress it completely.

To add a short text message to the chart, select Chart /Annotation. The resulting box allows you to type in the message and locate it at a set point defined by position on the vertical and horizontal axes.

To alter the layout or change the scales of the chart axes select Chart /Options and further dialogue boxes appropriate to the type of chart you are editing allow you to specify how you want the chart to be constructed. The options offered depend on the type of chart you are editing, but this menu gives great flexibility in chart design.

To have a normal curve added to a histogram or add a regression line to a scatterplot, use the menu Chart /Options.

You can swap axes, so that histograms, for example, are oriented horizontally rather than vertically, by selecting Format /Swap Axes, or by clicking on the icon in the icon bar which portrays a movement of the axes.

To alter the patterns used to fill areas of the chart, and similar features of the chart, select the Format menu.

To alter the text fonts and sizes, select Format /Text.

To suppress the display of some of the variables you have previously selected for inclusion in the chart, select Series /Displayed.

To alter the sequence in which variables are grouped in a clustered barchart or a stacked chart, select Series /Displayed and alter the order in which variables are listed in the Display text box of the Displayed Data dialogue box by removing variables from the list and then re-inserting them in the new sequence.

10.16 Saving and retrieving a chart

A chart is saved in the Output Viewer file, which has the filename extension .spo.

Select from the menu bar

```
File
      Save As
```

The name of the output file will appear in the Filename box. The directory in which it will be saved is shown, and you can alter this by clicking on the required alternative in the Save In drop-down list and navigating to the desired directory. To save the file to the floppy disk, you need to click on a:.

As charts are saved in the output file, retrieving them merely requires opening the output file containing the chart which had been saved previously. How to open an output file is described in section 7.6.

10.17 Transferring a chart to another application

When you are looking at a chart in the Output Viewer, it can be copied into other Windows applications, such as Word. Copy the chart to the windows clipboard by selecting it with a left click and then using the Edit /Copy menu. Open a document in Word and select Edit /Paste Special. A dialogue box is presented: select the Picture option and click OK. The chart will be pasted into the document as a picture and can be edited using Microsoft Draw.

Charts can be exported from SPSS in a variety of formats such as .bmp, .wmf, .tif for importing into other applications. To save the chart in one of these formats, use File /Export. A dialogue box illustrated in Figure 10.16 is presented. Open the drop-down list to show the alternatives which can be exported (Output Document, Output Document (No charts), or Charts Only). If Charts Only is selected, different graphic file formats become available in the File Type drop-down list.

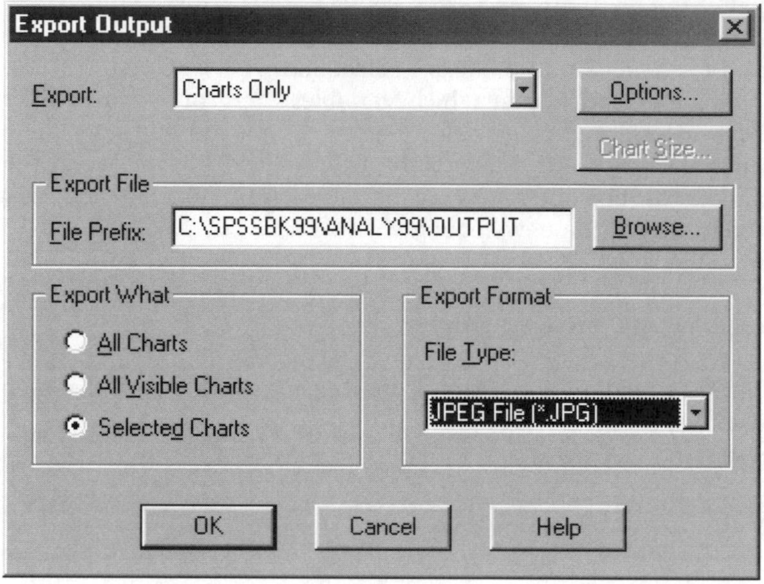

Figure 10.16   *The dialogue box for exporting charts*

10.18 Printing charts

If the chart is in the Output Viewer, it can be printed be selecting it with a click and then from the menu bar choosing

```
File
    Print
```

10.19 Chart templates

A chart template allows you to save the style of a chart so that it can be applied to other charts, so you do not have to go through the process of designing a chart every time. Essentially, when you save a chart, the features of that chart can be applied when you create a new chart or can be applied to a chart already in the chart window.

USING A TEMPLATE WHEN CREATING A CHART When you access the Define Chart dialogue box, it contains an area titled Template, with the option 'Use chart specifications from:'. If you select this and then click on the File button in the template area, a list of template files, with the filename extension .sct, is shown. Select the one you want from the list so its name appears in the Chart Template File text box and click on Open. The chart you are creating will be assigned the attributes of the chart you are using as a template.

ASSIGNING A TEMPLATE TO AN EXISTING CHART If you have a chart in the Chart Editor and want to apply a template to it, select from the menu Format /Apply Chart Template.

10.20 Adding grid lines to charts

You can ask for horizontal or vertical grid lines to be added to charts by selecting from the menu Edit /Options. Select the Charts tab, and there is the facility for adding grid lines: use the check boxes to request horizontal lines (Scale axis) and/or vertical lines (Category axis).

11

RANKING AND SORTING THE DATA

Summary

- To convert a set of scores into rank values, use Transform /Rank Cases.
- When a variable ve is ranked, you obtain a new variable called rve. Switch to the Data Editor window to see the scores on rve, the ranked variable.
- To rank within subgroups enter the variable name for forming subgroups into the By box of the Rank Cases dialogue box.
- To obtain rank correlations refer to section 17.3.
- To sort the cases into a new order, use Data /Sort Cases.

11.1 Ranking scores

If you want to convert a set of scores into rank values, select from the menu

```
Transform
    Rank Cases
```

The dialogue box shown in Figure 11.1 will be presented. Enter into the Variable(s) box the variables to be ranked. Ensure the option Display Summary Tables is ticked (clicking in the check box if necessary); this has the effect of putting a message in the output window to tell you what the procedure has done. An example of the message is shown in Figure 11.2.

To have rank values assigned in ascending order, so the lowest score has a rank value of 1, you need do nothing, but if you want the scores ranked in descending order so the largest value has the rank of 1 then you select Largest Value in the Assign Rank 1 To section of the dialogue box. Paste the command into the syntax window and run it.

The Rank procedure creates a new variable, which by default has the name of the variable being ranked preceded by the letter r. So when sales_1 are ranked, you obtain a new variable called rsales_1. When you

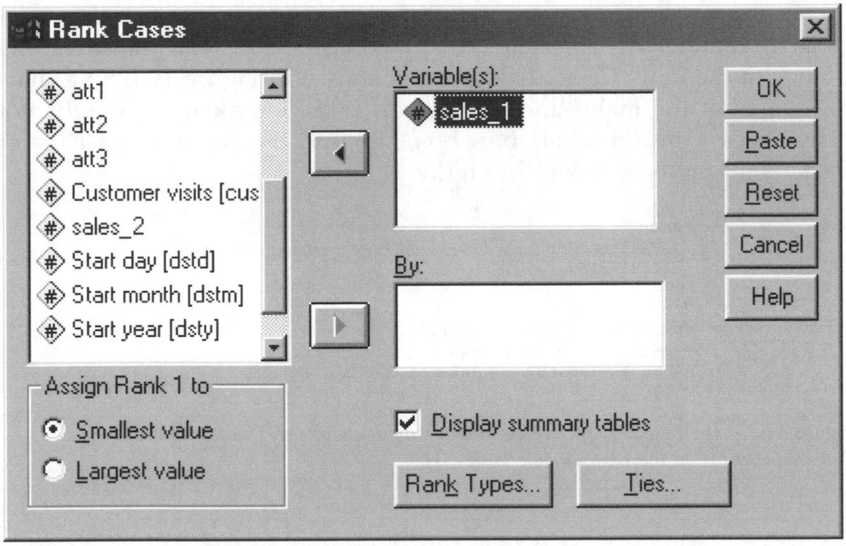

Figure 11.1   *The Rank Cases dialogue box*

have run Rank you will see the message illustrated in Figure 11.2 in the output window; switch to the Data Editor window and you will find that the new variable has been added to the data in the table. The name of the new variable must be used if you wish to list or analyse the ranked values.

```
RANK
   VARIABLES=sales_1  (A) /RANK /PRINT=YES
   /TIES=MEAN .

From      New
variable  variable  Label
--------  --------  -----
SALES_1   RSALES_1  RANK of SALES_1
```

Figure 11.2   *The output from the Rank procedure. (Switch to the Data window to see the new variable rsales_1)*

There are a number of options on how to assign ranks to tied values. Unless you specify otherwise, via the Ties button, tied values will be given the mean rank value of the scores. Alternative methods of ranking, unlikely to be used by the beginner, are available from the Rank Types button.

11.2 Ranking within subgroups

The basic Rank command ranks the whole set of scores on the variables specified. You frequently need the ranking of scores within subgroups;

for example, one may require the data for males and females to be ranked separately. This is achieved by entering a variable name into the By box of the Rank Cases dialogue box shown in Figure 11.1. So to have the scores of the males and females on sales_1 ranked separately, you insert sales_1 into the Variables box, sex into the By box and click on Paste. The syntax is shown in Figure 11.3.

```
RANK
   VARIABLES=sales_1  (A) BY sex  /RANK /PRINT=YES
   /TIES=MEAN .

From      New
variable  variable  Label
--------  --------  -----
SALES_1   RSALES_1  RANK of SALES_1 by SEX
```

Figure 11.3   *The output from ranking within subgroups of sex. (Switch to the Data window to see the new variable rsales_1)*

11.3 Rank correlation

Rank correlations are obtained from the Correlate entry of the Analyze drop-down menu, described in section 17.3. If the data is on an interval or ratio scale, you do not have to use the rank procedure before finding the rank correlation, as the ranking is done automatically.

11.4 Putting the cases in a different order: Sort Cases

There are occasions when you may wish to sort the cases into a new order. For example, if you were analysing just the first 50 cases in a large data file, you might want those first 50 cases to be all males, or all of a given level of income or having some other feature. You can have the cases sorted into a specified order using the Sort Cases procedure. The procedure is obtained from the menu

```
Data
     Sort Cases
```

Enter the variable(s) to be used for sorting the data into the Sort By box, and select ascending or descending Sort Order.

If you enter two variables in the Sort By box, the cases will be sorted first of all by the first one in the list and then by the second one in the list and so on. So if you wanted the data in salesq to be sorted so that all the males (sex = 1) from the North (area = 1) came first, followed by all the men from the South (area = 2), then all the women from the North and finally all the women from the South, you would put sex and area into the Sort By box. When the cases have been sorted, they are shown in the new order in the Data Editor window.

11.5 Restoring the original order after using Sort Cases

If the cases were originally ordered by some other variable, such as id, the original order can be restored by running the Sort Cases procedure again with id as the defining variable. (This is one reason why it is always worth having an identifying variable such as the variable id in salesq; you can restore the original order.) If, however, you do not have a variable with which you can sort to regain the original order, you can only get back to the original by reloading the data file from the disk. This makes it important that if you have sorted the data you should save the data file under a new filename so that the original order is preserved in the original data file on the disk.

12

CHANGING THE WAY DATA IS CODED AND GROUPED

Summary

- To calculate a new variable from the original data use the Transform /Compute procedure.
- To code the data in a different way from that used when the data file was initially created, use the Transform /Recode procedure. It is always wise to choose Recode /Into Different Variables.
- To obtain z scores use the Analyze /Descriptive Statistics /Descriptives procedure, explained in section 15.4.
- To collapse data across a set of cases and form a new 'case' which has scores derived from the collapsed data, use Data /Aggregate.

12.1 Why you might want to modify the data

In analysing data you may want to calculate a new variable from the original data. For example, from respondents' sales and the number of customers visited, you may want to create a new variable which is the average sales per customer visit or you may want to know the average of respondents' scores on a number of measures such as finding the mean for each person of their responses to att1, att2 and att3. This is achieved using the Compute procedure.

Sometimes you may want to code the data in a different way from that used when the data file was initially created. For example, the salesq file includes data on the number of customers visited. You may want to divide the respondents into just two groups: those who visited more than 40 customers, and those who visited less than 40. The Recode procedure will do this for you.

Another common situation is when you want to reverse the scoring of one of the variables. For example, in the Sales Personnel Questionnaire, there were three questions asking respondents about their attitude to their job. Questions 5 and 6 (named as att1 and att2) have the responses coded so that 1 indicates the respondent is very satisfied and 5 indicates dissatisfaction. But for question 7 (att3), 1 indicates dissatisfaction and 5 indicates satisfaction. Suppose you wanted the scores on att3 to be scored in the opposite direction, so they are consistent with att1 and att2, with a low score meaning very satisfied and a high score (5) meaning very dissatisfied. This kind of alteration is easily made using the Recode command.

12.2 Calculating 'new' scores and transforming scores: Compute

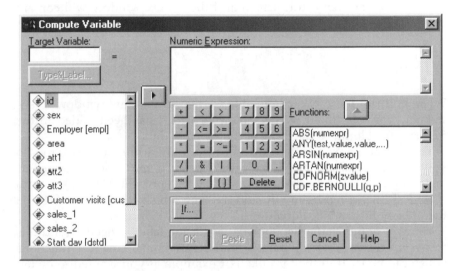

Figure 12.1   *The Compute Variable dialogue box*

Compute is found from the menu under

```
Transform
     Compute
```

It opens the dialogue box entitled Compute Variable shown in Figure 12.1. Type a name for the variable you are computing into the Target Variable text box: the name must not be more than eight characters long, must not contain a space, must not end in a full-stop. You can assign a label to the new variable name by pressing the Type&Label button from the dialogue box and responding to the box revealed.

The new variable will be calculated from some combination of the existing variables, linked by mathematical operators. For example, you might want to calculate a new variable, totatt, which is the total of the scores on att1, att2 and att3. The box headed Numeric Expression is where you indicate the formula that is used to calculate the new variable, and you select existing variables to enter into the formula by the usual process of clicking on their names in the left-hand list and then on the right-pointing arrow. Mathematical operators (the plus sign, multiplication sign, etc.) are entered into the formula by clicking on the appropriate button in the area which looks like a calculator key-pad. So the formula for calculating totatt is att1 + att2 + att3, and you enter this into the Numeric Expression box by clicking on att1 in the lefthand list and on the arrow, then on the + sign in the on-screen key-pad, then on att2 in the variable list and the right arrow, etc.

When you have created the formula you want, click on the Paste button at the bottom of the screen and the syntax window will contain these lines:

```
COMPUTE totatt = att1 + att2 + att3 .
EXECUTE .
```

When you run these two commands, switch to the data window to see the new variable (totatt in this example) which has been added in the first empty column to the right of the original data.

The key pad area allows you to use not only arithmetic operators in your formula, but also relational operators such as < and > as well as logical operators: the keypad has an & key to represent AND, a key with a vertical line to represent OR, and a ~ key which represents NOT. (So the ~= key means Not Equal to.)

You will notice that a list appears under the label Functions, and this allows access to a set of transformations and mathematical functions which can be used in the formula. For example, if you wanted to obtain the log of the scores on variable cust, you would enter a new variable name, logcust, and then scroll down the Functions list until the LG10 function was exposed. Click on that and then on the upward pointing arrow above the list of Functions. The function you selected will appear in the Numeric Expression list, with question marks to show that you still have to enter the arguments for the expression (i.e. the variables to be used when calculating the log, mean, square root or whatever you are asking for). Click on the first question mark in the expression in the Numeric Expression list, then click on the appropriate variable (cust, for example) in the variable list on the left of the dialogue box. The Numeric Expression will then read LG10[cust]. Click on Paste and run the Compute procedure, and the new variable logcust will be added to the Data Editor. It is important to realize that the Functions facility deals with missing values in a way that can be misleading. See section 12.4 below for an explanation and details on how to avoid being misled.

The Functions list allows you to select a number of transformations and statistics expressions. You can obtain the absolute value of scores with ABS, the SQRT provides square roots, arcsines are provided by ARSIN, and there are many others. The statistical functions allow you to

obtain the mean, sum, standard deviation, variance, minimum or maximum of a set of scores, but remember this refers to a set of scores
obtained by each respondent. Suppose you want to obtain the average
score on att1, att2 and att3 for each respondent: you would put a name for
the new variable in the Target Variable box and then from the Functions list
select MEAN(numexpr,numexpr,. . .). It appears in the Numeric Expression window, and you then click on the names of the variables for which
you want the mean by clicking on them in the variable list and then clicking
on the right arrow. In this example, you would select att1, att2 and att3
so that the formula in the Numeric Expressions text box read MEAN
(att1,att2,att3).

Clicking on the Paste button at the bottom of the screen will insert into
the syntax window these lines:

```
COMPUTE Meanatt = MEAN(att1,att2,att3) .
EXECUTE .
```

When these two commands have been run, switch to the data window to
see the new variable (Meanatt in this example) which has been added in
the first empty column to the right of the original data.

The earlier example of calculating the total of scores att1, att2 and att3
could be obtained more simply by using the function SUM(att1,att2,att3),
but do see section 12.4 below regarding the treatment of missing values
when functions are used.

The Functions list contains an entry ANY(test,value,value. . .), one of
the Logical Functions. What this does is to check whether the scores for
each respondent on a named variable (the one referred to as test) match
a specified value. For example, ANY(year,90,91) will examine the data
for each respondent to see whether the score on the variable year
matches the values given: 90 or 91. If there is a match, the new variable is
added to the Data Editor and a score of 1 is given.

Exercise 12.1

Use Compute to calculate a new score called avsales1 which is the
average sales_1 per customer visited for each respondent in the data file
salesq. The formula for avsales1 is sales_1/cust.

12.3 Using Compute with certain cases only: Compute If

You may want to compute a new variable for just some cases in your
data file, cases that meet certain criteria. For example, you might want to
calculate the sum of att1, att2 and att3 only for people from the North

area. To do this, you click on the If... button in the Compute Variable dialogue box shown in Figure 12.1, and this opens another box entitled Compute Variables: If Cases. The structure of this box resembles the previous Compute Variable one, but you can specify the conditions to apply before the Compute procedure takes place. For example, suppose you want to calculate a new variable called Northtot which is the total of att1, att2 and att3 but is only calculated for those respondents who had a score of 1 on the variable area (these are the respondents who worked in the North). To do this, you need the box in Compute Variables: If Cases to contain the expression area = 1.

The expression is created very much as the Numeric Expression in Compute Variables was obtained, by selecting variable names from the list, entering them into the box by clicking on the arrow button, and using the calculator key pad to obtain arithmetic or logical expressions and functions. Once the formula is entered in the box, click on the Include if Cases Satisfies Condition: button, and then on the Continue button at the bottom of the box. Once the Compute box has been completed, clicking on Paste will insert into the syntax window the lines:

```
IF (area = 1) Northtot = att1 + att2 + att3 .
EXECUTE .
```

When these commands are run, the variable Northtot will be added to the data window and the values inserted just for those respondents who have an entry of 1 on the variable area.

12.4 Missing values in Compute

If you are using compute with an arithmetic expression, such as att1+att2+att3, then any case which has a missing value on any of the variables included in the formula (in this example att1, att2, att3) will be classified as having a missing value on the new variable you are computing.

Statistical functions work differently: if you compute a new variable using the function MEAN(att1,att2,att3), then the new variable will have a missing value if the respondent has missing data on all of the variables in the expression. This could be misleading: you might ask for the mean of att1, att2 and att3 for a respondent who only has scores on att1 and att2. The mean that is given will be the mean of the two scores the respondent has, and you may be unaware that for this respondent the mean calculated is not the mean of three variables but only of two. To prevent this happening use MEAN.3(att1,att2,att3). You have to type the .3 in: before the opening bracket, put a decimal point and follow this with a number equal to the number of variables listed in the function.

With this formulation, any case that has a missing value on any one of the variables named between the brackets will have a missing value assigned on the computed variable.

12.5 Obtaining *z* scores

When a series of parametric data is transformed so that it has a mean of zero and a standard deviation of 1.00, the scores are known as z scores. To obtain z scores for any variable, use the Descriptives procedure and select the Save Standardized Values as Variables option in the Descriptives dialogue box. Details are given in section 15.4.

12.6 Changing the way data is coded: Recode

Recode is obtained from the menu by selecting

```
Transform
        Recode
                Into Different Variables
```

which yields the dialogue box shown in Figure 12.2. It is always wise to choose Recode /Into Different Variables. The recoded values make a new variable, which you have to name as described below, and the original variable and the scores on it are retained in the data file. If you choose Recode /Into Same Variables, the recoded values will replace the old values in the Data Editor. This is a dangerous thing to do, as you run the risk of losing the original values which you may need later. It is always possible to reload the original data file from disk so that you get the original scores back, but it is easy to make mistakes and save a version of the data which overwrites the original file. If this happens you can have lost the original scores for good.

Specify the variables to be recoded by entering them in the Variables list and provide a name for the variable when it has been recoded by typing in the new name in the Output Variable Name box and clicking on Change. The new name will be inserted next to the old name in the Input Variable → Output Variable list as shown in Figure 12.2. Next select the Old and New Values button to obtain the display shown in Figure 12.3. Specify the old value and the new value; for example, if you want a score of 5 to be recoded as a 1, 5 goes into the Old Value's Value box, and 1 into the New Value's Value box. You then click on the Add button.

As the lower left part of Figure 12.3 implies, you can specify a range of values to be recoded as a single value. Suppose we wanted to recode the data so that two groups are formed according to their standing on the

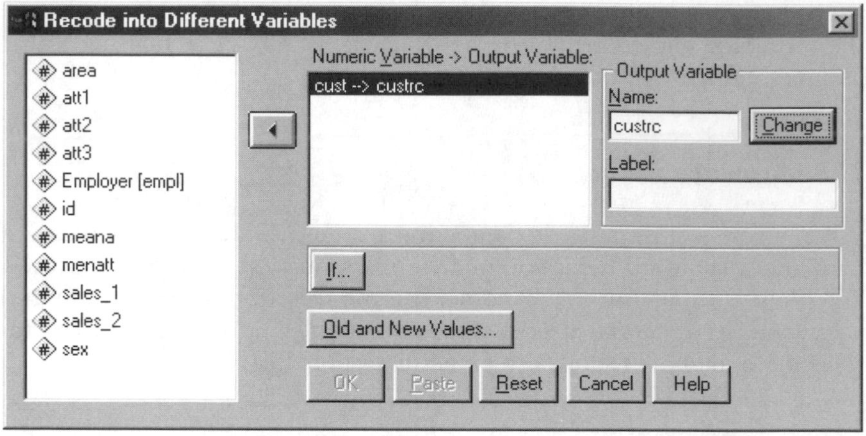

Figure 12.2   *The dialogue box for Recode. Note that the variable cust has been selected for recoding into the variable custrc*

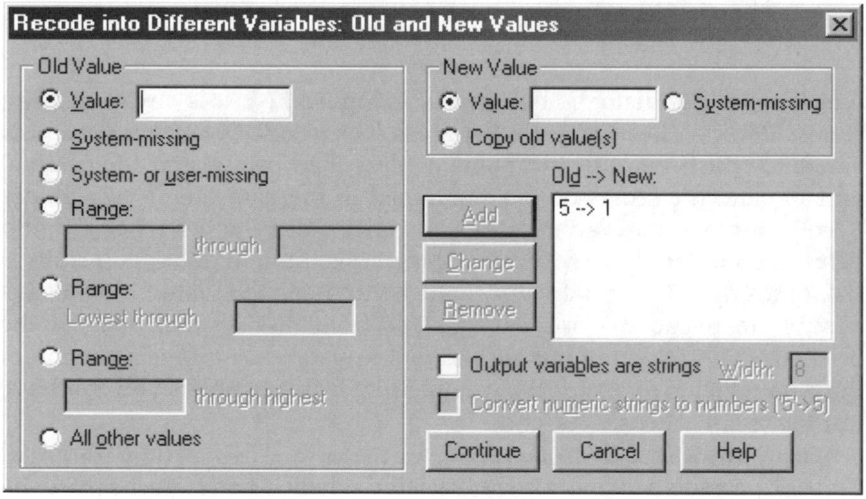

Figure 12.3   *The dialogue box for assigning new values in Recode. The current value 5 has been set to be recoded as 1*

cust variable, with all cases where cust is 40 or less being given a new, recoded score of 1 and all those with a cust score of 41 or more having a recoded score of 2. You could define one range as 0 through 40 and assign it the new value of 1, click on Add, and then define the second range as 41 through highest, assign it a new value of 2 and click on Add. Note that you can specify one category for recoding as lowest score to a specified value and another as from a specified value to the highest score, which is useful for forming two groups such as those scoring below and above the median.

When you have specified the old values to be recoded, it is necessary to decide how any unspecified values are to be treated. If you do nothing, they will all be given the system missing value, which is rarely what is needed. To ensure that any old values you do not want recoded are carried over into the new variable with the same values as before, make sure you select All Other Values in the Old and New Values dialogue box, and then select Copy Old Values in the New Value area of the box and finally press the Add button. The entry ELSE → COPY appears in the list to show that all unspecified values will be carried over into the new variable.

You can ask for only certain cases to be recoded: if you wanted only the men's scores (sex = 1 in salesq) recoded, for example, click on the If... button of Figure 12.2. This opens the If dialogue box which is explained in section 12.3.

When all selections have been made from the dialogue boxes, Paste the syntax into a syntax window. An example of the Recode syntax is shown in Figure 12.4.

When the commands are run, switch to the Data window to see the new recoded variables which have been added to the data. To save the new variables, save the contents of the Data Editor as a data file.

```
RECODE
  cust
  (Lowest thru 40=1) (41 thru 60=2) (61 thru Highest=3) INTO custrc.
EXECUTE .
```

Figure 12.4   *Examples of the syntax for Recode*

Recode /Into Same Variables operates in a similar way to Recode /Into Different Variables, except that as noted above it runs unnecessary dangers.

Recode only applies to the data in the active file. The original data file is not affected by running the Recode command, so there is no risk of making permanent (and non-reversible) changes to the entries in the data file. To store a copy of the data to which the Recode has been applied, carry out the recode, and then save the data file. It is a wise precaution to save it under a different name from the original data file (use File /Save As...) just in case there are any catastrophes later.

Exercise 12.2

Recode the scores on the variable sales_1 in the data file salesq so that values of 8000 or over are coded as 3, values of 4000 or less are coded as 1 and values between 4000 and 8000 are coded as 2.

12.7 Automatic Recode

This procedure automatically recodes all the scores on a variable into consecutive integers. For example, the customers-visited scores in salesq include a 28, a 29, a 30, a 33 and the largest figure is 83. If you use

```
Transform
    Automatic Recode
```

the scores will be modified so that the lowest score is changed to 1, the second-lowest to 2, the third-lowest to 3 and so on. The procedure creates a new variable for the recoded scores, which must be given a new name by highlighting the variable entered in the Variable → New Name list, typing the new name in the text box to the right of the New Name button, then clicking on that button. When Automatic Recode runs, switch to the data window to see the new variable. The values on the new variable are automatically given value labels corresponding to the original values on the variable which has been recoded. Figure 12.5 illustrates the effect of using Automatic Recode.

```
AUTORECODE
  VARIABLES=cust   /INTO custautr
  /PRINT.

              CUST        CUSTAUTR   Number customer visits
           Old Value     New Value   Value Label
                 28            1      28
                 30            2      30
                 33            3      33
                 36            4      36
                 38            5      38
                 39            6      39
                 40            7      40
                 41            8      41
                 42            9      42
                 43           10      43
                 46           11      46
                 48           12      48
                 58           13      58
                 60           14      60
                 68           15      68
                 71           16      71
                 72           17      72
                 76           18      76
                 79           19      79
                 83           20      83
```

Figure 12.5   *Example of the effects of Automatic Recode*

12.8 Multiple responses

Surveys often use questions with non-exclusive responses: suppose that instead of asking the people who completed the sales questionnaire described in chapter 4 which employer they worked for now, we asked them to indicate which of the employers they had ever worked for. We might find individuals who had worked for employer 1 (Jones) only,

others who had worked for 1 (Jones) and 2 (Smith), others who had
worked for 2 (Smith) and 3 (Tomkins), and so on. There are alternative
ways of dealing with such data. One method would be to have a variable
for each employer and use a score of 1 to indicate 'yes' and 2 to indicate
'no'. This is referred to as the multiple dichotomy method.

The alternative method is known as the multiple category method.
Here one would have three variables, and the score on each one would
indicate which employer had been mentioned. In our example, a score of
1 would represent Jones, 2 Smith and 3 Tomkins. So a respondent who
had been employed by Jones and by Tomkins would score 1 on varia-
ble1, 3 on variable2 and have a missing value on variable3.

Whichever method one chose, the responses on the variables need to
be combined either into a multiple dichotomy set or into a multiple
category set. This is achieved by selecting from the menu

```
Analyze
    Multiple Response
        Define Sets
```

The dialogue box allows you to specify the variables to be entered into a
set. You have to indicate for each variable whether the scores are
dichotomies (the scores represent yes or no) or whether the scores have
more than two alternatives. The former is used for the multiple dichotomy method, the latter for the multiple category method. You have to
enter a name for the set and Add it to the list, where the name you gave
will be preceded with a $ sign.

The analysis of multiple response sets is achieved by selecting either

```
Analyze
    Multiple Response
        Frequencies
```

or

```
Analyze
    Multiple Response
        Tables
```

Frequencies produces tables which show the number of respondents
giving each possible response (i.e. each employer, in our example)
collapsed across the variables in the set. The Tables subcommand is used
to produce cross-tabulations, in which the responses are collapsed across
the variables in the defined set and then tabulated against scores on
another variable.

12.9 Collapsing data across cases: Aggregate

You may wish to collapse data across a set of cases, and form a new 'case' which has scores which are derived from the collapsed data. As an example, you could collapse the scores for each of the sexes and have one case representing 'men' and a second case representing 'women'. (This procedure should be used only rarely and after some thought about whether it is justified. This example is merely to allow me to explain what Aggregate achieves.)

To obtain an aggregation, select

```
Data
      Aggregate
```

Specify in the Break Variable(s) box the variable to be used to identify the groups to be formed. In the example I am using, this would be sex. In the Aggregate Variable(s) box you enter the variables to be aggregated; SPSS will create a new variable. You have to indicate the function to be used in making the aggregation: do you want the aggregate score to be the mean of the individual cases or their sum or the percentage of cases falling between certain limits or some other function? The mean is used by default; if you want any other function, you have to select the Functions button and fill in the dialogue box.

The Aggregate procedure creates a new data file, aggr.sav, in the current directory. If you want a different name or the file to be saved elsewhere, click on the File button and complete the dialogue box.

13

SELECTING SUBGROUPS FOR ANALYSIS

Summary

- Analysing subgroups is needed to carry out an analysis on a subset of cases such as just the males.
- To form subgroups based on each level of a variable use Data /Split File.
- To form subgroups based on scores on a variable use Data /Select Cases.
- To select a random sample of cases of data use Data /Select Cases.
- Turn off both Split File and Select Cases after use.

13.1 When analysing subgroups is needed

If you have data from different groups, such as males and females, you may want to carry out some analyses on each group separately. For example, in the data file salesq we have a record of the number of sales (sales_1) by male and female respondents from the North and from the South. Imagine you want to analyse separately the sales_1 scores for the two sexes. Split File allows you to do so and you can then return to analysing all the cases by turning Split File off.

13.2 Selecting subgroups based on each level of a variable: Split File

From the menu select

```
Data
     Split File
```

In the dialogue box revealed (Figure 13.1) select either Compare Groups or Organize Output by Groups. (Both of these have the effect of invoking the Split File procedure. The difference is in the way the output is

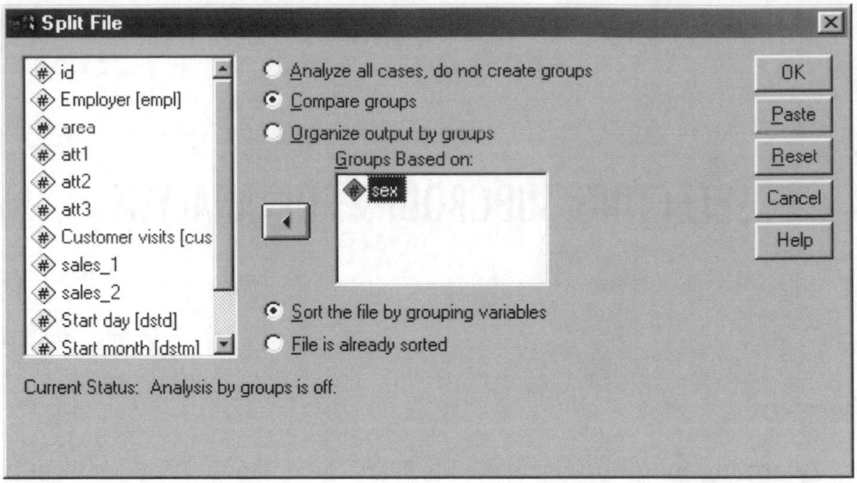

Figure 13.1   *The dialogue box for Split File*

organized, as explained in section 13.3 below.) Then select the variable to be used to divide the cases into subgroups and enter it in the Groups Based On text box. Suppose that we want to take each sex separately and compare people from the North with those from the South on their scores on the variable sales_1. We want to select people according to their sex, so the variable sex would need to be entered in this box. When Pasted, the syntax window contains these lines:

```
SORT CASES BY sex .
SPLIT FILE
  LAYERED BY sex .
```

or

```
SORT CASES BY sex .
SPLIT FILE
  SEPARATE BY sex .
```

To carry out a *t*-test comparing people from the North with those from the South on sales_1 data, one then selects the necessary commands from the menu and pastes them into the syntax window, and then turns Split File off by returning to the Split File dialogue box, selecting Analyze All Cases, Do Not Create Groups and pressing Paste. The complete syntax is included in Figure 13.2. (The first section of the syntax uses the Select Cases command, explained in 13.4 below, to exclude from the analysis those cases where sex is not known, where the respondent has a score more than 2 on the variable sex. You will be able to understand it better when you have read section 13.4.)

The output from running this syntax is shown in Figure 13.2. Two separate *t*-tests have been performed, one on males and one on females. Each *t*-test compares the sales_1 scores for respondents from the North with those for respondents from the South.

Once invoked the Split File command continues to be operative throughout an SPSS run of commands unless you turn it off by going back to the Split File box and selecting Analyze All Cases, Do Not Create Groups.

When it is operating, Split File sorts the data in the data file so that it has all cases with the same value on the grouping variables in the correct sequence. (This is done automatically, but if the data is already sorted in the appropriate order, the sorting can be omitted by selecting the button marked File Is Already Sorted.)

13.3 Compare Groups or Organize Output by Groups in Split File

Either of these options invokes the splitting of the file. The difference between them is in the way the output is organized. Figures 13.2 and 13.3 illustrate the formats. In Figure 13.2, the file was split by sex with the Compare Groups option chosen (leading to the syntax Layered by Sex). The tables of Group Statistics and of Independent Samples Test both have sex as a layer in the table. By contrast, Figure 13.3 shows the output when the file was split with the Organize Output by Groups option (yielding the syntax Separate by Sex). This gives separate tables for each level of the sex variable.

13.4 Selecting subgroups using Select Cases

Select Cases resembles Split File but applies a filter to the data file and then only analyses those cases which have been filtered. Select Cases is needed if you want to form a subset of cases based on their standing on a continuous variable, or you want a more sophisticated way of selecting cases than can be achieved by using Split File. Select Cases was used to exclude some cases from the analysis in Figures 13.2 and 13.3. You also use Select Cases if you want to analyse the results from a random sample of the cases.

As an example, suppose you wanted to analyse the data only for those cases which had a value of 5000 or more on the variable sales_1 in the data file salesq. Select Cases allows you to do this.

It is possible to tell the program to delete from the data file those cases which have not been filtered; if this happens the deleted cases cannot be retrieved unless you have kept a copy of the original data file on a disk. So be wary of using the Delete cases option!

```
USE ALL.
COMPUTE filter_$=(sex < 3).
VARIABLE LABEL filter_$ 'sex < 3 (FILTER)'.
VALUE LABELS filter_$  0 'Not Selected' 1 'Selected'.
FORMAT filter_$ (f1.0).
FILTER BY filter_$.
EXECUTE .
SORT CASES BY sex .
SPLIT FILE
  LAYERED BY sex .
T-TEST
  GROUPS=area(1 2)
  /MISSING=ANALYSIS
  /VARIABLES=sales_1
  /CRITERIA=CIN(.95) .
FILTER OFF.
```

Group Statistics

SEX		AREA	N	Mean	Std. Deviation	Std. Error Mean
male	SALES_1	North	3	5321.3433	3134.3666	1809.6274
		South	7	6220.3343	2823.4992	1067.1824
female	SALES_1	North	6	6577.0533	2284.4114	932.6070
		South	5	4700.3280	1409.6785	630.4274

Independent Samples Test

SEX			Levene's Test for Equality of Variances		t-test for Equality of Means					95% Confidence Interval of the Difference	
			F	Sig.	t	df	Sig. (2-tailed)	Mean Difference	Std. Error Difference	Lower	Upper
male	SALES_1	Equal variances assumed	.104	.755	-.449	8	.666	-898.9910	2004.1831	-5520.65	722.6635
		Equal variances not assumed			-.428	3.492	.694	-898.9910	2100.8640	-7082.14	284.1583
female	SALES_1	Equal variances assumed	3.088	.113	1.594	9	.145	1876.7253	1177.6561	-787.3178	4540.7685
		Equal variances not assumed			1.667	8.417	.132	1876.7253	1125.6974	-696.9346	4450.3853

```
SPLIT FILE
  OFF.
```

Figure 13.2   *Example of using Split File to analyse males and females separately*

When you choose from the menu

```
Data
    Select Cases
```

it opens a dialogue box shown in Figure 13.4, which has a number of paths through it. Suppose you want to compare (using a *t*-test) the sales_2 scores of men and women but only for those respondents who had a score of at least 5000 on sales_1. To select respondents with a sales_1 score of at least 5000, click on the If Condition is Satisfied option and then on the If... button, which opens another box, entitled Select Cases: If. This requires you to enter the variables to be used for selecting cases and mathematical or logical expressions and is described in section 12.3.

```
USE ALL.
COMPUTE filter_$=(sex < 3).
VARIABLE LABEL filter_$ 'sex < 3 (FILTER)'.
VALUE LABELS filter_$  0 'Not Selected' 1 'Selected'.
FORMAT filter_$ (f1.0).
FILTER BY filter_$.
EXECUTE .
SORT CASES BY sex .
SPLIT FILE
  SEPARATE BY sex .
T-TEST
  GROUPS=area(1 2)
  /MISSING=ANALYSIS
  /VARIABLES=sales_1
  /CRITERIA=CIN(.95) .
SPLIT FILE
  OFF.
FILTER OFF.
```

Group Statistics^a

	AREA	N	Mean	Std. Deviation	Std. Error Mean
SALES_1	North	3	5321.3433	3134.3666	1809.6274
	South	7	6220.3343	2823.4992	1067.1824

a. SEX = male

Independent Samples Test^a

		Levene's Test for Equality of Variances		t-test for Equality of Means						
									95% Confidence Interval of the Difference	
		F	Sig.	t	df	Sig. (2-tailed)	Mean Difference	Std. Error Difference	Lower	Upper
SALES_	Equal variances assumed	.104	.755	-.449	8	.666	-898.9910	2004.1831	5520.65	722.6635
	Equal variances not assumed			-.428	3.492	.694	-898.9910	2100.8640	-7082.14	284.1583

a. SEX = male

Group Statistics^a

	AREA	N	Mean	Std. Deviation	Std. Error Mean
SALES_1	North	6	6577.0533	2284.4114	932.6070
	South	5	4700.3280	1409.6785	630.4274

a. SEX = female

Independent Samples Test^a

		Levene's Test for Equality of Variances		t-test for Equality of Means						
									95% Confidence Interval of the Difference	
		F	Sig.	t	df	Sig. (2-tailed)	Mean Difference	Std. Error Difference	Lower	Upper
SALES_1	Equal variances assumed	3.088	.113	1.594	9	.145	1876.7253	1177.6561	-787.3178	4540.7685
	Equal variances not assumed			1.667	8.417	.132	1876.7253	1125.6974	-696.9346	4450.3853

a. SEX = female

Figure 13.3 *Example of output from Split File with the Organize Output by Groups option*

So for the example of selecting the cases where sales_1 is 5000 or more, you need to have this formula (sales_1 >= 5000) in the main text box of this dialogue box. Click on Continue to return to the Select Cases box and then press Paste to insert the syntax into a syntax window. The syntax is shown in Figure 13.5, and illustrates the way a filter is applied. The *t*-test can then be requested from the Statistics menu, and will be applied only to those cases included when the Select Cases command has run.

When you have used Select Cases and want to return to using all the cases in the data file, turn Select Cases off by selecting the All Cases option from Figure 13.4 and pasting that into the syntax window, where it will show, as illustrated in Figure 13.5, the commands

```
Filter off.
Use all.
Execute.
```

Running these commands turns Select File off.

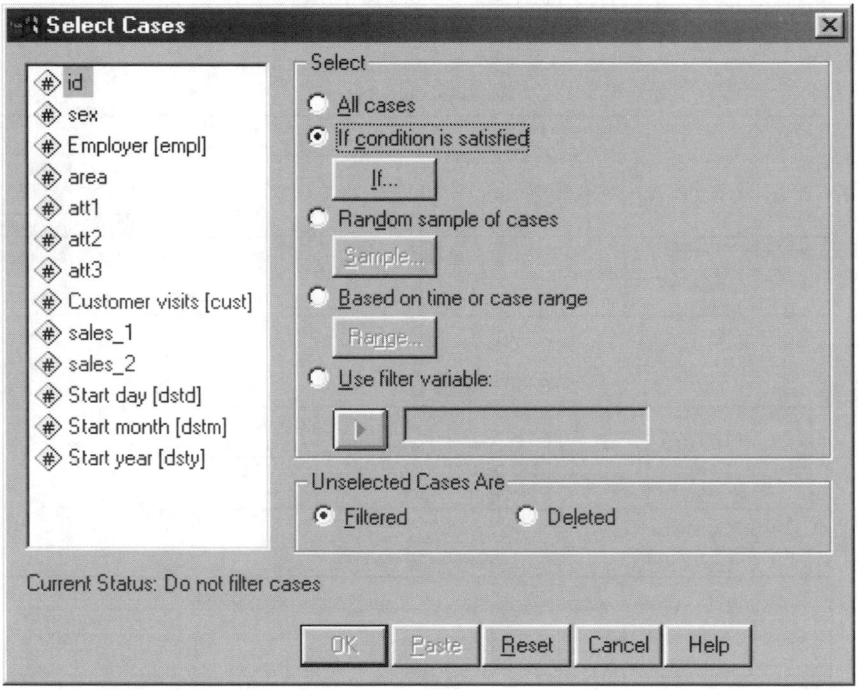

Figure 13.4   *The dialogue box for Select Cases*

13.5 Selecting a subset of cases based on case number or id number

The option in Figure 13.4 to select cases based on Time or Case Range allows you to select subsets of cases. If you select this entry and then

```
* Using Select Cases to select respondents who scored 5000
or more on sales_1.
USE ALL.
COMPUTE filter_$=(sales_1 >= 5000).
VARIABLE LABEL filter_$ 'sales_1 >= 5000 (FILTER)'.
VALUE LABELS filter_$ 0 'Not Selected' 1 'Selected'.
FORMAT filter_$ (f1.0).
FILTER BY filter_$.
EXECUTE .
* statistical procedures would follow here.
*The following lines turn off Select Cases.
FILTER OFF.
USE ALL.
EXECUTE .
```

Figure 13.5   *Example of the syntax for Select Cases. Note that this example selects cases with a score of 5000 or more on the variable sales_1*

press the Range. . . button, you can type into textboxes the numbers of the first and last cases you want to use in the analysis. Remember that the casenumber is the number of the row in the table you see when you are looking at the Data Editor. The actual data which is in any row may change; for example you might start with respondent 1, a male, in the first row. But if you then sort the data by sex, this respondent's data may move and be in a different row of the Data Editor. Bear this in mind if you are thinking of using this way of selecting cases.

You may want to select certain cases, knowing just which cases they are. For example, you might want to analyse the data from respondents 1 to 10 only. This can easily be done if you have entered an identification number as a variable, which is always to be recommended. (In the data file salesq, the variable id was used for this purpose.) To analyse only the data from respondents 1 to 10, i.e. with identification numbers below 11, and assuming the variable id is the identification number variable that was entered for each respondent, select

Data
    Select Cases

and then click on the If Condition is Satisfied option and the If. . . button. By clicking on the appropriate buttons, get the entry in the text box to read id<11, and then press the Continue button and then the Paste button to put the command into your syntax file. Run the syntax to have Select Cases operating. When you have run the analyses you require, remember to turn off Select Cases by selecting the All Cases option from Figure 13.4, pasting that into your syntax file and running it.

13.6 Selecting a random sample of cases

With very large data file, you may wish to select a sample of cases for analysis. To select a 10% random sample, use from the menu

```
Data
        Select Cases...
```

In the Select Cases dialogue box (Figure 13.4) select Random Sample of Cases and click on the Sample button. Another box is revealed and allows you to specify a percentage of the cases or an exact number of cases selected randomly from the data file.

14

HOW MANY RESPONDENTS GAVE A PARTICULAR ANSWER? FREQUENCY DATA

Summary

- To obtain tables and histograms or barcharts showing how many people gave each response use Analyze /Descriptive Statistics /Frequencies.
- To find out how often a respondent used a particular response category use Transform /Count.
- Obtain cross-tabulations from Analyze /Descriptive Statistics /Crosstabs.
- The two-sample chi-square is made available from the Statistics button of the Analyze /Descriptive Statistics /Crosstabs dialogue box. Do not confuse this two-sample chi-square with the one obtained from the chi-square option of the Analyze /Nonparametric Tests menu, which gives the one-sample chi-square.

14.1 Obtaining tables showing how many people gave each response: Frequencies

Probably the first question you ask of your data is: how many people gave each alternative response to a particular question? The answer is obtained using the Frequencies command. If you want cross-tabulations, showing how many people with a particular score on one variable obtained a particular score on another variable, the procedure needed is Crosstabs described in section 14.4.

Obtain the frequencies procedure by selecting

```
Analyze
    Descriptive Statistics
        Frequencies
```

The dialogue box shown in Figure 14.1 is presented. Select each variable to be analysed by clicking on its name, which will then be highlighted.

Then click in the button marked with a right-pointing arrow, and the variable will appear in the right-hand box, the one headed Variable(s).

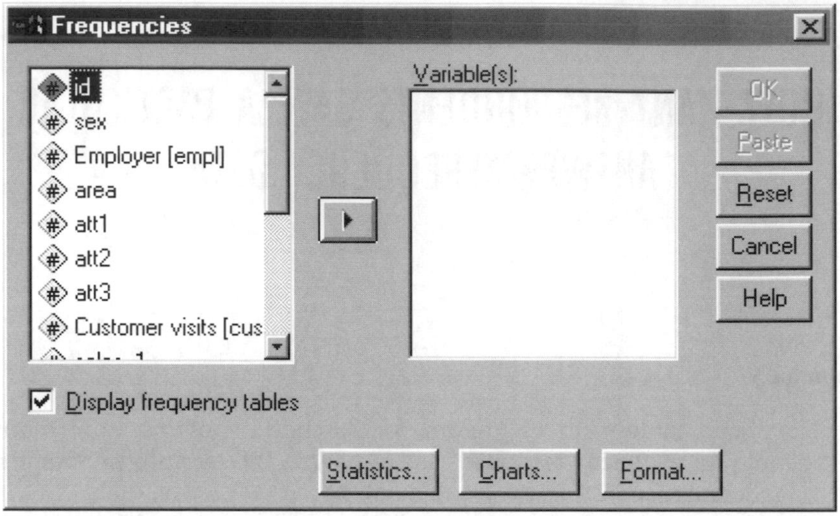

Figure 14.1   *The dialogue box for Frequencies*

The result of running Frequencies on the variable sex in salesq is shown in Figure 14.2. The first table shows the number of valid cases and the number of cases in the data file where data on the variable sex was missing. The main table shows the frequency of each score on the variable sex. In the data file salesq, the scores are 1 for male, 2 for female and 3 which was defined as a missing value and represents sex unknown. In the output table the scores 1 and 2 have been given their value labels 'male' and 'female'. The frequencies are shown as percentages in the Percent column. Valid Percent gives the percentages when missing values are excluded, so for males there are 10 cases, which is 45.5% of 22 (the total number of cases in the data file) but 47.6% of 21 (the number of cases where sex is known). The Cum Percent column shows the cumulative percentages of the valid percent column.

To obtain the means or other statistics using Frequencies, request them by clicking on the button labelled Statistics. . . at the bottom left of the dialogue box shown in Figure 14.1, which reveals another dialogue box illustrated in chapter 7 (Figure 7.6).

14.2 Histograms, bar charts and piecharts showing distributions of scores

The Frequencies procedure provides histograms, bar charts and piecharts showing the distribution of the scores on any variable. These are useful

```
FREQUENCIES
   VARIABLES=sex
   /ORDER   ANALYSIS .
```

Statistics

SEX

N	Valid	21
	Missing	1

SEX

		Frequency	Percent	Valid Percent	Cumulative Percent
Valid	male	10	45.5	47.6	47.6
	female	11	50.0	52.4	100.0
	Total	21	95.5	100.0	
Missing	3.00	1	4.5		
Total		22	100.0		

Figure 14.2   *Output from the Frequencies procedure*

for seeing whether the distribution approximates a normal one, whether it is likely that some of the data has been miskeyed. Details on how to obtain these types of data plot are given in section 10.7.

14.3 How many times did a respondent give a particular answer? Count

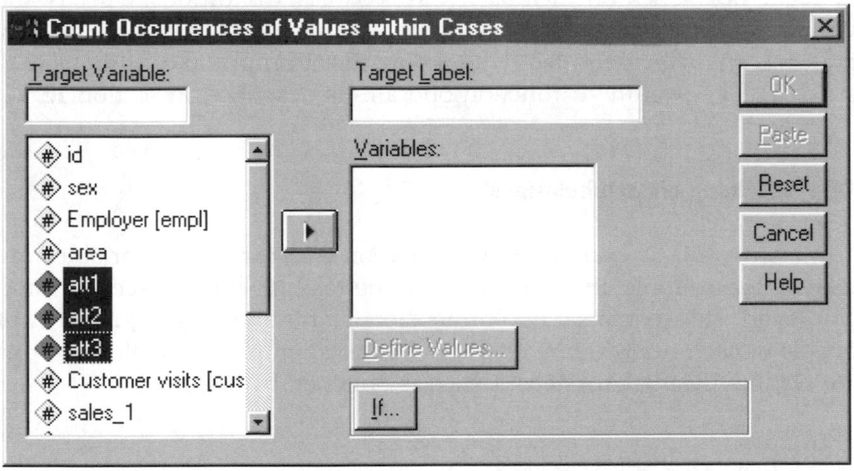

Figure 14.3   *The dialogue box for Count*

You may wish to know how often a respondent used a particular response category. For example, in salesq, how often did the respondents use the response 3 on the attitude questions? This kind of question can be answered by using the Count procedure, obtained from the menu by selecting

```
Transform
      Count
```

Count creates a new variable, and the dialogue box shown in Figure 14.3 asks you to enter a name for this in the Target Variable text box. You then specify the variables to be analysed, and click on the Define Values button, which opens another box, shown in Figure 14.4, in which you indicate the value or range of values to be counted. To count how many times the response 3 was given to att1, att2 and att3 in salesq, you would enter these variables into the Variables list in Figure 14.3, enter a name such as num3 for the Target variable, and put a label such as 'Number of 3 responses on att questions' in the Target Label text box. Click on Define Values, and in the Value text box shown in Figure 14.4 you would enter 3, click on the Add button, and then on Continue, which takes you back to the Count Occurrences box. Clicking on Paste puts the syntax illustrated in Figure 14.5 into a syntax window. When the procedure is run, the new variable is added to the data in the Data Editor. Switch to the data window to see the new variable.

It is possible to perform Count on specified cases, such as only those which have a score of 1 on sex. This is achieved by selecting the If... button, and entering requirements in the Count Occurrences: If Cases dialogue box. Click on Include if Cases Satisfy Conditions:, specify the variable to be used to identify the cases (e.g. sex) and then indicate how the cases are to be identified by inserting the appropriate conditions (e.g. sex = 1). The way the If function operates is described in section 12.3.

14.4 Obtaining cross-tabulations

You often want to examine how scores on two (or more) variables are related; for example, in salesq, what is the relationship between sex and employer? This requires a two-dimensional table showing the number of people of each sex who are employed by each employer. Tables like this are obtained using Crosstabs, which is obtained by selecting

```
Analyze
      Descriptive Statistics
            Crosstabs
```

The dialogue box shown in Figure 14.6 asks you to enter a variable to form the rows of the table and a variable to form the columns from the variable list. If you insert more than one variable into the Row(s) or

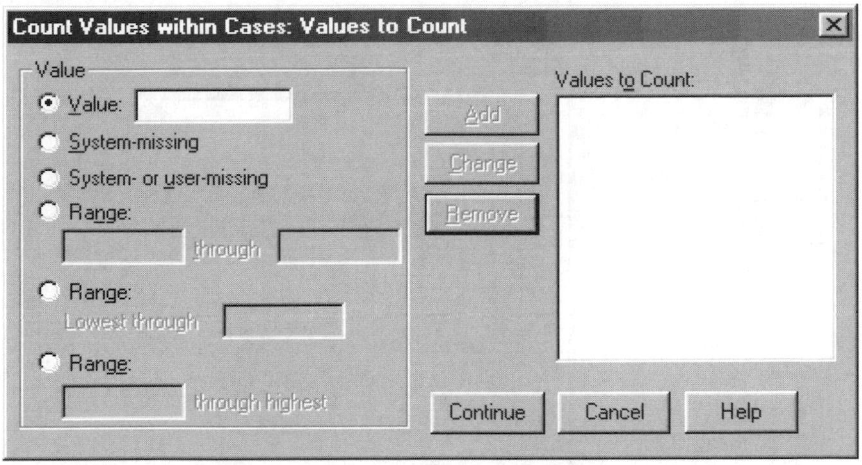

Figure 14.4   *The Count Values: Values to Count dialogue box*

```
COUNT
  num3 = att1 att2 att3   (3)   .
VARIABLE LABELS num3 'Number of 3 responses on att
questions' .
EXECUTE .
```

Figure 14.5   *Example of the syntax for the Count procedure*

Column(s) boxes, you will obtain a set of cross-tabulations. An example of the output when a cross-tabulation of sex by employer was requested is shown in Figure 14.7.

Note that in Figure 14.7, the total shown in the Case Processing Summary is 21 and one missing observation is indicated; this is because the original data had one case where sex was coded as 3, which had been defined as a missing value indicating the sex of that respondent was unknown. Consequently there are only 21 cases that can be used in the sex by employer table.

The contents of the Crosstabs table are set by clicking on the Cells button in Figure 14.6, which opens a box in which you can ask for Expected frequencies, and for the observed frequencies to be expressed as percentages of the row, column and/or total number of cases in the table. Figure 14.8 shows the output when all statistics are requested: there are the actual frequency of cases in each cell (Count), the expected value if there were no relationship between the two variables tabulated (Expected Count), the frequencies as a percentage of the total in the row, as a percentage of the total in the column, and as percentage of the overall total. There are also figures for Residual, Std Residual and Adjusted Residual which are associated with the chi-square test and are

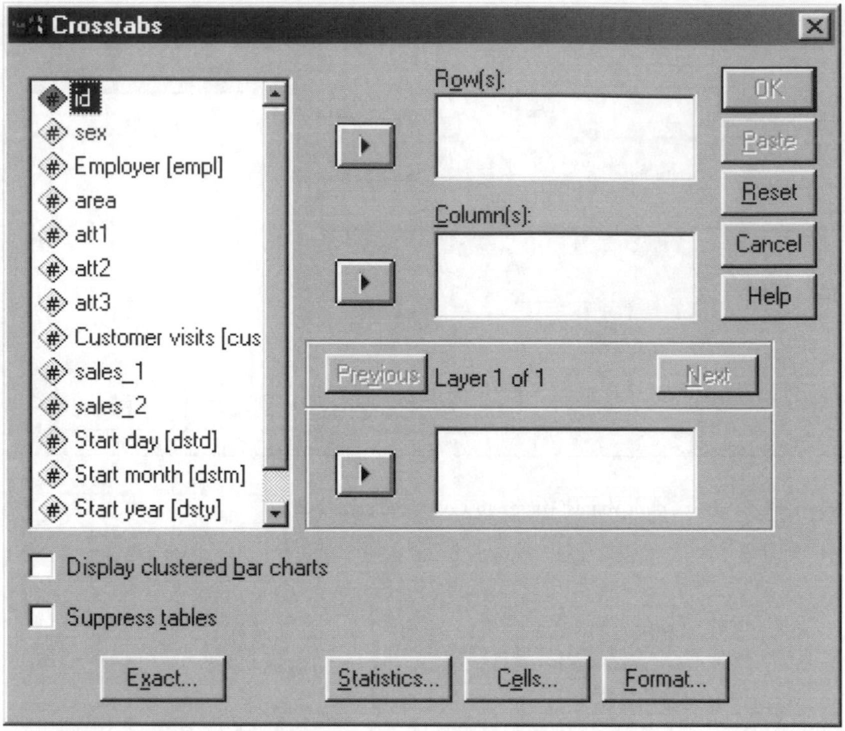

Figure 14.6   *The dialogue box for Crosstabs*

```
CROSSTABS
  /TABLES=sex  BY empl
  /FORMAT= AVALUE TABLES
  /CELLS= COUNT .
```

Case Processing Summary

	Cases					
	Valid		Missing		Total	
	N	Percent	N	Percent	N	Percent
SEX * Employer	21	95.5%	1	4.5%	22	100.0%

SEX * Employer Crosstabulation

Count

		Employer			
		Jones and Son	Smith and Co	Tomkins	Total
SEX	male	4	3	3	10
	female	4	4	3	11
Total		8	7	6	21

Figure 14.7   *Output from the command Crosstabs Tables sex By empl*

unlikely to be needed. (Residual is the difference between the observed frequency and the expected frequency.)

```
CROSSTABS
  /TABLES=sex  BY empl
  /FORMAT= AVALUE TABLES
  /CELLS= COUNT EXPECTED ROW COLUMN TOTAL RESID SRESID
ASRESID .
```

Case Processing Summary

	Cases					
	Valid		Missing		Total	
	N	Percent	N	Percent	N	Percent
SEX * Employer	21	95.5%	1	4.5%	22	100.0%

SEX * Employer Crosstabulation

			Employer			
			Jones and Son	Smith and Co	Tomkins	Total
SEX	male	Count	4	3	3	10
		Expected Count	3.8	3.3	2.9	10.0
		% within SEX	40.0%	30.0%	30.0%	100.0%
		% within Employer	50.0%	42.9%	50.0%	47.6%
		% of Total	19.0%	14.3%	14.3%	47.6%
		Residual	.2	-.3	.1	
		Std. Residual	.1	-.2	.1	
		Adjusted Residual	.2	-.3	.1	
	female	Count	4	4	3	11
		Expected Count	4.2	3.7	3.1	11.0
		% within SEX	36.4%	36.4%	27.3%	100.0%
		% within Employer	50.0%	57.1%	50.0%	52.4%
		% of Total	19.0%	19.0%	14.3%	52.4%
		Residual	-.2	.3	-.1	
		Std. Residual	-.1	.2	-.1	
		Adjusted Residual	-.2	.3	-.1	
Total		Count	8	7	6	21
		Expected Count	8.0	7.0	6.0	21.0
		% within SEX	38.1%	33.3%	28.6%	100.0%
		% within Employer	100.0%	100.0%	100.0%	100.0%
		% of Total	38.1%	33.3%	28.6%	100.0%

Figure 14.8   *Output from the command Crosstabs Tables sex By empl with additional cell contents*

You may want a further breakdown of the figures, with separate tables of variable1 by variable2 for each level of variable3; for example, suppose we want a sex by employer table, like that shown in Figure 14.7 but for each area group separately. The variable area is referred to as control variable, and you have to enter it in the box under the heading Layer 1 of 1 in the dialogue box shown in Figure 14.6. You can have further control variables by clicking on the Next button.

If you wish to have the table organised in descending order of variable scores, or to obtain an index of the tables you are requesting, these can be set by using the Format button in the Crosstabs dialogue box.

14.5 Obtaining the two-sample chi-square test

The chi-square test is used when respondents have been allocated to categories on two variables (e.g. sex, area). The test compares the number of cases falling into each cell of the table with the frequency that would be expected if there were no association between the two variables that form the table. (The expected frequencies are calculated for each cell in the table by multiplying the appropriate row and column totals and dividing by N.)

Chi-square and other tests of association such as the contingency coefficient, and also correlations are available from the Statistics button of the Crosstabs dialogue box (Figure 14.6).

The output from the chi-square test for two samples is shown in Figure 14.9. The Cross-tabulation table shows the number of cases in each cell of the table. It is followed by the Chi-square Tests table showing the value of chi-square (labelled Pearson Chi-square), with the degrees of freedom (df) and the probability (Asymp. Sig.). If the Significance value is equal to or less than 0.05, you can conclude that the chi-square test indicates that there is a significant association between the two variables. The output also gives you the figures for Likelihood Ratio chi-square and the Fisher Exact Test which should be used if more than 20% of cells have an expected frequency count of less than 5. (The number of cells having an expected frequency less than 5 is shown below the table.) The Linear-by-Linear Association tests whether there is a linear relationship between the row and column variables. It is only applicable to ordinal data, and should not be used if the data is nominal.

The chi-square test is only valid if three conditions are met. First, the data must be independent: no respondent can appear in more than one cell of the table. Secondly, no cell should have an expected frequency of less than 1. The footnote under the Chi-square Tests table tells you the minimum expected frequency, so it is simple to check whether this condition has been met. If the test is not valid, you must either alter the data table by amalgamating categories (using the Recode procedure explained in section 12.6) to remove cells with small expected frequencies, or collect more data.

The third requirement is that no more than 20% of the Expected Frequencies in the table can be less than 5. So if you have a 2 × 5 table which has 10 cells, the test will be invalid if three expected frequencies are below 5. If your data fails to meet this criterion, you have to collect more data or it may be possible to change the table; for example you could merge groups together.

With a 2 × 2 table, there are two further points to bear in mind. For a 2 × 2 table, one should use the correction for continuity rather than the simple chi-square: you will see that there is a Continuity Correction value shown in the output table, and this rather than the chi-square value should be used for this 2 × 2 table. Also, with a 2 × 2 table, if the smallest expected frequency for any cell is less than 5, then one should use the Fisher Exact Test. As Figure 14.9 illustrates, the result of this test is provided if it is needed, as it is in this case. The chi-square test is not valid on this table, as more than 20% of cells have an expected frequency smaller than 5; so you would use the Fisher Exact Test, and conclude that there is no relationship between sex and area of work.

```
CROSSTABS
  /TABLES=sex   BY area
  /FORMAT= AVALUE TABLES
  /STATISTIC=CHISQ
  /CELLS= COUNT TOTAL .
```

Case Processing Summary

	Cases					
	Valid		Missing		Total	
	N	Percent	N	Percent	N	Percent
SEX * AREA	21	95.5%	1	4.5%	22	100.0%

SEX * AREA Crosstabulation

			AREA		Total
			North	South	
SEX	male	Count	3	7	10
		% of Total	14.3%	33.3%	47.6%
	female	Count	6	5	11
		% of Total	28.6%	23.8%	52.4%
Total		Count	9	12	21
		% of Total	42.9%	57.1%	100.0%

Chi-Square Tests

	Value	df	Asymp. Sig. (2-sided)	Exact Sig. (2-sided)	Exact Sig. (1-sided)
Pearson Chi-Square	1.289[b]	1	.256		
Continuity Correction[a]	.481	1	.488		
Likelihood Ratio	1.307	1	.253		
Fisher's Exact Test				.387	.245
Linear-by-Linear Association	1.227	1	.268		
N of Valid Cases	21				

a. Computed only for a 2x2 table

b. 2 cells (50.0%) have expected count less than 5. The minimum expected count is 4.29.

Figure 14.9   *Output from Crosstabs Tables sex By area Statistics Chisq*

14.6 Loglinear analysis

Loglinear analysis is a technique for analysing multiway contingency tables of frequency counts (cross tabulations) which are more complex than the two-dimensional tables shown in Figures 14.7, 14.8 and 14.9. It involves transforming the frequency values into their natural logs, and has the benefit of allowing tests for interactions in the classifications. Accounts can be found in texts on multivariate statistics such as Stevens (1996). It is available from the Analyze /Loglinear drop-down menu.

15

WHAT IS THE AVERAGE SCORE? MEASURES OF CENTRAL TENDENCY AND DISPERSION

Summary

- To obtain the mean, sum and standard deviation of all respondents on any of the variables use the Analyze /Descriptive Statistics /Explore, Frequencies or Descriptives procedures.
- To obtain the means of subgroups of respondents use the Analyze /Compare Means /Means procedure.
- To obtain the median or mode use Analyze /Descriptive Statistics /Frequencies.
- Obtain z scores using Analyze /Descriptive Statistics /Descriptives.

15.1 Finding the mean and standard deviation

Note that when you require the means of subgroups of respondents, such as the mean of males and then separately the mean of females, you need the Means procedure (see section 15.3), which also provides the mean score of all the respondents on any of the variables. But the simple way to obtain the mean, sum and standard deviation of all respondents on any of the variables in the data file, is to use the Explore (which appears in the syntax file as Examine), Frequencies or Descriptives procedures which are accessed by selecting

```
Analyze
     Descriptive Statistics
```

Specify the variables to be analysed by clicking on their names in the list and then on the button with the right-pointing arrow. The mean and standard deviation are provided automatically. To obtain the sum, variance, range, standard error and indices of kurtosis or skew, if you are using Descriptives select the Options button and if you are using Frequencies select the Statistics button. Then specify the statistics required. You can have the means listed in alphabetical order of the variable names if you use Descriptives, select Options and in the dialogue box which is then presented select Name display order.

When carrying out parametrical statistical tests, such as the *t*-test, the output will give the means and variances of the data, so there is no need to obtain them using a separate procedure.

15.2 Finding median or mode

The median and mode are obtained if you use

```
Analyze
     Descriptive Statistics
          Frequencies
```

When presented with the dialogue box, click on the Statistics button, and check the appropriate boxes.

The median is also provided by the Explore procedure, described in chapter 9 or the Table procedure described in chapter 21.

15.3 Finding the means of subgroups of respondents

To obtain the means of subgroups of respondents, use the Means procedure, which is obtained by selecting

```
Analyze
     Compare Means
          Means
```

This reveals the dialogue box shown in Figure 15.1. Suppose you want the mean scores of males and females on the sales_1 variable in the salesq data file. Having selected Analyze /Compare Means /Means from the window menu, insert the dependent variable (sales_1) in the Dependent List text box of the Means dialogue box, and then insert sex into the Independent List text box, and click on Paste. The output is shown in Figure 15.2. It shows the mean and standard deviation on sales_1 for each of the two sex groups from the data file salesq. Observe that the respondent whose sex is unknown, who was given a sex score of 3 (missing value), is not included in the table.

The Means dialogue box allows you to subdivide the respondents into further subgroups by using the unhelpfully-titled Layer 1 of 1 option. To find the mean scores on the sales_1 variable of males and females from each area (North and South), enter sales_1 as the Dependent List variable, enter sex as the Independent List variable, then click on the

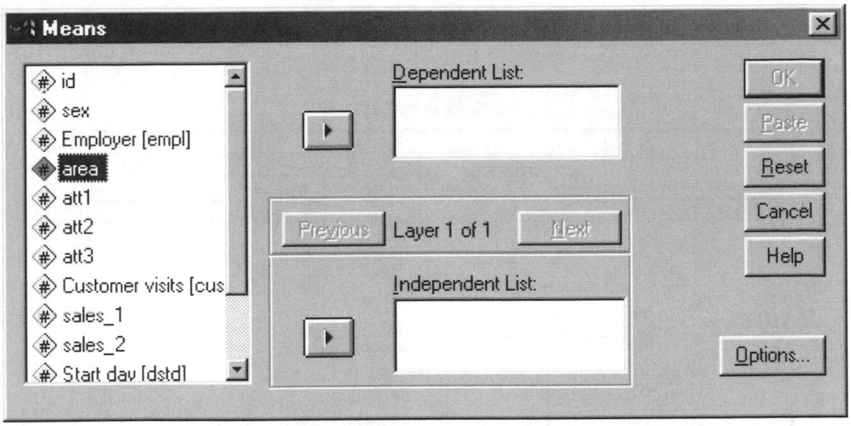

Figure 15.1 *The Means dialogue box*

Next button and insert area in the Independent List box. The output is shown in Figure 15.3 and gives the means of the subgroups.

```
MEANS
    TABLES=sales_1  BY sex
    /CELLS MEAN COUNT STDDEV  .
```

Case Processing Summary

	Cases					
	Included		Excluded		Total	
	N	Percent	N	Percent	N	Percent
SALES_1 * SEX	21	95.5%	1	4.5%	22	100.0%

Report

SALES_1

SEX	Mean	N	Std. Deviation
male	5950.6370	10	2772.4555
female	5723.9964	11	2089.1906
Total	5831.9205	21	2377.9699

Figure 15.2 *Example of the output from the Means procedure*

If you want the mean scores on sales_1 for the separate sex groups and then for the separate area groups, edit the syntax in the syntax window to read

```
MEANS /TABLES sales_1 BY sex area .
```

One-way analysis of variance (described more fully in chapter 16) to compare the means of the subgroups is obtained by selecting the Options

```
MEANS
  TABLES=sales_1  BY sex  BY area
  /CELLS MEAN COUNT STDDEV  .
```

Case Processing Summary

	Cases					
	Included		Excluded		Total	
	N	Percent	N	Percent	N	Percent
SALES_1 * SEX * AREA	21	95.5%	1	4.5%	22	100.0%

Report

SALES_1

SEX	AREA	Mean	N	Std. Deviation
male	North	5321.3433	3	3134.3666
	South	6220.3343	7	2823.4992
	Total	5950.6370	10	2772.4555
female	North	6577.0533	6	2284.4114
	South	4700.3280	5	1409.6785
	Total	5723.9964	11	2089.1906
Total	North	6158.4833	9	2472.2156
	South	5586.9983	12	2384.0451
	Total	5831.9205	21	2377.9699

Figure 15.3   *Output from requesting means of subgroups using Means*

button from Figure 15.1 and checking the box labelled ANOVA Table and Eta.

15.4 Obtaining *z* scores

The Descriptives procedure is used to obtain z scores for any variable, by selecting the Save Standardized Values as Variables option in the Descriptives dialogue box. This option creates a new variable which is added to the data file, and is named as z + the first 7 letters of the variable name so that the z scores of sales_1 are labeled zsales_1. When the syntax is run, switch to the data editor window to see the new column of z scores.

16

PARAMETRIC STATISTICAL TESTS COMPARING MEANS

Summary

- When using parametric tests, to compare the scores of two groups of different subjects on one variable, use the between-subjects or independent-samples *t*-test.
- Remember that it is the absolute value of *t* which is important: ignore any minus sign.
- To compare the mean of a sample with a specified test value, use the one-sample *t*-test.
- To compare the mean scores of three or more sets of data use the analysis of variance.
- Use Table 16.1 to decide which type of analysis of variance is needed.
- Remember that right-clicking over items in the dialogue boxes presents an explanation of what the item is.

16.1 Basic preliminaries about the parametric tests

This chapter describes the commands needed to obtain the commoner parametric statistical tests used to compare the means of sets of scores. Guidance on selecting which test to use is provided in section 2.9. To compare the means of two sets of scores, use the *t*-test. If you are comparing the scores of the same respondents on two variables, use the within-subjects (paired-samples) *t*-test. To compare the scores of two groups of different subjects on one variable, use the between-subjects or independent-samples *t*-test. To compare the mean of a sample with a specified test value, use the one-sample *t*-test. If you wish to compare more than two sets of scores, you need the analysis of variance and should refer to section 16.5.

The printouts for the parametric tests show two-tailed significance (probability) levels which are appropriate for testing non-directional hypotheses. If you have a directional hypothesis you can halve the probability values which SPSS prints out. For example, a significance

level of 0.08 for a two-tailed (non-directional) test equates to a significance level of 0.04 for a one-tailed (directional) test.

Except for section 16.12, the examples shown in this chapter use the
names of the variables in the salesq file; if you are applying the
commands to a set of data with different variable names, you must of
course use those variable names.

16.2 Within-subjects (paired-samples) t-test

The dialogue box for the paired-samples *t*-test, shown in Figure 16.1, is
obtained by selecting

```
Analyze
      Compare Means
            Paired-Samples T Test
```

Indicate the two variables to be compared by clicking on each of them;
the first one will appear as the Current Selections Variable 1, and the
second one will appear as Current Selections Variable 2. To insert these
into the Paired Variables list, click on the right-pointing arrow button:
the two variables will then be shown as a linked pair. You can create
further pairs in the same way. The Options button of the T Test box
allows you to alter the confidence intervals shown in the output by
entering a number (such as 99 for the 99% interval) in the text box.

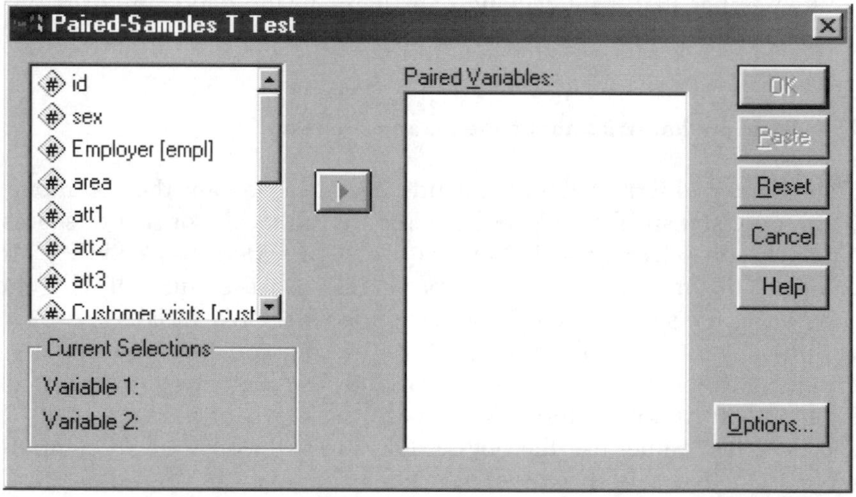

Figure 16.1   *The dialogue box for the paired-samples t-test*

Clicking on Paste will put into the Syntax window the procedure
commands shown in Figure 16.2, where the scores on att1 and att2 have

been selected for comparison. When the procedure is run, the output shown in Figure 16.2 appears in the output viewer. The first table shows the means, standard deviations and standard errors of the scores on the two variables. The second table shows the correlation between them (0.700 in this example). The significance of the correlation is provided: the value of .000 in Figure 16.2 indicates that the correlation is significant beyond the 0.001 level.

The paired t-test involves taking the difference between the two scores for each respondent and finding the mean of these difference scores. The Paired Samples Test table in the output gives this mean difference, its standard deviation and standard error and the confidence intervals of the difference. The value of the t statistic is then shown, with its degrees of freedom (df) and its probability level (Sig. 2-tail): if the probability is less than 0.05 (in Figure 16.2 it is .004), you can conclude there was a statistically significant difference between the means of the two sets of scores. In Figure 16.2, the mean on att2 at 3.0909 is significantly different from the mean on att1, which is 2.5455.

```
T-TEST
  PAIRS= att1  WITH att2 (PAIRED)
  /CRITERIA=CIN(.95)
  /MISSING=ANALYSIS.
```

Paired Samples Statistics

		Mean	N	Std. Deviation	Std. Error Mean
Pair 1	ATT1	2.5455	22	1.1010	.2347
	ATT2	3.0909	22	.9211	.1964

Paired Samples Correlations

		N	Correlation	Sig.
Pair 1	ATT1 & ATT2	22	.700	.000

Paired Samples Test

		Paired Differences							
					95% Confidence Interval of the Difference				
		Mean	Std. Deviation	Std. Error Mean	Lower	Upper	t	df	Sig. (2-tailed)
Pair 1	ATT1 - ATT2	-.5455	.8004	.1707	-.9003	-.1906	-3.196	21	.004

Figure 16.2   *Output from a paired-sample t-test*

16.3 Between-subjects (independent-samples) *t*-test

The dialogue box for the independent-samples t-test, shown in Figure 16.3, is obtained by selecting

```
Analyze
     Compare Means
          Independent Samples T Test
```

The dependent variables to be compared have to be inserted into the Tests Variable(s) text box. The independent (grouping) variable used to divide the respondents into the two groups to be compared has to be inserted into the Grouping Variable text box, and you then have to click the Define Groups button, which opens the dialogue box shown in Figure 16.4. The normal procedure is to enter into the Group 1 and Group 2 windows the values on the grouping variable which define the two groups to be compared. For example, if you wanted to compare the scores on sales_1 for respondents of employer 2 with those for respondents on employer 3, you would insert the variable (empl) in the Grouping Variable box of the Independent Samples T Test dialogue box (Figure 16.3). Then you would click on the Define Groups button and when presented with the Define Groups dialogue box shown in Figure 16.4, enter 2 into the Group 1 window and 3 into the Group 2 window. Click on Continue to return to the T-Test box, and click on Paste to transfer the commands to the syntax window.

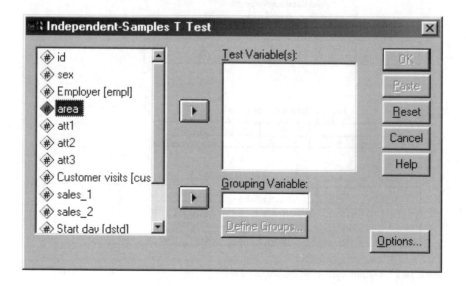

Figure 16.3   *The dialogue box for the independent-samples t-test*

An example of the syntax for the independent groups *t*-test and the output provided is shown in Figure 16.5. The Group Statistics table shows that the variable being tested was sales_1, and that the groups of

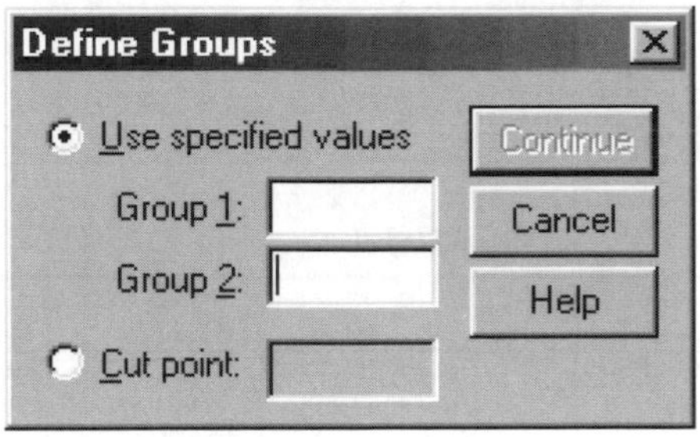

Figure 16.4   *The Define Groups dialogue box*

scores being compared were those for the two employers Smith and Co and Tomkins. (The variable labels which were assigned earlier are printed.) The mean score on sales_1 for each group is shown, with the standard deviations and standard errors. The table entitled Independent Samples Test gives the outcome of Levene's test for equality of variance, and then *t* values, degrees of freedom, two-tailed probability (Sig.) of *t*, mean difference, standard errors for the difference and 95% confidence intervals for the difference. If the Levene test shows a Significance (Sig.) level less than 0.05, the populations from which the two groups are samples had unequal variances and you should use the *t* value for unequal variances (the final line of the table). If the Levene test has a probability value greater than 0.05 (as here), you are entitled to use the *t* value for equal variances. Remember that it is the absolute value of *t* which is taken: ignore the negative sign. You do not need a table of *t* values, as the printout shows the significance value. In Figure 16.5 the significance is shown as .000 indicating that the means differ at less than the 0.001 level.

FORMING TWO GROUPS ACCORDING TO THEIR SCORES ON AN INDEPENDENT VARIABLE   When the Define Groups dialogue box (Figure 16.4) is presented, it has an option Cut Point, and a text window into which a value can be entered. This has the effect of dividing the cases into two groups, one which has scores below the value entered as the cut point and the other having scores equal to or above the cut point. This can be useful if, for example, you wanted to compare the means of two groups formed by dividing them into those scoring below and above a certain value on one of the variables.

An example of the syntax and printout using the Cut Point facility is shown in Figure 16.6, where two groups were formed according to whether they scored below 3 or above or equal to 3 on the variable att2 and their scores on the variable cust were compared. The Levene test was not significant (Significance = 0.266), so the *t* value for equal variances is the one to consider. In Figure 16.6, $t = -1.915$ and $p = .070$ so there is no significant difference between the two means.

```
T-TEST
  GROUPS=empl(2 3)
  /MISSING=ANALYSIS
  /VARIABLES=sales_1
  /CRITERIA=CIN(.95) .
```

Group Statistics

	Employer	N	Mean	Std. Deviation	Std. Error Mean
SALES_1	Smith and Co	8	4625.1713	1089.7836	385.2967
	Tomkins	6	8207.4150	925.1783	377.7025

Independent Samples Test

		Levene's Test for Equality of Variances		t-test for Equality of Means					95% Confidence Interval of the Difference	
		F	Sig.	t	df	Sig. (2-tailed)	Mean Difference	Std. Error Difference	Lower	Upper
SALES_1	Equal variances assumed	.322	.581	-6.475	12	.000	-3582.2437	553.2487	-4787.67	-2376.82
	Equal variances not assumed			-6.639	11.740	.000	-3582.2437	539.5486	-4760.71	-2403.77

Figure 16.5   *Output for an independent t-test*

```
T-TEST
  GROUPS=att2(3)
  /MISSING=ANALYSIS
  /VARIABLES=cust
  /CRITERIA=CIN(.95) .
```

Group Statistics

	ATT2	N	Mean	Std. Deviation	Std. Error Mean
Customer visits	>= 3.00	16	46.8125	14.8199	3.7050
	< 3.00	6	61.5000	19.1911	7.8348

Independent Samples Test

		Levene's Test for Equality of Variances		t-test for Equality of Means					95% Confidence Interval of the Difference	
		F	Sig.	t	df	Sig. (2-tailed)	Mean Difference	Std. Error Difference	Lower	Upper
Customer visits	Equal variances assumed	1.307	.266	-1.915	20	.070	-14.6875	7.6713	-30.6896	1.3146
	Equal variances not assumed			-1.695	7.364	.132	-14.6875	8.6666	-34.9775	5.6025

Figure 16.6   *Examples of use of Cut Point in the independent t-test*

16.4 One-sample *t*-test

The one-sample *t*-test is used to compare the mean of a sample with a specified test value. For example, it could be used to see whether the mean of the scores on the variable att1 is significantly different from 3, the neutral point of the scale for att1 which ran from 1 to 5.

Obtain the one-sample t-test by selecting it from the Analyze /Compare Means menu. Select the variable to be tested and type into the text box the test value with which the mean is to be compared. An example of the syntax and output is illustrated in Figure 16.7. In the One-Sample Test table, the test value is shown and the t-value and significance (probability) are printed. Here, $t = -1.936, p = .066$. As 0.066 is larger than 0.05, the mean on att1 (shown in the One-Sample Statistics table to be 2.5455) is not significantly different from 3.

```
T-TEST
  /TESTVAL=3
  /MISSING=ANALYSIS
  /VARIABLES=att1
  /CRITERIA=CIN (.95) .
```

One-Sample Statistics

	N	Mean	Std. Deviation	Std. Error Mean
ATT1	22	2.5455	1.1010	.2347

One-Sample Test

	Test Value = 3					
					95% Confidence Interval of the Difference	
	t	df	Sig. (2-tailed)	Mean Difference	Lower	Upper
ATT1	-1.936	21	.066	-.4545	-.9427	3.359E-02

Figure 16.7   *Syntax and output for the one-sample t-test*

16.5 Dealing with cases that have missing data when using a *t*-test

The t-test procedures will exclude any case which has missing data on either the variable used to create the groups being compared or on the variable which is being subjected to the t-test. This is referred to as Exclude Cases Analysis-by-Analysis. If you are requesting a number of t-tests on a series of variables, the package will omit those cases which have missing data on the variable being analysed and do this separately for each test. You can ask the program to omit, from all t-tests, any cases which have missing values on either the grouping variable or on any of the variables being t-tested. This is obtained by clicking on the Options button in the T Test dialogue box and then selecting the Exclude Cases Listwise alternative.

16.6 Basic principles of the analysis of variance

When you have three or more sets of parametric data, you may want to test the hypothesis that the means of the sets differ. You cannot use the *t*-test, as that only compares two sets, so the parametric analysis of variance is the technique to employ.

As the name implies, analysis of variance examines the variance within the whole sets of scores. Imagine we have sets of data from three separate groups of subjects, and want to know whether there is a difference between the three groups. If there were no difference between the groups (the null hypothesis is true) their data would all come from the same population, and the three sets of data would all have the same means and the same variances. The variance of each group would be an estimate of the population variance (variance due to random fluctuations between respondents, known as error variance because it arises due to chance alterations in the data). Our best estimate of the population variance is given by calculating the mean of the variances of the three groups. So by looking at the average variance of the three groups, we can get an estimate of the error variance.

Again, if the null hypothesis is true, the means of the three groups will be the same, and the variance of the means (i.e. how much the means differ from each other) will be very small. (We would expect it to be the same as the population variance.) The variance of the means of the three groups is known as the treatment variance. So if the null hypothesis were true, and the three groups did not differ from each other, the variance between the means (the treatment variance) would equal the error variance; if we divided the treatment variance by the error variance, the answer would be 1.00. The result of dividing the treatment variance by the error variance is denoted as *F*.

If the null hypothesis is not true, there is a difference between the three groups. The variance of the means will be larger than the error variance. If we divide the variance of the means (the treatment variance) by the error variance, we shall get a number (*F*) bigger than 1.00.

In the analysis of variance, we compare the treatment variance with the error variance to test the hypothesis that there is a significant difference between the means. There are different types of analysis of variance, and you need to ensure you apply the procedure which is appropriate for the situation you are analysing. When you want to compare three or more levels of one between-subjects variable, use a one-way analysis of variance. But analysis of variance can be extended to situations in which there are two or more independent variables. Imagine we have measured the performance of young (under 30) and old (over 50) subjects at two different times of day (2 am and 2 pm), and used different subjects in each group so there were four separate groups altogether. We might be interested in knowing whether performance differed according to the subject's age, differed according to time of day, and whether there was an interaction between these variables. Interaction means that the effect of one variable was influenced by the other; for example, we might find that the difference between performance at 2 pm and 2 am was less for the younger subjects than for the older ones. If this were so, the analysis of variance would show a significant interaction term.

In the example just given, both variables are between-subjects, as different people were used in each of the four groups. But analysis of variance can be applied to within-subjects (repeated measures) studies, where the same subjects are used in different conditions. For example, we would have a repeated measures study if we had carried out our time-of-day/age of subjects experiment, and tested the same respondents at 2 am and 2 pm.

FIXED AND RANDOM FACTORS When you are asking SPSS to carry out analysis of variance, you will usually be asked to indicate whether the independent variables or factors are fixed or random ones. If the levels of the independent variable are taken to be a random sample of possible levels, then the variable is a random factor. But if the levels of the independent variable are not taken to be a random sample of possible levels, the variable is a fixed factor. An example might make this clear. Imagine you were comparing the two sexes in an analysis of variance. The possible levels on the variable sex, male and female, cannot be thought of as a random sample from a whole series of other possible levels, so sex would be a fixed factor. But if you had respondents from different employers, as we do in the datafile salesq, you might want to take the employers who were included in the study as a random sample from all the other employers who could have been included, so that you could generalize any results and say they were not true only for the employers studied but would also be true for any other random sample of employers. Then employers would be a random factor. Or suppose you had investigated people's memory for short and long words, using words of 6, 8 and 14 letters. You might want to generalize the results to other possible word lengths which could have been used, in which case word length would be a random factor.

If a factor called vname has been identified as a random factor, rather than a fixed one, the syntax includes the subcommand

```
/RANDOM = vname
```

and some of the output numbers differ since the calculations of error terms for random factors are different from those used for fixed factors.

A PRIORI AND POST HOC TESTS Analysis of variance can tell you that there is a difference between the means of the three or more groups of respondents, but it does not tell you just where the differences occur: is group 1 different from both group 2 and group 3, does group 2 differ from both group 1 and group 3? Questions like this are answered by comparing the means of the subgroups, and there are two types of procedure. One is referred to as a priori comparisons, and these are ones that were planned before the data was collected: you might, for example, have predicted that group 3 differs significantly from group 1 but not from group 2. Post hoc tests, on the other hand, are comparisons suggested after you have examined the data.

A priori contrasts, including orthogonal contrasts, can be obtained by clicking the Contrasts. . . button in the dialogue box presented when you are requesting an analysis of variance. How to use this is best explained with a simple example. Suppose we are using a one-way analysis of variance to compare the scores on sales_1 for the three employers in salesq, and had predicted that there would be a significant difference between the scores for employer 1 and the combined scores for employers 2 and 3. To test this prediction we would use linear contrasts: the coefficient for employer 1's data can be set at -1 and the coefficients for employers 2 and 3 each set to 0.5. When the Contrasts button has been pressed, the coefficient of -1 for group 1 is entered in the box marked Coefficient, and the Add button used to insert it into the list. The coefficient of 0.5 for group 2 is then entered in the Coefficient box and Add used to insert it in the list, and finally the coefficient for group 3 is inserted in the list by using the Add button. The order of the coefficients is crucial, as they are applied in sequence to the ascending order of values on the factor variable: the first coefficient is assigned to the lowest value, the second to the next-to-lowest value and so on. Coefficients can be removed or altered by highlighting them and using the Remove or Change buttons. Further sets of contrasts can be entered if you click on the Next button. An example of the output obtained when a priori contrasts were requested in a one-way analysis of variance is shown in Figure 16.11.

Post hoc tests such as Duncan's test, Tukey's test, Scheffe's test (and others) are obtained if you click on the Post Hoc. . . button in the dialogue box for requesting analysis of variance. Select the tests required from the list provided in the dialogue box which is presented. Figure 16.10 shows how the output of the Tukey test is presented in a one-way analysis of variance.

ETA-SQUARED   This statistic is a measure of the strength of the experimental effect, indicating the proportion of the variance accounted for by the experimental variable or factor. It can be obtained from the dialogue boxes used in requesting analysis of variance, by pressing the Options button to reveal a screen such as that shown in Figure 16.13, and checking the Estimates of Effect Size entry. It is added to the analysis of variance output, usually as a separate column of the ANOVA table.

TEST OF SPHERICITY   The output from an analysis of variance will often include a test of sphericity, which shows whether there is heterogeneity of covariance. Advanced textbooks on statistics such as Howell (1992) or Stevens (1996) discuss the meaning of sphericity, but non-experts can take comfort from Stevens (1996): 'There are various tests of sphericity . . . we don't recommend using these tests' (p. 460). Nevertheless, a simplified explanation may be useful. One test of sphericity is Mauchly's test. The values of the Greenhouse–Geisser epsilon and the Huynh–Feldt epsilon are also indications of whether the data shows sphericity: if sphericity is met, the Greenhouse–Geisser epsilon equals 1. The worst possible violation gives epsilon $= 1/(k-1)$. If the test of sphericity is significant, then some adjustment to the degrees of freedom used in calculating the mean square can be made. There are different recommendations about the adjustment which should be applied and how to use the Greenhouse–Geisser epsilon to modify the degrees of freedom. Stevens (1996) says that one should adjust the degrees of freedom from $(k-1)$ and $(k-1)(n-1)$ by multiplying each of these by epsilon, which will reduce the degrees of freedom and mean that a higher value of F is needed before it is taken as statistically significant. In the output, SPSS gives the epsilon values and in the familiar analysis of variance table shows the degrees of freedom, mean squares and values of F which occur if they are used.

OBTAINING HELP   The various help facilities have been mentioned in section 3.11. Remember that when you have a table of output, you can access some help on it by double-clicking on it so it is activated and then putting the cursor over a row or column heading and right-clicking. This opens a menu, one entry of which is What's this? Clicking on this menu entry will reveal a brief explanation of that part of the table.

16.7 Which ANOVA do you require?

Which analysis of variance you need is determined by the design of your study. For most situations, there are two points you need to know: (1) how many independent variables were there (one or more than one)? (2) taking each independent variable in turn, was it a between-subjects (independent samples) variable or a within-subjects (repeated measures) one? If you have more than one independent variable and all variables are between subjects, you need SPSS's UNIANOVA procedure. If any of the independent variables is within subjects (repeated measures), you need SPSS's GLM procedure.

In some cases, you may have two or more dependent variables to be analysed together. In such cases, you require the MANOVA procedure which is described in section 16.14. Table 16.1 will help you decide which type of ANOVA you need.

Table 16.1   *Deciding between the various types of analysis of variance*

How many independent variables?*	Between or within subjects?	SPSS procedure required	See section
I	Between	Means/ANOVA or Oneway or UNIANOVA	16.9.1 16.9.2 16.9.3
I	Within	GLM	16.10
2 or more	All between	UNIANOVA	16.11
2 or more	One or more between and one or more within	GLM	16.12
2 or more	All within	GLM	16.13

*If you have two or more *dependent* variables which you want to analyse together, use the MANOVA procedure described in section 16.14

16.8 Obtaining the ANOVA

The following sections describe how to obtain the ANOVA for each of the situations described in Table 16.1, and explain how to interpret the printout. SPSS has three separate procedures for calculating the analysis of variance: Oneway, UNIANOVA and GLM. If you have one independent between-subjects variable, Oneway or UNIANOVA can be used. If you have two or more independent between-subjects variables, use UNIANOVA. If any of the variables is within-subjects, you need GLM. For each procedure, dialogue boxes are used to tell the program which are the dependent variables and how any subgroups of respondents are identified. When necessary the system will present dialogue boxes so you can tell it which variables are within subjects and which are between subjects.

Note that in the analysis of variance summary tables which appear in the output, the column headed Sig shows the probability of getting the observed F value by chance. If the entry is .0000, this means the finding is significant beyond the 0.0001 (0.01%) level.

16.9 One independent variable, between-subjects

This form of analysis of variance can be obtained in three ways. If you use the Means procedure described in section 15.3, one-way analysis of variance (ANOVA) can be requested via the Options button and selecting ANOVA Table and Eta (section 16.9.1). Alternatively, you can request Oneway from the Analyze /Compare Means menu entry (section 16.9.2). A one-way analysis of variance (UNIANOVA) is also available from the Analyze /General Linear Model entry (section 16.9.3). Oneway and UNIANOVA are basically the same and give similar output.

16.9.1 One-way analysis of variance from Means

The Means procedure is described in chapter 15. One-way analysis of variance to compare the means of subgroups is obtained by selecting

```
Analyze
    Compare Means
```

Then press the Options button from Figure 15.1 and check the box labelled ANOVA Table and Eta. So if you have used sales_1 as the dependent variable and empl (employer) as the independent variable, selecting the Options button and requesting the ANOVA Table and Eta will give a one-way analysis of variance on the sales_1 scores of the subgroups of the employer variable. The output is illustrated in Figure 16.8. The Report shows the mean and standard deviation for each employer group and then there is an analysis of variance summary table. Here F is 6.838, which is significant ($p = 0.006$), so there is a significant difference between the groups on the sales_1 scores. The final table shows the value of eta and eta-squared. Part of the output shown in Figure 16.8 is expressed in scientific notation: if you are unsure about this, see section 4.5.

One-way analysis of variance obtained from the Analyze /Compare Means menu will exclude any case which has a missing value on the dependent or on the factor variables. If you are requesting a number of analyses, you can ask for any case that has missing values on any of the variables involved to be excluded from all analyses. This is done by clicking on the Options button of the dialogue box and selecting the Exclude Cases Listwise option.

16.9.2 One-way analysis of variance using Oneway

Select from the menu system

```
Analyze
    Compare Means
        One-way ANOVA
```

The dialogue box shown in Figure 16.9 will be presented.

Suppose you want to compare the scores on sales_1 for respondents from the three different employers in the file salesq. This involves the one-way analysis of variance and can be achieved by following the stages listed here:

1 *Identify the dependent variable.* In this example, the variable sales_1 is the dependent variable. Click on its name and then on the right-pointing arrow button so that sales_1 appears in the box headed Dependent List.

```
MEANS
  TABLES=sales_1  BY empl
  /CELLS MEAN COUNT STDDEV
  /STATISTICS ANOVA .
```

Means

Case Processing Summary

	Cases					
	Included		Excluded		Total	
	N	Percent	N	Percent	N	Percent
SALES_1 * Employer	22	100.0%	0	.0%	22	100.0%

Report

SALES_1

Employer	Mean	N	Std. Deviation
Jones and Son	5333.2313	8	2761.3599
Smith and Co	4625.1712	8	1089.7836
Tomkins	8207.4150	6	925.1783
Total	5859.6232	22	2324.2958

ANOVA Table

			Sum of Squares	df	Mean Square	F	Sig.
SALES_1 * Employer	Between Groups	(Combined)	47480439	2	23740219.42	6.838	.006
	Within Groups		65968934	19	3472049.165		
	Total		1.13E+08	21			

Measures of Association

	Eta	Eta Squared
SALES_1 * Employer	.647	.419

Figure 16.8   *Output of analysis of variance obtained from the Means procedure*

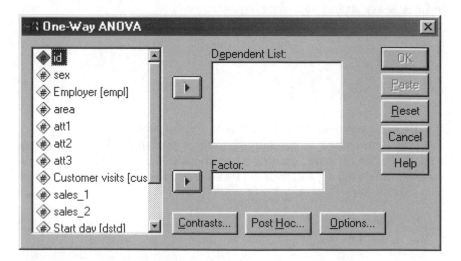

Figure 16.9   *The dialogue box for Oneway*

2 *Identify the variable (Factor) which distinguishes the subgroups of respon-*
   dents. In the example, this is the variable empl, the variable name for
   employer. Click on its name in the variable list and then click on the
   right-arrow button next to the box headed Factor. The variable name
   will then appear as the Factor.
3 *Request the means of the subgroups.* If you want the output to show you
   the means on the dependent variable (sales_1 in this example) for the
   various levels of the independent variable, click on the Options
   button; yet another dialogue box is revealed, and you select Descriptive. A plot of the means can also be requested. When you have
   finished with the Options window, click on Continue, to be returned
   to Figure 16.9.
4 *Request any a priori tests* by pressing the Contrasts button *and any post
   hoc tests* by pressing the Post Hoc button and completing the dialogue
   boxes revealed.

Figure 16.10 shows the output of the Oneway procedure, in which the
scores on the variable sales_1 were compared for the three employers,
and descriptive statistics were requested. A plot of the means was asked
for and a Tukey post hoc test was specified. The first table shows the
descriptive statistics, and this is followed by the conventional ANOVA
summary table, showing the Sum of Squares, degrees of freedom, Mean
Square, F ratio and significance (Sig.) of F for the between-groups
variable. The F ratio is the between-groups mean square divided by the
within-groups mean square. The probability associated with F is given in
the final column: if it is less than 0.05 (in Figure 16.10 it is .006), this
shows there is a significant difference between the groups being compared. In our example, it indicates that there was a significant difference
between the employers in the sales_1 scores. Remember that if the entry
is .0000, this means the finding is significant beyond the 0.0001 (0.01%)
level.

The additional output obtained by including the subcommand
/POSTHOC = TUKEY is given in the Multiple Comparisons table of
Figure 16.10. The first part of this table indicates that the Jones and Son
group does not differ significantly from the Smith and Co group: the
mean difference between the two groups is 708.06 and the significance is
shown as 0.731. It also shows that the Jones and Son group is significantly different from the Tomkins group: the mean difference is
−2874.1837 and the significance is 0.026. The other lines of the table can
be read in a similar way: the Smith and Co group differs significantly
from the Tomkins group; the Tomkins group differs significantly from
both the Jones and Son group and the Smith and Co group.

The section of the output entitled Homogeneous Subsets lists in each
column the subset of means which do not differ from each other. In this
example, the Smith and Co and the Jones and Son groups do not differ,

and so are listed in one column; both of these differ from the Tomkins group, so that is listed in a separate column.

The plot of the means in Figure 16.10 was obtained by making the appropriate selection from the window which is presented when the Options button of Figure 16.9 is pressed.

In Figure 16.11, Oneway was run with a priori contrasts requested. The Contrast Coefficients table shows that coefficients were set at −1, 0.5 and 0.5. The Contrast Tests printout shows that the *t* probability (Sig.) was greater than 0.05, so you would conclude that the Jones and Son group is not significantly different from the pooled value of the other two groups. If you look at the means of the three subgroups included in Figure 16.10, you will see that a more sensible comparison would be to compare the Tomkins group (mean = 8207.415) with the pooled mean of the other two groups (means = 5333.2313 and 4625.1713). You might like to carry out this analysis to confirm that you understand how it is done.

16.9.3 One-way analysis of variance using the General Linear Model menu

Select from the menu system

```
Analyze
     General Linear Model
          Univariate
```

A dialogue box will appear (Figure 16.12). Suppose you want to compare the scores on sales_1 for respondents from the three different employers in the file salesq. This involves the one-way analysis of variance and can be achieved by following the stages listed here:

1 *Identify the dependent variable.* You have to tell SPSS which is the dependent variable by clicking on its name (sales_1 in this example) and then on the right arrow button so that it appears in the box headed Dependent Variable.

2 *Identify the variable that distinguishes the groups you are comparing (Factor).* In this example, this is called empl, for employer. Click on empl and then either on the right arrow next to the box headed Fixed Factor(s) or on the right arrow next to the box headed Random Factor(s). The variable name will appear in the appropriate box. If you need reminding about the distinction between fixed and random factors, refer to section 16.6. For the data being used here, employer is not being taken as a random sample from all possible employers, so empl would be a fixed factor.

3 *Request the means of the subgroups.* To obtain the mean scores of each of the subgroups of respondents (each level on the Factor), click on Options in Figure 16.12. Another box is shown, reproduced in Figure 16.13, in which you can request Descriptive Statistics and a number of other measures including eta-squared (Estimate of effect size).

```
ONEWAY
  sales_1 BY empl
  /STATISTICS DESCRIPTIVES
  /PLOT MEANS
  /MISSING ANALYSIS
  /POSTHOC = TUKEY ALPHA(.05).
```

Oneway

Descriptives

SALES_1

	N	Mean	Std. Deviation	Std. Error	95% Confidence Interval for Mean		Minimum	Maximum
					Lower Bound	Upper Bound		
Jones and Son	8	5333.2313	2761.3599	976.2882	3024.6766	7641.7859	2005.30	10432.82
Smith and Co	8	4625.1713	1089.7836	385.2967	3714.0893	5536.2532	3124.20	6441.38
Tomkins	6	8207.4150	925.1783	377.7025	7236.4999	9178.3301	6497.05	8914.50
Total	22	5859.6232	2324.2958	495.5415	4829.0881	6890.1582	2005.30	10432.82

ANOVA

SALES_1

	Sum of Squares	df	Mean Square	F	Sig.
Between Groups	47480439	2	23740219.42	6.838	.006
Within Groups	65968934	19	3472049.165		
Total	1.13E+08	21			

Post Hoc Tests

Multiple Comparisons

Dependent Variable: SALES_1

Tukey HSD

(I) Employer	(J) Employer	Mean Difference (I-J)	Std. Error	Sig.	95% Confidence Interval	
					Lower Bound	Upper Bound
Jones and Son	Smith and Co	708.0600	931.6718	.731	-1658.8156	3074.9356
	Tomkins	-2874.1837*	1006.3205	.026	-5430.7015	-317.6660
Smith and Co	Jones and Son	708.0600	931.8718	.731	-3074.9356	1658.8156
	Tomkins	-3582.2437*	1006.3205	.006	-6138.7615	-1025.7260
Tomkins	Jones and Son	2874.1837*	1006.3205	.026	317.6660	5430.7015
	Smith and Co	3582.2437*	1006.3205	.006	1025.7260	6138.7615

*. The mean difference is significant at the .05 level.

Homogeneous Subsets

SALES_1

Tukey HSD[a,b]

Employer	N	Subset for alpha = .05	
		1	2
Smith and Co	8	4625.1713	
Jones and Son	8	5333.2313	
Tomkins	6		8207.4150
Sig.		.754	1.000

Means for groups in homogeneous subsets are displayed.

a. Uses Harmonic Mean Sample Size = 7.200.

b. The group sizes are unequal. The harmonic mean of the group sizes is used. Type I error levels are not guaranteed.

Continued on next page

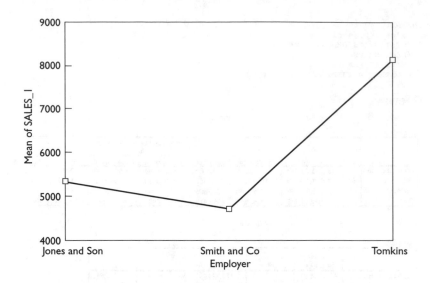

Figure 16.10   *Output from Oneway with a priori contrasts requested*

```
ONEWAY
   sales_1 BY empl
   /CONTRAST= -1 .5 .5
   /MISSING ANALYSIS .
```

ANOVA

SALES_1

	Sum of Squares	df	Mean Square	F	Sig.
Between Groups	47480439	2	23740219	6.838	.006
Within Groups	65968934	19	3472049.2		
Total	1.13E+08	21			

Contrast Coefficients

	Employer		
Contrast	Jones and Son	Smith and Co	Tomkins
1	-1	.5	.5

Contrast Tests

		Contrast	Value of Contrast	Std. Error	t	df	Sig. (2-tailed)
SALES_1	Assume equal variances	1	1083.0619	828.9610	1.307	19	.207
	Does not assume equal	1	1083.0619	1012.8755	1.069	8.082	.316

Figure 16.11   *Output from Oneway with a priori contrasts requested*

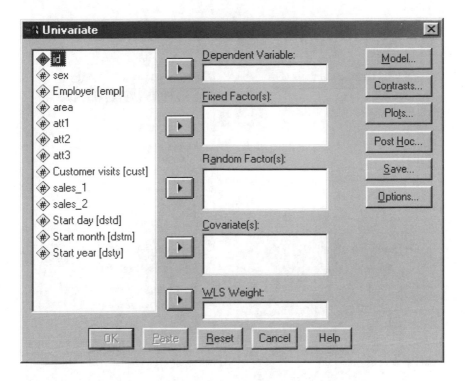

Figure 16.12 *The dialogue box for General Linear Model Univariate*

If you want the printout to show the estimated marginal means for the different levels of the between-subjects factor, click on the names of the variable or variables listed under Factors(s) and Factor Interactions: and then on the arrow button so the variable names appear in the Display Means For list. If you ask for the estimated marginal means, the syntax will include the subcommands

```
/EMEANS TABLES(variablename)
```

where variablename is the name of the variables specified. The printout will show the estimated means of the subgroups after the ANOVA summary tables, as shown in Figure 16.19.

4 Request any a priori tests by pressing the Contrasts button and any post hoc tests by pressing the Post Hoc button and completing the dialogue boxes revealed.

The syntax and output for this UNIANOVA command is shown in Figure 16.14. As the command included the subcommand /PRINT = DESCRIPTIVE, the Descriptive Statistics table is provided, showing the means, standard deviations and *n* for each subgroup and for the total set of scores.

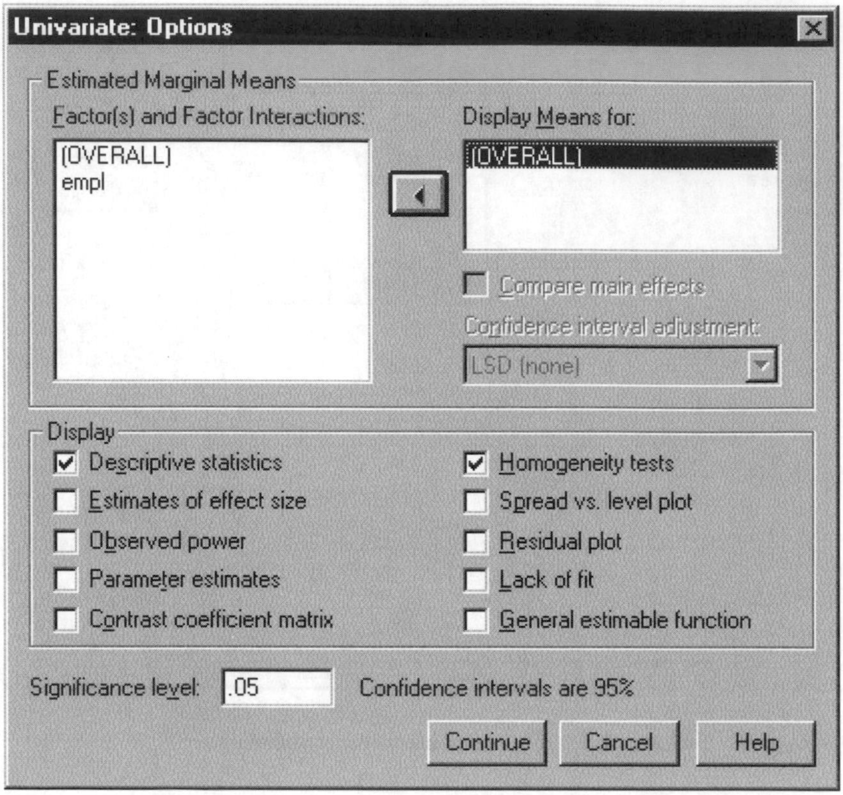

Figure 16.13   *The dialogue box for Univariate Options. Note that Descriptive Statistics and Homogeneity Tests have been requested*

The analysis of variance table Tests of Between-Subjects Effects is then given. Here, *F* for the empl variable is 6.838, and the significance is shown as .006.

Figure 16.10 and Figure 16.14 show the outputs for analyses of the same set of data. There are slight differences in their layout: using Oneway (Figure 16.10) gives a less cluttered appearance as fewer details are shown than when UNIANOVA is used (Figure 16.14).

16.10 One independent variable, within-subjects

When you have one independent within-subjects variable with more than two levels and want to compare the scores on the levels, the GLM /Repeated Measures procedure is needed. For an example of one independent within-subjects variable, suppose that we had carried out a study involving the effects of different types of praise on employees'

```
UNIANOVA
  sales_1  BY empl
  /METHOD = SSTYPE(3)
  /INTERCEPT = INCLUDE
  /PRINT = DESCRIPTIVE
  /CRITERIA = ALPHA(.05)
  /DESIGN = empl .
```

Univariate Analysis of Variance

Between-Subjects Factors

		Value Label	N
Employer	1.00	Jones and Son	8
	2.00	Smith and Co	8
	3.00	Tomkins	6

Descriptive Statistics

Dependent Variable: SALES_1

Employer	Mean	Std. Deviation	N
Jones and Son	5333.2313	2761.3599	8
Smith and Co	4625.1712	1089.7836	8
Tomkins	8207.4150	925.1783	6
Total	5959.6232	2324.2958	22

Tests of Between-Subjects Effects

Dependent Variable: SALES_1

Source	Type III Sum of Squares	df	Mean Square	F	Sig.
Corrected Model	47480439[a]	2	23740219	6.838	.006
Intercept	7.92E+08	1	7.92E+08	228.105	.000
EMPL	47480439	2	23740219	6.838	.006
Error	65968934	19	3472049.2		
Total	8.69E+08	22			
Corrected Total	1.13E+08	21			

a. R Squared = .419 (Adjusted R Squared = .357)

Figure 16.14   Syntax and output for the GLM Univariate UNIANOVA

attitude to their employer. We might, perhaps, have given no praise for one week, irregular praise for one week and regular praise for another week. These three conditions are levels of an independent variable. If we arranged all participants to experience all three conditions, we would have a within-subjects variable. Although the data in the data file salesq is not really like this, we can use the scores on the three attitude statements (att1, att2 and att3) to illustrate how to analyse a single, within-subjects variable with more than two levels.

To obtain the repeated-measures ANOVA select from the menu system

```
Analyze
     General Linear Model
          Repeated Measures
```

This presents the dialogue box shown in Figure 16.15.

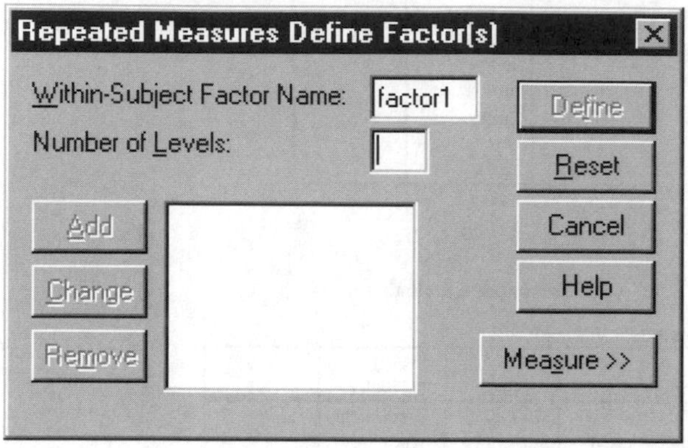

Figure 16.15   *The dialogue box for GLM Model Repeated Measures*

1   *Name the within-subject factor.* The within-subject factor is initially labelled factor1, and you need to enter a more meaningful title for it. In our example, the factor is made up from the three scores on measures of attitude (att1, att2 and att3), so we can label the within-subjects variable attitude by typing it in to replace the name factor1.
2   *Identify the number of levels of the within-subjects factor.* You need to type the appropriate number into the Number of Levels box: in this example there are three levels. Only when you have inserted the number of levels can you click on the Add button, and the untitled box will have inserted into it the factor name and number of levels; here it is attitude(3).
3   *Identify the variables which make up the within-subject factor.* You still have to tell SPSS which are the variables in the data which make up the factor. To do this, ensure the factor name in the list is highlighted and click on the Define button: the Repeated Measures ANOVA dialogue box shown in Figure 16.16 will be revealed. Select the data variables (in this example they are att1, att2 and att3) by clicking on them and then on the right-arrow button. They will then be added to the box headed Within-Subjects Variables.
4   *Request a table of means and a graph of estimated marginal means.* To obtain a table showing the mean scores on each variable use the

Options button of Figure 16.16 to open a dialogue box similar to that shown in Figure 16.13. Check the Descriptive Statistics option. Eta-squared is obtained if you check the Estimates of Effect Size option.

If you want the printout to show the estimated marginal means for the different levels of the between-subjects factor, click on the names of the variable or variables listed under Factors(s) and Factor Inter-actions: and then on the arrow button so the variable names appear in the Display Means For list. If you ask for the estimated marginal means, the syntax will include the subcommands

```
/EMEANS TABLES(variablename)
```

where variablename is the name of the variables specified. The printout will show the estimated means of the subgroups after the ANOVA summary tables, as shown in Figure 16.19.

To obtain a graph of the estimated marginal means, press the Plots button of Figure 16.16 and request the graph by completing the Profile Plots dialogue box then revealed and pressing the Add button.

5   Request any a priori tests by pressing the Contrasts button and any post hoc tests by pressing the Post Hoc button and completing the dialogue boxes revealed.

The syntax and output for this analysis is shown in Figure 16.17, when descriptive statistics and a graph of marginal means were requested.

The first section of the output in Figure 16.17 shows that the factor Attitude was made up of the variables att1, att2 and att3. The Descriptive Statistics table provides the means and standard deviations on each variable, and this is followed by the Multivariate Tests section which shows the results of multivariate tests (Pillais, Wilks', etc.) (which can be ignored as they are only relevant when there are a number of dependent variables). The table for the Mauchly Test of Sphericity follows, and in this example shows a highly significant value.

The main part of the output, the Tests of Within-Subjects Effects table, is a conventional ANOVA table. In Figure 16.17 it shows that, with sphericity assumed, the Mean Square for the variable attitude was 4.197, F was 2.831 and the probability (Sig.) was 0.070. Adjusted values are given for the various corrections one can make because the sphericity test was significant; they involve adjusting the degrees of freedom, so that the same F values (shown in the column headed F) have different significance levels. As the significance here is in all cases larger than 0.05, there was no significant difference between the scores for the different levels of the variable i.e. the scores on att1, att2 and att3 do not differ significantly.

The Test of Within-Subject Contrasts and the Test of Between-Subjects Effects can be ignored. The graph Profile Plots displays the estimated

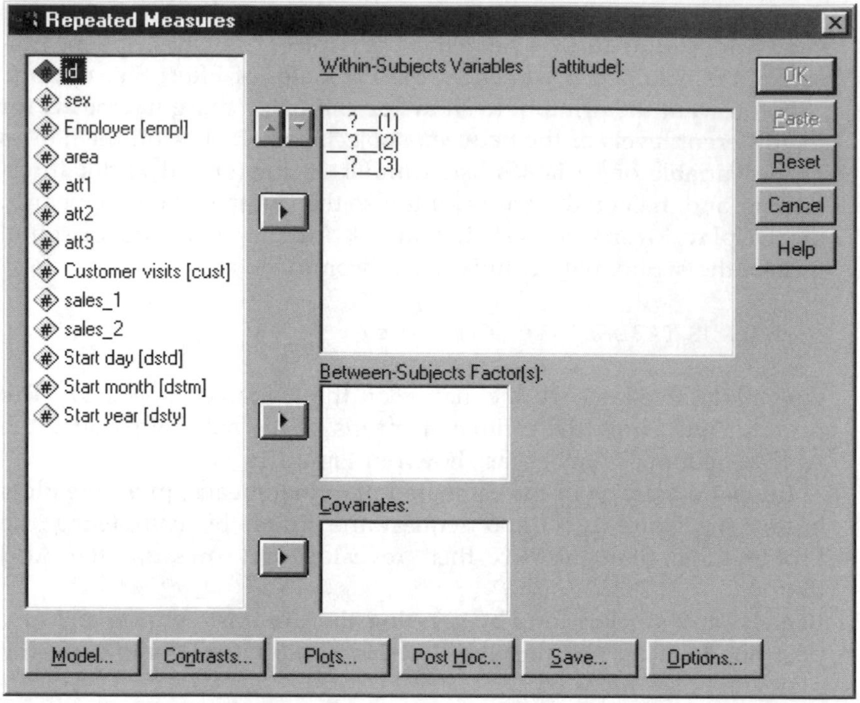

Figure 16.16   *The dialogue box for GLM Repeated Measures, to identify the variables making up the within-subjects factor*

marginal means, but note that the axes give an exaggerated picture of the differences.

16.11 Two-way analysis of variance with two (or more) independent variables, all between-subjects

When you have more than one independent variable and they are all between-subjects factors, you can analyse the effects of each variable and the interaction between them using the GLM procedure. Suppose that for the data in salesq we wanted to see whether there is a difference on sales_2 for people from different areas and of different sexes, and whether there is an interaction between these two factors. Is it the case, for example, that men sold more than women in the North but women sold more than men in the South?

To apply the analysis of variance for two (or more) between-subjects variables, select from the menu system

```
Analyze
     General Linear Model
          Univariate
```

The dialogue box shown in Figure 16.12 is presented.

1 *Identify the dependent variable.* Click on its name (sales_2 in this example) in the variable list and insert it in the Dependent Variable list by clicking on the arrow button next to that list.

```
GLM
   att1 att2 att3
   /WSFACTOR = attitude 3 Polynomial
   /METHOD = SSTYPE(3)
   /PLOT = PROFILE( attitude )
   /PRINT = DESCRIPTIVE
   /CRITERIA = ALPHA(.05)
   /WSDESIGN = attitude .
```

General Linear Model

Within-Subjects Factors

Measure: MEASURE_1

ATTITUDE	Dependent Variable
1	ATT1
2	ATT2
3	ATT3

Descriptive Statistics

	Mean	Std. Deviation	N
ATT1	2.5455	1.1010	22
ATT2	3.0909	.9211	22
ATT3	3.4091	1.1816	22

Multivariate Tests^a

Effect		Value	F	Hypothesis df	Error df	Sig.
ATTITUDE	Pillai's Trace	.332	4.968^a	2.000	20.000	.018
	Wilks' Lambda	.668	4.968^a	2.000	20.000	.018
	Hotelling's Trace	.497	4.968^a	2.000	20.000	.018
	Roy's Largest Root	.497	4.968^a	2.000	20.000	.018

a. Exact statistic

b.
   Design: Intercept
   Within Subjects Design: ATTITUDE

Mauchly's Test of Sphericity^b

Measure: MEASURE_1

Within Subjects Effect	Mauchly's W	Approx. Chi-Square	df	Sig.	Epsilon^a		
					Greenhouse-Geisser	Huynh-Feldt	Lower-bound
ATTITUDE	.352	20.901	2	.000	.607	.624	.500

Tests the null hypothesis that the error covariance matrix of the orthonormalized transformed dependent variables is proportional to an identity matrix.

a. May be used to adjust the degrees of freedom for the averaged tests of significance. Corrected tests are displayed in the layers (by default) of the Tests of Within Subjects Effects table.

b.
   Design: Intercept
   Within Subjects Design: ATTITUDE

Continued on next page

Tests of Within-Subjects Effects

Measure: MEASURE_1

Source		Type III Sum of Squares	df	Mean Square	F	Sig.
ATTITUDE	Sphericity Assumed	8.394	2	4.197	2.831	.070
	Greenhouse-Geisser	8.394	1.213	6.918	2.831	.099
	Huynh-Feldt	8.394	1.248	6.726	2.831	.097
	Lower-bound	8.394	1.000	8.394	2.831	.107
Error(ATTITUDE)	Sphericity Assumed	62.273	42	1.483		
	Greenhouse-Geisser	62.273	25.480	2.444		
	Huynh-Feldt	62.273	26.208	2.376		
	Lower-bound	62.273	21.000	2.965		

Tests of Within-Subjects Contrasts

Measure: MEASURE_1

Source	ATTITUDE	Type III Sum of Squares	df	Mean Square	F	Sig.
ATTITUDE	Linear	8.205	1	8.205	3.568	.073
	Quadratic	.189	1	.189	.285	.599
Error(ATTITUDE)	Linear	48.295	21	2.300		
	Quadratic	13.977	21	.666		

Tests of Between-Subjects Effects

Measure: MEASURE_1
Transformed Variable: Average

Source	Type III Sum of Squares	df	Mean Square	F	Sig.
Intercept	600.015	1	600.015	1221.176	.000
Error	10.318	21	.491		

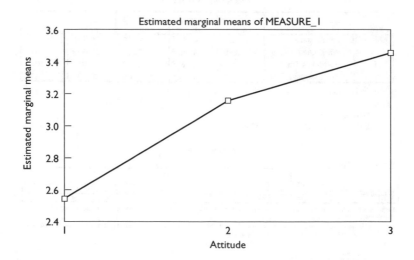

Figure 16.17   *Syntax and output for GLM with one within-subjects variable*

2   *Define each of the Factors (independent variables).* The Factors are what divide the respondents into subgroups, and in this example they are area and sex. When faced with Figure 16.12, click on the relevant variable (such as area) in the variable list and then on the right arrow next to the box headed Fixed Factor(s) or on the right-arrow next to the box headed Random Factor(s). The variable name will appear in the appropriate box. If you need reminding about the distinction between fixed and random factors, refer to section 6.5 above. For the data being used here, area is not being taken as a random sample from all possible areas, so area would be a fixed factor.

3   *Request the means of the subgroups.* To obtain the mean scores of each of the subgroups of respondents (each level on the Factor), click on Options in Figure 16.12 to reveal the dialogue box shown in Figure 16.13 and select Descriptive Statistics. Eta-squared is obtained if you check the Estimates of effect size option. When you have made the choices you want, click on Continue to return to Figure 16.12.

   If you want the printout to show the estimated marginal means for the different levels of the between-subjects factor, click on the names of the variable or variables listed under Factors(s) and Factor Interactions: and then on the arrow button so the variable names appear in the Display Means For list. If you ask for the estimated marginal means, the syntax will include the subcommands

   `/EMEANS TABLES(variablename)`

   where variablename is the name of the variables specified. The printout will show the estimated means of the subgroups after the ANOVA summary tables, as shown in Figure 16.19.

   To obtain a graph of the estimated marginal means, use the Plots button of Figure 16.12 and request the plot from the window then revealed.

4   Request any a priori tests by pressing the Contrasts button and any post hoc tests by pressing the Post Hoc button and completing the dialogue boxes revealed.

The syntax and output for this two-way analysis of variance with independent groups, where means and a graph were requested, is shown in Figure 16.18. The first table shows the variables being analysed and their value labels. The Descriptive Statistics table is the result of including /PRINT = DESCRIPTIVE in the command. It gives the mean scores on the dependent variable for all subsets of respondents together with the number of respondents in each subgroup.

   The table Tests of Between-Subjects Effects shows the ANOVA table listing the sources of variation, divided into main effects and interactions, and for each one there is the sum of squares, the degrees of freedom, the Mean Square (the sum of squares divided by the degrees of freedom), the value of F and the probability of F (Sig.). If any value in this final column is smaller than .05, there is an effect significant at the 0.05 (5%) level. The F value for sex is .917 and the probability is .352, so there is no overall difference between the two sexes. F for the area factor is 3.040 and the probability is .099 which means there was no overall difference between the two areas. The interaction between the two factors, Sex * Area, has $F = 4.612$ and has a probability of .046. So the area × sex interaction is significant at the 0.05 level. To see what this means, look at the mean scores of the four area/sex subgroups. For area 1, males (sex = 1) sold less (6115.15) than females (sex = 2) who sold 7362.41. But for area 2, the men sold 6538.56 and the women sold 3283.35. So the difference between the sexes differs according to which area one examines.

The graph included in Figure 16.18 was obtained by using the Plots button of Figure 16.16. It demonstrates the interaction between the sex and area variables, since the lines are not parallel. Note that the graph is of the estimated marginal means; to obtain a plot of the actual means, see section 10.6.

16.12 Two (or more) independent variables, with at least one between-subjects and at least one within-subjects (mixed design)

In the data set salesq, we have two figures (sales_1 and sales_2) showing amount sold by each respondent, and data on the respondents' sex. Suppose we varied the amount of commission the people received so that in one situation they received 1% and in the other situation they received 2% commission, and that the amounts in sales_1 and sales_2 indicate their sales under these two conditions. So there is one within-subjects independent variable (amount sold) which has two levels (sales_ 1 and sales_2), and one between-subjects variable (sex). Suppose we want to know whether there is a difference between sales_1 and sales_2 and whether any difference that there is varies according to the respondent's sex. To answer the question, we need to use the GLM procedure.

To obtain the mixed ANOVA, from the menu system select

```
Analyze
      General Linear Model
            Repeated Measures
```

You will be presented with the GLM Repeated Measures /Define Factors dialogue box (Figure 16.15).

1 *Define the within-subjects factor.* The within-subject factor is initially labelled factor1 (as shown in Figure 16.15), and you need to enter a

more meaningful title for it. In our example we are taking the two scores (sales_1 and sales_2) of each respondent on the sales questions as the within-subjects variable, and we can call it amsold, standing for 'amount sold'. Type in the name amsold so that it replaces the name factor1. You then need to type the appropriate number into the

```
UNIANOVA
    sales_2  BY sex area
    /METHOD = SSTYPE(3)
    /INTERCEPT = INCLUDE
    /PLOT = PROFILE( sex*area )
    /PRINT = DESCRIPTIVE
    /CRITERIA = ALPHA(.05)
    /DESIGN = sex area sex*area .
```

Between-Subjects Factors

		Value Label	N
SEX	1.00	male	10
	2.00	female	11
AREA	1.00	North	9
	2.00	South	12

Descriptive Statistics

Dependent Variable: SALES_2

SEX	AREA	Mean	Std. Deviation	N
male	North	6115.1533	3245.6768	3
	South	6538.5557	2689.7886	7
	Total	6411.5350	2684.4217	10
female	North	7362.4133	1978.1940	6
	South	3283.3500	1074.4614	5
	Total	5508.2936	2637.4715	11
Total	North	6946.6600	2338.4399	9
	South	5182.2200	2678.7668	12
	Total	5938.4086	2633.3544	21

Tests of Between-Subjects Effects

Dependent Variable: SALES_2

Source	Type III Sum of Squares	df	Mean Square	F	Sig.
Corrected Model	50028370[a]	3	16676123	3.197	.050
Intercept	6.44E+08	1	6.44E+08	123.494	.000
SEX	4783546.1	1	4783546.1	.917	.352
AREA	15855424	1	15855424	3.040	.099
SEX * AREA	24051760	1	24051760	4.612	.046
Error	88662741	17	5215455.4		
Total	8.79E+08	21			
Corrected Total	1.39E+08	20			

a. R Squared = .361 (Adjusted R Squared = .248)

Continued on next page

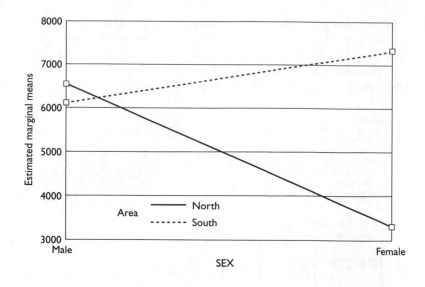

Figure 16.18 *Syntax and output for GLM Simple Factorial ANOVA with two between-subjects independent variables*

Number of Levels box: here it is 2 as there were two items of data per respondent. Then click on the Add button, and the untitled box will have inserted into it the factor name and number of levels; here it is amsold(2).

2 *Identify the variables which make up the within-subjects factor.* You still have to tell SPSS which are the variables in the data which make up the factor. To do this, click on the variable name (amsold(2) in this example) and then on the Define button of the dialogue box shown in Figure 16.15, which will lead to the screen showing the GLM Repeated Measures dialogue box illustrated in Figure 16.16. Select the data variables (sales_1, sales_2) by clicking on them and then on the right-arrow button. These variable names will be inserted into the Within-Subjects Variables list as the different levels of the within-subjects factor. Do not press Paste yet: you still have to define the between-subjects factor!

3 *Define the between-subjects factor.* While you are faced with the Repeated Measures ANOVA dialogue box (Figure 16.16), click on the name of the between-subjects variable (in the example we are describing, it will be sex), and then on the right-pointing arrow next to the box headed Between-Subjects Factor(s). The variable will be inserted into that list.

4 *Request the means of the subgroups.* To obtain the means for the different levels of the between-subjects factor, click on the Options button of the GLM Repeated Measures box (Figure 16.16), to open a window

similar to Figure 16.13. Select the Descriptive Statistics option. Eta-squared is obtained if you check the Estimates of Effect Size option.

If you want the printout to show the estimated marginal means for the different levels of the between-subjects factor, click on the names of the variable or variables listed under Factors(s) and Factor Interactions: and then on the arrow button so the variable names appear in the Display Means For list. If you ask for the estimated marginal means, the syntax will include the subcommands

```
/EMEANS TABLES(variablename)
```

where variablename is the name of the variables specified. The printout will show the estimated means of the subgroups after the ANOVA summary tables.

A graph of the estimated marginal means is obtained by pressing the Plots button of Figure 16.16. In the window then shown, specify the variable for the horizontal axis, the variable for Separate Lines and then press the Add button. Note that the graph is of the estimated marginal means.

5   Request any a priori tests by pressing the Contrasts button and any post hoc tests by pressing the Post Hoc button and completing the dialogue boxes revealed.

The syntax and output for this mixed ANOVA analysis with the request for the descriptive statistics of the subgroups is shown in Figure 16.19. Note that in the syntax the subcommand /WSFACTORS is included when a within-subjects variable has been identified.

The first table shows the variables making up the within-subjects factor Measure_1, and the second one identifies the between-subjects factor. The Descriptive Statistics table gives the means and standard deviations on each level of the within-subjects factor for each level of the between-subjects factor.

The Multivariate Tests table can be ignored as it is only relevant when there are a number of dependent variables. The table for the Mauchly Test of Sphericity follows; it can be ignored in this analysis since it does not apply with only two levels of the independent variable. (You will notice that no significance level is indicated, and that the values in the table of Within Subjects Effects are the same for the rows with Sphericity Assumed and for the other rows such as Greenhouse–Geisser.)

The analysis of variance output is in separate sections. In the table headed Tests of Within-Subject Effects, the line Sphericity Assumed shows that comparing the levels of amsold (the within-subjects variable) gave $F = 0.319$, Significance $= 0.579$ showing no significant difference between the levels of amsold i.e. between sales_1 and sales_2. The interaction between the two variables (amsold * sex) gave $F = 2.427, p =$

0.136. So for this data there is also no significant interaction between the two variables of amount sold and sex. The table headed Tests of Between-Subjects Effects compares the means for the different levels on the between-subjects variable (sex, in this example): here $F = 0.267$, $p = 0.611$ so there is no overall difference between the sexes on the amount sold.

When there are two or more variables being analysed and any significant F is obtained, it often helps to gain an understanding of the data if the means of the subsets of scores are plotted on a graph. A plot of the estimated marginal means can be obtained by using the Plots button in Figure 16.16. Specify the variable for the horizontal axis, the variable for Separate Lines and then press the Add button and the Continue button.

```
GLM
    sales_1 sales_2 BY sex
    /WSFACTOR = amsold 2 Polynomial
    /METHOD = SSTYPE(3)
    /PLOT = PROFILE( sex*amsold )
    /EMMEANS = TABLES(OVERALL)
    /EMMEANS = TABLES(sex)
    /EMMEANS = TABLES(amsold)
    /EMMEANS = TABLES(sex*amsold)
    /PRINT = DESCRIPTIVE
    /CRITERIA = ALPHA(.05)
    /WSDESIGN = amsold
    /DESIGN = sex .
```

Within-Subjects Factors

Measure: MEASURE_1

AMSOLD	Dependent Variable
1	SALES_1
2	SALES_2

Between-Subjects Factors

		Value Label	N
SEX	1.00	male	10
	2.00	female	11

Descriptive Statistics

	SEX	Mean	Std. Deviation	N
SALES_1	male	5950.6370	2772.4555	10
	female	5723.9964	2089.1906	11
	Total	5831.9205	2377.9699	21
SALES_2	male	6411.5350	2684.4217	10
	female	5508.2936	2637.4715	11
	Total	5938.4086	2633.3544	21

Continued on facing page

Multivariate Tests[b]

Effect		Value	F	Hypothesis df	Error df	Sig.
AMSOLD	Pillai's Trace	.016	.319[a]	1.000	19.000	.579
	Wilks' Lambda	.984	.319[a]	1.000	19.000	.579
	Hotelling's Trace	.017	.319[a]	1.000	19.000	.579
	Roy's Largest Root	.017	.319[a]	1.000	19.000	.579
AMSOLD * SEX	Pillai's Trace	.113	2.427[a]	1.000	19.000	.136
	Wilks' Lambda	.887	2.427[a]	1.000	19.000	.136
	Hotelling's Trace	.128	2.427[a]	1.000	19.000	.136
	Roy's Largest Root	.128	2.427[a]	1.000	19.000	.136

a. Exact statistic

b. Design: Intercept+SEX
   Within Subjects Design: AMSOLD

Mauchly's Test of Sphericity[b]

Measure: MEASURE_1

Within Subjects Effect	Mauchly's W	Approx. Chi-Square	df	Sig.	Epsilon[a] Greenhouse-Geisser	Huynh-Feldt	Lower-bound
AMSOLD	1.000	.000	0	.	1.000	1.000	1.000

Tests the null hypothesis that the error covariance matrix of the orthonormalized transformed dependent variables is proportional to an identity matrix.

a. May be used to adjust the degrees of freedom for the averaged tests of significance. Corrected tests are displayed in the layers (by default) of the Tests of Within Subjects Effects table.

b. Design: Intercept+SEX
   Within Subjects Design: AMSOLD

Tests of Within-Subjects Effects

Measure: MEASURE_1

Source		Type III Sum of Squares	df	Mean Square	F	Sig.
AMSOLD	Sphericity Assumed	157459.033	1	157459.033	.319	.579
	Greenhouse-Geisser	157459.033	1.000	157459.033	.319	.579
	Huynh-Feldt	157459.033	1.000	157459.033	.319	.579
	Lower-bound	157459.033	1.000	157459.033	.319	.579
AMSOLD * SEX	Sphericity Assumed	1198970.0	1	1198970.0	2.427	.136
	Greenhouse-Geisser	1198970.0	1.000	1198970.0	2.427	.136
	Huynh-Feldt	1198970.0	1.000	1198970.0	2.427	.136
	Lower-bound	1198970.0	1.000	1198970.0	2.427	.136
Error(AMSOLD)	Sphericity Assumed	9387076.5	19	494056.657		
	Greenhouse-Geisser	9387076.5	19.000	494056.657		
	Huynh-Feldt	9387076.5	19.000	494056.657		
	Lower-bound	9387076.5	19.000	494056.657		

Tests of Within-Subjects Contrasts

Measure: MEASURE_1

Source	AMSOLD	Type III Sum of Squares	df	Mean Square	F	Sig.
AMSOLD	Linear	157459.033	1	157459.033	.319	.579
AMSOLD * SEX	Linear	1198970.0	1	1198970.0	2.427	.136
Error(AMSOLD)	Linear	9387076.5	19	494056.657		

Tests of Between-Subjects Effects

Measure: MEASURE_1
Transformed Variable: Average

Source	Type III Sum of Squares	df	Mean Square	F	Sig.
Intercept	1.46E+09	1	1.46E+09	116.467	.000
SEX	3343563.5	1	3343563.5	.267	.611
Error	2.38E+08	19	12518753		

Figure 16.19 *Syntax and output for analysis of variance with one within-subjects variable and one between-subjects variable*

16.13 Two (or more) independent variables, all within-subjects (repeated measures)

To explain this analysis, we shall have a rest from the salesq data file and use a separate example. An investigator studied people's ability to recognize faces in upright and inverted orientation, and when the faces were shown in black-and-white (b/w) or colour. There were two independent variables, orientation and colour, both with two levels (upright or inverted; b/w or colour) so there were four conditions: upright b/w, inverted b/w, upright colour, inverted colour. The researcher used one group of respondents; everyone took part in all of the four conditions. Both independent variables are within-subjects, as each person saw both levels of every variable. So the two-way analysis of variance for repeated measures is needed.

The data, and the order in which it should be entered into SPSS, is shown in Table 16.2.

Table 16.2 *Data from an experiment on facial recognition*

Subject	INVBW	INVCOL	UPBW	UPCOL
1.00	1.25	2.33	1.67	2.18
2.00	1.82	2.56	1.48	2.04
3.00	1.59	2.69	1.58	2.58
4.00	1.73	3.01	1.63	2.21
5.00	1.72	2.87	1.88	2.73
6.00	1.49	3.23	1.22	3.20
7.00	1.03	3.78	0.94	3.71
8.00	1.35	3.22	1.21	3.15
9.00	1.47	3.21	1.20	3.40
10.00	1.02	3.26	1.02	3.11

When entering the data into SPSS for a within-subjects factorial design, it is vital that the order of columns is correct: all the subconditions at one level of one variable occur before the subconditions at the second level of that variable. In Table 16.2, the first two columns both refer to the Inverted condition, one with black-and-white faces and the other with colour. Then the data for the Upright condition is given, again with two columns since there has to be one for black-and-white and one for colour. You will also see that the order of the two levels of the colour condition is consistent: for both Inverted and Upright faces, they are in the same order (BW followed by COL).

To obtain the repeated-measures ANOVA, select from the menu system

```
Analyze
      General Linear Model
            Repeated Measures
```

This presents the dialogue box shown in Figure 16.15.

1   *Identify the within-subjects factors.* The within-subjects factor is initially
    labelled factor1, and you need to enter a more meaningful title for it.
    In the faces experiment, the variables were position (upright or
    inverted) and colour (b/w or colour). You need to give these vari-
    ables names, which should be different from those used as variable
    names (column headings) in the data file. We shall call them downup
    and colour. So when presented with Figure 16.15, type in the name
    downup so that it replaces factor1 in the box and enter the appro-
    priate number in the Number of Levels box. In the experiment, there
    were two levels of downup, so enter 2. Then click on the Add button,
    and the untitled box will have inserted into it the factor name and
    number of levels; here it is downup(2).
        The second within-subjects factor is defined in a similar way. Type
    the name (in this example it is colour) into the box where factor
    names appear, the number of levels into the appropriate box, and
    then click on Add. The factor list then reads:

    ```
    downup(2)
    colour(2)
    ```

2   *Identify the variables which make up the within-subjects factors.* You still
    have to tell SPSS which are the variables (columns) in the data which
    make up the factors. Click on one of the factor names (downup(2))
    and then on the Define button. You will be presented with the
    Repeated Measures ANOVA dialogue box shown in Figure 16.20. The
    variables from the data file are listed on the left-hand side. You have
    to select the data variables so that they are matched correctly with the
    names and levels of the within-subject variables.
        In this example, the first factor, which appears in the brackets after
    the Within-Subjects Variables title is downup; the second factor is
    colour. You will see that there are entries in the central box: __?__[1,1]
    etc. The first of these has to be paired with the first level on downup
    and the first level on colour, i.e. the variable INVBW: click on this
    name in the variable list and then on the right-pointing arrow. The
    second entry in the within-subjects variable list, __?__[1,2] has to be
    paired with the data variable corresponding to the first level on the
    first factor (downup) and the second level on the second factor
    (colour): the INVCOL data. The third entry is paired with second
    level on the first factor (downup is the factor and the second level is
    UP) and the first level on the second factor (colour is the factor and
    the level is BW) so the variable needed is UPBW. The fourth entry is
    paired with the second level of the first factor and the second level of
    the second factor: the variable UPCOL.
        This is a little confusing, but it is vital to appreciate that the first
    level of the first factor is entered first, with the levels of the second
    factor entered sequentially. Then the second level of the first factor is

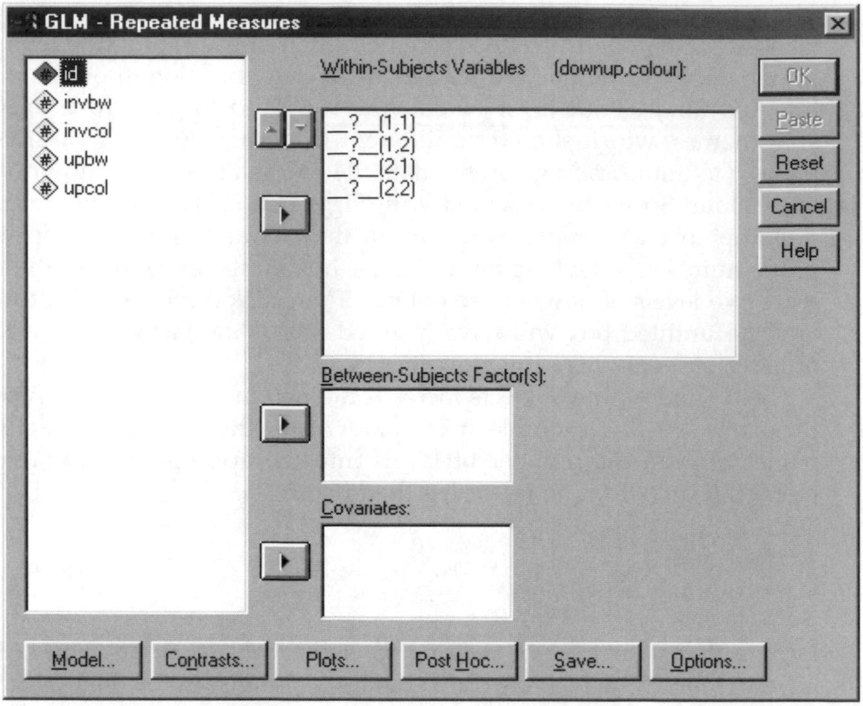

Figure 16.20 *The dialogue box for GLM Repeated Measures for two within-subjects variables (downup, colour)*

entered with the levels of the second factor entered sequentially. So if you have two factors, A and B, with three levels of A (A1, A2 and A3) and two levels of B (B1 and B2), the final sequence which has to appear in the Within Subjects Variables list is: A1 B1; A1 B2; A2 B1; A2 B2; A3 B1; A3 B2.

3   *Request the means of the subgroups.* To obtain the means for the different levels of the between-subjects factor, click on the Options button of the GLM Repeated Measures box (Figure 16.20), to open a window similar to Figure 16.13. Select the Descriptive Statistics option. This will give in the output the means etc. for each column of the data set of Table 16.2. It is worth running this procedure, if only to check that you have completed Figure 16.20 correctly! Eta-squared is obtained if you check the Estimates of Effect Size option.

If you want the printout to show the estimated marginal means for the different levels of the between-subjects factor, click on the names of the variable or variables listed under Factors(s) and Factor Interactions: and then on the arrow button so the variable names appear in the Display Means For list. If you ask for the estimated marginal means, the syntax will include the subcommands

```
/EMEANS TABLES(variablename)
```

where variablename is the name of the variables specified. The printout will show the estimated means of the subgroups after the ANOVA summary tables.

To obtain a plot of the means of the various conditions, choose the Plots button from Figure 16.20. A dialogue box will be revealed in which you specify which factor to use for the horizontal axis and which to use for separate lines on the graph.

4   Request any a priori or post hoc tests by pressing the Contrasts or Post Hoc buttons and completing the dialogue box revealed.

The syntax and output for this analysis is shown in Figure 16.21. The first table shows how the dependent variables have been allocated to the within-subject factors, and is followed by the Descriptive Statistics table.

The table for the Mauchly Test of Sphericity follows, and in this example shows a highly significant value. The Multivariate Tests table shows the results of multivariate tests (Pillais, Wilks' etc.); it can be ignored as it is only relevant when there are a number of dependent variables. It is followed by the table for Mauchly's Test of Sphericity, which can also be ignored; such tests are of questionable value, as explained in section 16.6.

The main part of the output is the table Tests of Within-Subjects Effects. This shows that the test of the DOWNUP effect has $F = 4.627$, $p = 0.060$; the COLOUR effect has $F = 45.10$ and p is 0.000 while the interaction of the two variables has $F = 1.200$ and p is 0.302. So in this set of data, only colour has a significant effect. The effect of orientation is not significant ($p = 0.06 > 0.05$). The full output includes tables of Tests of Within-Subjects Contrasts and Tests of Between-Subjects Effects, but these can be ignored.

16.14 Analysing two or more dependent variables together: MANOVA

Multivariate analysis (MANOVA) is used when you have a number of dependent variables to be analysed together. Tabachnick and Fidell (1996) give an example in which a researcher studies the effects of different types of treatment on anxiety, and measures three kinds of anxiety: test anxiety, minor life stress anxiety and free-floating anxiety. Each participant is given one of the types of treatment and assessed on all three kinds of anxiety, so they each yield three scores. MANOVA is used to determine whether a combination of the three anxiety measures varies according to the treatment the participant received. 'MANOVA tests whether mean differences among groups on a combination of DVs (dependent variables) are likely to have occurred by chance' (Tabachnick and Fidell, 1996: 375).

In the data file salesq, there are three measures of attitude for each respondent and these can be used to illustrate how the MANOVA procedure operates. Suppose we want to compare the two sexes on their responses to the three attitude measures, and are taking the three measures as indicative of three types of attitude in a similar way to the three kinds of anxiety mentioned in the previous paragraph.

```
GLM
    invbw invcol upbw upcol
    /WSFACTOR = downup 2 Polynomial colour 2 Polynomial
    /METHOD = SSTYPE(3)
    /PRINT = DESCRIPTIVE
    /CRITERIA = ALPHA(.05)
    /WSDESIGN = downup colour downup*colour .
```

Within-Subjects Factors

Measure: MEASURE_1

DOWNUP	COLOUR	Dependent Variable
1	1	INVBW
	2	INVCOL
2	1	UPBW
	2	UPCOL

Descriptive Statistics

	Mean	Std. Deviation	N
INVBW	1.4470	.2830	10
INVCOL	3.0160	.4183	10
UPBW	1.3830	.3085	10
UPCOL	2.8310	.5696	10

Multivariate Tests[b]

Effect		Value	F	Hypothesis df	Error df	Sig.
DOWNUP	Pillai's Trace	.340	4.627[a]	1.000	9.000	.060
	Wilks' Lambda	.660	4.627[a]	1.000	9.000	.060
	Hotelling's Trace	.514	4.627[a]	1.000	9.000	.060
	Roy's Largest Root	.514	4.627[a]	1.000	9.000	.060
COLOUR	Pillai's Trace	.834	45.105[a]	1.000	9.000	.000
	Wilks' Lambda	.166	45.105[a]	1.000	9.000	.000
	Hotelling's Trace	5.012	45.105[a]	1.000	9.000	.000
	Roy's Largest Root	5.012	45.105[a]	1.000	9.000	.000
DOWNUP * COLOUR	Pillai's Trace	.118	1.200[a]	1.000	9.000	.302
	Wilks' Lambda	.882	1.200[a]	1.000	9.000	.302
	Hotelling's Trace	.133	1.200[a]	1.000	9.000	.302
	Roy's Largest Root	.133	1.200[a]	1.000	9.000	.302

a. Exact statistic

b.

Design: Intercept

Within Subjects Design: DOWNUP+COLOUR+DOWNUP*COLOUR

Continued on facing page

Mauchly's Test of Sphericity[b]

Measure: MEASURE_1

Within Subjects Effect	Mauchly's W	Approx. Chi-Square	df	Sig.	Epsilon[a]		
					Greenhouse-Geisser	Huynh-Feldt	Lower-bound
DOWNUP	1.000	.000	0	.	1.000	1.000	1.000
COLOUR	1.000	.000	0	.	1.000	1.000	1.000
DOWNUP * COLOUR	1.000	.000	0	.	1.000	1.000	1.000

Tests the null hypothesis that the error covariance matrix of the orthonormalized transformed dependent variables is proportional to an identity matrix.

  a. May be used to adjust the degrees of freedom for the averaged tests of significance. Corrected tests are displayed in the layers (by default) of the Tests of Within Subjects Effects table.

  b.

    Design: Intercept

    Within Subjects Design: DOWNUP+COLOUR+DOWNUP*COLOUR

Tests of Within-Subjects Effects

Measure: MEASURE_1

Source		Type III Sum of Squares	df	Mean Square	F	Sig.
DOWNUP	Sphericity Assumed	.155	1	.155	4.627	.060
	Greenhouse-Geisser	.155	1.000	.155	4.627	.060
	Huynh-Feldt	.155	1.000	.155	4.627	.060
	Lower-bound	.155	1.000	.155	4.627	.060
Error(DOWNUP)	Sphericity Assumed	.301	9	3.350E-02		
	Greenhouse-Geisser	.301	9.000	3.350E-02		
	Huynh-Feldt	.301	9.000	3.350E-02		
	Lower-bound	.301	9.000	3.350E-02		
COLOUR	Sphericity Assumed	22.756	1	22.756	45.105	.000
	Greenhouse-Geisser	22.756	1.000	22.756	45.105	.000
	Huynh-Feldt	22.756	1.000	22.756	45.105	.000
	Lower-bound	22.756	1.000	22.756	45.105	.000
Error(COLOUR)	Sphericity Assumed	4.541	9	.505		
	Greenhouse-Geisser	4.541	9.000	.505		
	Huynh-Feldt	4.541	9.000	.505		
	Lower-bound	4.541	9.000	.505		
DOWNUP * COLOUR	Sphericity Assumed	3.660E-02	1	3.660E-02	1.200	.302
	Greenhouse-Geisser	3.660E-02	1.000	3.660E-02	1.200	.302
	Huynh-Feldt	3.660E-02	1.000	3.660E-02	1.200	.302
	Lower-bound	3.660E-02	1.000	3.660E-02	1.200	.302
Error(DOWNUP*COLOUR)	Sphericity Assumed	.274	9	3.050E-02		
	Greenhouse-Geisser	.274	9.000	3.050E-02		
	Huynh-Feldt	.274	9.000	3.050E-02		
	Lower-bound	.274	9.000	3.050E-02		

Figure 16.21 *Syntax and excerpt of output for analysis of variance with two repeated-measures independent variables, including a request for descriptive statistics*

To obtain the mutivariate procedure, select

```
Analyze
        General Linear Model
                Multivariate
```

The dialogue box similar to that shown in Figure 16.12 is presented, but you can enter a number of dependent variables and there is no provision for entering any random factors. For this example, the three attitude responses were entered as Dependent Variables, and sex was entered as a Fixed Factor.

The outcome of this analysis is shown in Figure 16.22. The Multivariate Tests table indicates that there is a significant difference between the two sexes ($F = 3.541$, $p = 0.037$). Note that this difference is on a combination of the three attitude measures. In the Tests of Between-Subjects table, the scores of the two sexes are compared on each of the three attitude measures. On none of them is there a significant difference:

```
GLM
    att1 att2 att3  BY sex
    /METHOD = SSTYPE(3)
    /INTERCEPT = INCLUDE
    /CRITERIA = ALPHA(.05)
    /~~~GN = sex .
```

General Linear Model

Multivariate Tests[b]

Effect		Value	F	Hypothesis df	Error df	Sig.
Intercept	Pillai's Trace	.992	678.471[a]	3.000	17.000	.000
	Wilks' Lambda	.008	678.471[a]	3.000	17.000	.000
	Hotelling's Trace	119.730	678.471[a]	3.000	17.000	.000
	Roy's Largest Root	119.730	678.471[a]	3.000	17.000	.000
SEX	Pillai's Trace	.385	3.541[a]	3.000	17.000	.037
	Wilks' Lambda	.615	3.541[a]	3.000	17.000	.037
	Hotelling's Trace	.625	3.541[a]	3.000	17.000	.037
	Roy's Largest Root	.625	3.541[a]	3.000	17.000	.037

a. Exact statistic

b. Design: Intercept+SEX

Tests of Between-Subjects Effects

Source	Dependent Variable	Type III Sum of Squares	df	Mean Square	F	Sig.
Corrected Model	ATT1	9.740E-02[a]	1	9.740E-02	.074	.789
	ATT2	.471[b]	1	.471	.556	.465
	ATT3	3.352[c]	1	3.352	2.488	.131
Intercept	ATT1	138.193	1	138.193	104.836	.000
	ATT2	207.900	1	207.900	245.348	.000
	ATT3	242.210	1	242.210	179.765	.000
SEX	ATT1	9.740E-02	1	9.740E-02	.074	.789
	ATT2	.471	1	.471	.556	.465
	ATT3	3.352	1	3.352	2.488	.131
Error	ATT1	25.045	19	1.318		
	ATT2	16.100	19	.847		
	ATT3	25.600	19	1.347		
Total	ATT1	164.000	21			
	ATT2	224.000	21			
	ATT3	269.000	21			
Corrected Total	ATT1	25.143	20			
	ATT2	16.571	20			
	ATT3	28.952	20			

a. R Squared = .004 (Adjusted R Squared = -.049)

b. R Squared = .028 (Adjusted R Squared = -.023)

c. R Squared = .116 (Adjusted R Squared = .069)

Figure 16.22 *Syntax and excerpt of output for multivariate analysis of variance with three dependent variables*

on att1, $F = 0.074$, $p = 0.789$; on att2, $F = 0.556$, $p = 0.465$ and on att3 $F = 2.488$, $p = 0.131$. This appears rather odd: how can there be an overall difference between the sexes, but no difference between them on each of the three attitude measures taken individually? Remember that the Multivariate Test is on a combination of the three separate scores calculated so as to maximize the probability of distinguishing the groups (sexes in this example). 'In MANOVA, a new DV that maximizes group differences is created from the set of DVs. The new DV is a linear combination of measured DVs, combined so as to separate the groups as much as possible' (Tabachnick and Fidell, 1996: 375).

17

CORRELATIONS AND MULTIPLE REGRESSION

Summary

- When calculating correlations, always plot the two variables in a scattergram using Graph /Scatter to see whether there is evidence of a curvilinear relationship.
- Obtain the mean and standard deviations of the variables being correlated from the Options button of the Bivariate Correlations dialogue box.
- Partial correlation allows you to examine the correlation between two variables when the effect of a third variable has been partialled out.
- Multiple regression uses a number of independent variables to predict the dependent variable. The Enter method forces all the predictor variables to be included in the analysis. The Stepwise method is more often used.

17.1 The concept of correlation

A correlation expresses the extent to which two variables vary together. A positive correlation means that as one variable increases so does the other. For example, there is a strong positive correlation between size of foot and height, and a weak positive correlation between how much one is paid and one's job satisfaction. A negative correlation is when one variable increases as the other decreases; for example, there is a negative correlation between job satisfaction and absenteeism: the more satisfied people are with their job, the lower the amount of absenteeism they show.

Correlations vary between −1.00 and +1.00; a correlation of 0.00 means there is no relationship between the two variables. For example, one would expect the correlation between size of foot and job satisfaction to be about 0.00 (although I have never seen any data on this relationship!).

If two variables have both been measured on an interval scale, use the Pearson product moment correlation coefficient. When data is ordinal, use the Spearman Rank (rho) correlation coefficient.

Whichever coefficient is chosen, you should always plot a scattergram of the relationship between the two variables to check that the relationship can be reasonably assumed to be linear. Simple correlations indicate how far there is a linear relationship between the two variables. In a curvilinear relationship, low scores on x are associated with low scores on y, medium scores on x are associated with high scores on y and high scores on x are associated with low scores on y. This relationship would not appear in a correlation coefficient, which would have a low value (about 0), but will be revealed if the two sets of data are plotted graphically.

When you have a scattergram it is possible to draw-in the best-fitting straight line that represents the relationship between x and y. The best-fitting line is known as the regression line and it can be expressed as an equation of the form $x = c + by$, where c is the intercept and b the slope.

The correlation coefficient squared (r^2) indicates how much of the variance in y is explained by x. So if x correlates with y 0.6, then 0.36 (36%) of the variance in y is explained by the variance in x.

Always bear in mind the aphorism 'Correlation does not equal causation': if variables A and B are correlated, one cannot say that A causes B. It could be that B causes A, or they may both be related to some other factor that produces the variation in A and B. Some examples: absenteeism and job satisfaction are negatively correlated, but one cannot conclude that low job satisfaction causes absenteeism; it is possible that being absent a lot causes the feelings of low job satisfaction. The positive correlation between foot size and height does not mean that having a large foot makes you grow; foot size and overall height are both caused by a common genetic factor. However, correlations are used to predict one variable from another. Knowing someone's foot size, one can predict better how tall they are than one could if you did not know their foot size.

Partial correlation is used when the correlation between two variables may arise because both are correlated with a third variable. Partial correlation is a technique which allows you to examine the correlation between two variables when the effect of the third variable has been partialled out.

Multiple regression refers to using more than one variable to predict the dependent variable. Job satisfaction is correlated with pay and with level of occupation. So one can predict job satisfaction from pay and one can predict it from job level; but one may get a better prediction if one uses both pay and job level as predictors. So one would have an equation of the form:

job satisfaction = pay (multiplied by a) + level of job (multiplied by b).

Each predictor variable is multiplied by a weighting, reflecting its importance in determining the dependent, or predicted, variable. The weighting is known as the regression coefficient for that variable. In multiple regression analysis, one investigates which variables add to one's ability to predict the dependent variable, and the weighting they should have.

17.2 Obtaining a scattergram

To get a scattergram between two variables, select from the menu

```
Graphs
        Scatter
```

The option Simple will be the default offered, so click the Define button, which opens a dialogue box in which you can specify which variable is to be on the Y axis and which on the X axis. Pressing the Titles button allows you to give a title to the graph. An example of the syntax and the scattergram it produces in the Output Viewer are shown in Figure 17.1.

```
GRAPH
    /SCATTERPLOT(BIVAR)=att2 WITH att1
    /MISSING=LISTWISE
    /TITLE= 'Scattergram of att1 versus att2'.
```

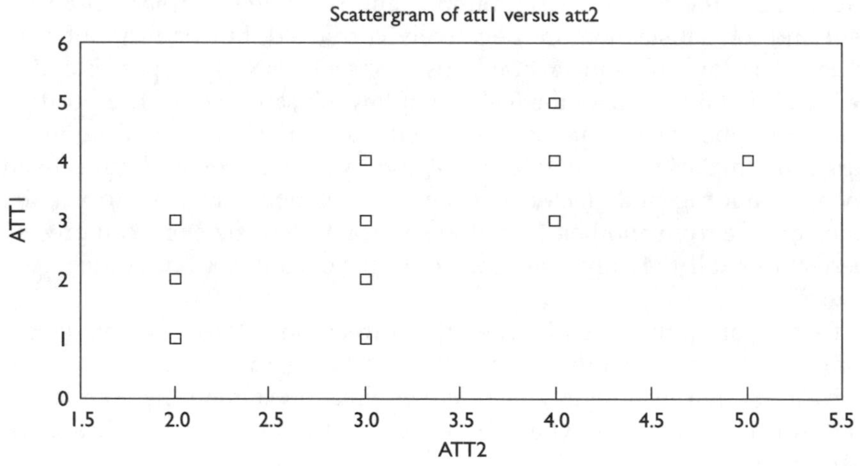

Figure 17.1   *Example of a scattergram and the syntax for obtaining it*

You can separate the plots for subgroups of respondents: for example, one could plot att1 versus att2 for all the respondents in salesq, but have the data for females indicated by a different marker from those used to plot males' data. This is achieved by entering sex as the variable in the Set Markers By text box.

If you wish the graph to include the best-fitting straight line, while viewing the scattergram in the Output Viewer double-click on it so that it appears in the Chart Editor. (The title of the window will change to Chart1 – SPSS Chart Editor.) Select from the menu bar

```
Chart
     Options
```

In the dialogue box revealed, shown in Figure 17.2, click on the Total option in the section entitled Fit Line and then on the button marked Fit Options. You will then be faced with the window shown in Figure 17.3; select the Linear Regression option.

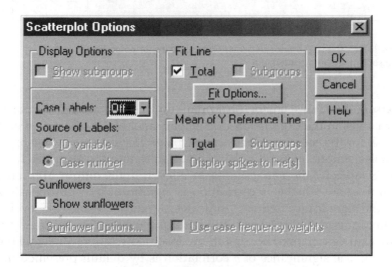

Figure 17.2 *The screen presented from Chart Options for selecting options for a scattergram*

17.3 Parametric (Pearson) and rank (Spearman) correlation

To obtain the correlation coefficient between two variables, select from the menus

```
Analyze
     Correlate
          Bivariate
```

The variables to be analysed have to be inserted in the Variables list in the usual manner. Specify which correlation coefficients you require

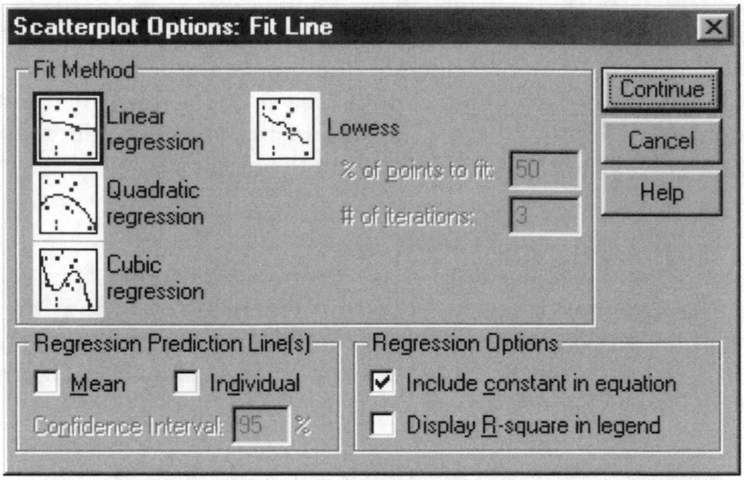

Figure 17.3   *The screen presented from Chart Options for obtaining the best-fitting straight line in a scattergram*

(Pearson, Kendall's tau or Spearman rank) by checking the relevant alternatives in the Correlation Coefficients area of the dialogue box. You can ask for the correlation between all possible pairings of three or more variables simply by inserting all the variables into the Variables list.

SPSS indicates the actual significance levels in the output. You can also ask it to show whether a correlation is significant by printing asterisks with the significance figures: * indicates significant at the 0.05 level, and ** significant at the 0.01 level. To obtain these asterisks, ensure the Flag Significant Correlations box in the Bivariate Correlations dialogue box is checked. The significance of a correlation is by default presented in the output using a non-directional (two-tailed) probability. If you have predicted in advance the direction of the relationship between the variables, you are entitled to use a directional (one-tailed) probability, and this can be requested in the Bivariate Correlations dialogue box.

Requesting Pearson correlations yields the output illustrated in Figure 17.4, where the correlations between scores on sales_1, sales_2, att1, att2 and att3 in the salesq file were requested. In Figure 17.4, the correlation between sales_2 and att2 is −.310 (Do not forget the minus sign indicates a negative correlation.) If the Sig (significance) value is less than .05, the correlation is statistically significant.

The Correlations procedure will exclude any case which has missing data on either of the variables being correlated. This is referred to as Exclude Cases Pairwise. If you are requesting a number of correlations, with three or more variables entered in the Variables list, you can ask SPSS to exclude from all the analyses any case that has a missing value on any of the variables: this is Exclude Cases Listwise, and is available via the Options button of the Bivariate Correlations dialogue box.

```
CORRELATIONS
 /VARIABLES=sales_1 sales_2 att1 att2 att3
 /PRINT=TWOTAIL NOSIG
 /MISSING=PAIRWISE .
```

Correlations

		SALES_1	SALES_2	ATT1	ATT2	ATT3
SALES_1	Pearson Correlation	1.000	.921**	-.273	-.437*	.274
	Sig. (2-tailed)	.	.000	.219	.042	.217
	N	22	22	22	22	22
SALES_2	Pearson Correlation	.921**	1.000	-.270	-.310	.217
	Sig. (2-tailed)	.000	.	.224	.161	.332
	N	22	22	22	22	22
ATT1	Pearson Correlation	-.273	-.270	1.000	.700**	-.765**
	Sig. (2-tailed)	.219	.224	.	.000	.000
	N	22	22	22	22	22
ATT2	Pearson Correlation	-.437*	-.310	.700**	1.000	-.648**
	Sig. (2-tailed)	.042	.161	.000	.	.001
	N	22	22	22	22	22
ATT3	Pearson Correlation	.274	.217	-.765**	-.648**	1.000
	Sig. (2-tailed)	.217	.332	.000	.001	.
	N	22	22	22	22	22

**. Correlation is significant at the 0.01 level (2-tailed).
*. Correlation is significant at the 0.05 level (2-tailed).

Figure 17.4   *Output from the correlation procedure showing Pearson correlation coefficients*

Spearman rank correlations are displayed as shown in Figure 17.5. The correlation coefficient is shown (.684 in Figure 17.5), followed by the significance level (.000 in Figure 17.5) and finally the number of cases, N. If the Sig (significance) value is less than .05, the correlation is statistically significant. In Figure 17.5, Sig = .000 which indicates a significant correlation between att1 and att2 because .000 is less than .05 or .01.

17.4 Obtaining means and standard deviations of the variables being correlated

To have the mean and standard deviations of the scores on the variables being correlated shown in the printout, select the Options button from the Bivariate Correlations dialogue box and check the Means and Standard Deviations box. This will add into the syntax the line

```
/STATISTICS DESCRIPTIVES
```

and when the procedure is run a table showing the statistics requested will be provided.

```
NONPAR CORR
  /VARIABLES=att1 att2
  /PRINT=SPEARMAN TWOTAIL NOSIG
  /MISSING=PAIRWISE .
```

Correlations

			ATT1	ATT2
Spearman's rho	ATT1	Correlation Coefficient	1.000	.684**
		Sig. (2-tailed)	.	.000
		N	22	22
	ATT2	Correlation Coefficient	.684**	1.000
		Sig. (2-tailed)	.000	.
		N	22	22

**. Correlation is significant at the .01 level (2-tailed).

Figure 17.5 *Output from the correlation procedure showing Spearman rank correlation coefficient*

17.5 Partial correlation

The correlation between two variables may arise because both are correlated with a third variable. Partial correlation is a technique which allows you to examine the correlation between two variables when the effect of other variable(s) has been partialled out. Partial correlation analysis is obtained from the menu

```
Analyze
    Correlate
        Partial
```

Enter into the Variables list the two variables to be correlated, and into the Controlling For: list the control variables, the ones whose influence on the correlation between the two variables is to be partialled out.

To obtain the means and standard deviations on each variable, and/or a matrix showing the zero-order correlations between all the variables, request them via the Options button. (A zero-order correlation is the usual correlation, with no partialling out for the effects of a control variable.)

Figure 17.6 illustrates the output from the Partial Correlations procedure. In this example, the correlation between sales_1 and att2 was examined, with number of customers visited (cust) as the control variable. Be careful in reading this old-style table: the correlation between the variables shown in a column and a row is shown where the column and row intersect. In Figure 17.6, the correlation is −.1062. (Do not forget the negative sign!) The degrees of freedom used in the calculation are shown in brackets below the correlation (19) and the probability value is given last as $p =$. In Figure 17.6 $p = .647$, which indicates the correlation is not significant. Do not make the common mistake of taking the p value as the correlation value!

Previously in Figure 17.4, the correlation between sales_1 and att2 was found to be negative and significant at −.437. But now, in Figure 17.6, after the effect of customer visits has been partialled out, the correlation is only −.1062. This suggests that the original correlation value was spurious, and arose because att2 correlates with customers visited and sales_1 and customers visited are also highly correlated. (The correlation is .727.) Once the effects of customers visited are removed by the partial correlation procedure, the low correlation between att2 and sales_1 is revealed.

```
PARTIAL CORR
  /VARIABLES= att2 sales_1 BY cust
  /SIGNIFICANCE=TWOTAIL
  /MISSING=LISTWISE .

- - - PARTIAL    CORRELATION    COEFFICIENTS
- - -

Controlling for..    CUST

                ATT2      SALES_1

ATT2          1.0000      -.1062
             (     0)    (    19)
             P= .        P= .647

SALES_1       -.1062      1.0000
             (    19)    (     0)
             P= .647     P= .

(Coefficient / (D.F.) / 2-tailed Significance)

" . " is printed if a coefficient cannot be computed
```

Figure 17.6   Output from the partial correlation procedure

17.6 Multiple regression

In multiple regression, you use a number of independent variables to predict the dependent variable. For example, you can predict sales_1 from cust (number of customers visited), since the correlation between these two variables is 0.727, significant at the 0.001 level. But will the prediction be better if you also consider the person's response to the att1, att2 and att3 questions? It is with this type of problem that multiple regression is concerned.

Multiple regression is obtained by selecting

```
Analyze
     Regression
          Linear
```

This opens the Linear Regression dialogue box shown in Figure 17.7. Enter the dependent variable in the Dependent box, and the predictor variables in the Independent box using the normal procedure of clicking on the variables in the source list and then on the appropriate arrow button.

You can specify the regression method to be used from Enter, Stepwise, Forward, Backward and Remove. Stepwise is probably the most frequently used method, although Enter is the default and enters all the variables in one step. Forward enters variables one at a time depending on whether they meet statistical criteria, Backward enters all the variables and then removes them one at a time depending on a removal criterion, while Stepwise which is a combination of forward and backward procedures examines each variable for entry or removal. Remove means that variables in a block are removed in one step. It is possible to specify one method for one block of variables and another method for another block; to do this, you have to create a second block of predictor variables by clicking on the Next button and then enter the predictor variables for this set. To move between the blocks of variables, use the Previous and Next buttons.

The Options button permits you to alter the criteria used when the stepwise, forward or backward methods are used, by inserting your own values for F or for the probability of F. You can also force the suppression of a constant term in the regression equation, by deselecting the Include Constant in Equation option.

Figure 17.8 illustrates the output from multiple regression when sales_1 was the dependent variable, cust, att1, att2 and att3 were used as predictor (independent) variables, and the Enter method was chosen.

Various statistics can be requested from the Statistics button of Figure 17.7. When it is clicked, a dialogue box is revealed allowing various options to be requested. If you select Descriptives, the output will include the means and standard deviations of the variables being analysed as well as a correlation matrix, as shown in Figure 17.8.

The Plots button will allow you to obtain a scatterplot of the dependent variable (Dependent in the source variable list) with standardized predicted values or one of a number of other predicted or residual variables which are calculated by the Regression procedure. These newly calculated variables can be saved from the Save button and its associated dialogue box.

The WLS button in the Linear Regression dialogue box allows you to obtain a weighted least-squares model.

The program will exclude from the analysis any case that has a missing value on any of the variables being analysed; this is referred to as Exclude Cases Listwise. You can have any missing values replaced with the mean of the scores on that variable, or you can ask the program to calculate correlations for all cases which have no missing value for the two variables being correlated (Exclude Cases Pairwise). These alternative treatments for missing values are obtained from the Options button of the Linear Regression dialogue box.

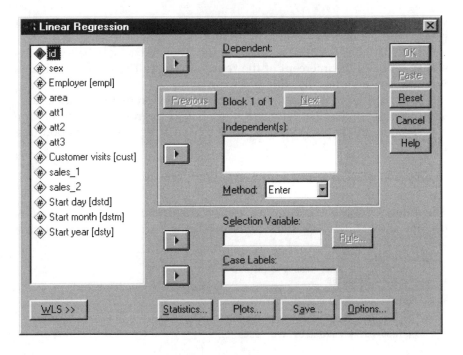

Figure 17.7   The Linear Regression dialogue box

The first part of the output shown in Figure 17.8 shows means and standard deviations of the variables included in the analysis, and this is followed by the correlations between them, all with one-tailed significance levels. In the table Variables Entered/Removed, the dependent variable is identified as sales_1, and the multiple regression method used is shown as 'Enter'.

The Model Summary table gives the multiple r (R = .734 in Figure 17.8) which is the correlation between the predictor variables combined and the dependent variable. R Square indicates the proportion of the variability in the dependent variable which is accounted for by the multiple regression equation. The figure labelled Adjusted R Square is an estimate of r^2 for the population (rather than the sample from which the data was obtained), and includes a correction for shrinkage.

The analysis of variance (ANOVA) table shown in Figure 17.8 shows the sum of squares explained by the regression equation and the 'residual' sum of squares. The residual sum of squares is the variability in the dependent variable which is left unexplained by the regression equation. The F statistic (4.953 in Figure 17.8) is obtained by dividing the Mean Square regression by the Mean Square residual. If F is significant (the probability value labelled Sig is less than 0.05), one can conclude that r^2 is significantly different from zero. This means that one can assume there is a linear relationship between the predictor and the dependent variables and that the regression equation allows you to predict the dependent variable at greater than chance level.

The final table is entitled Coefficients. The first row, labelled (Constant), refers to the intercept of the regression line. The *t* value indicates whether it is significantly different from zero.

The remainder of the Coefficients table lists the predictor variables and some statistics associated with each one. B is the regression coefficient for the variable. In the present example, we have a regression equation like this:

$$sales\_1 = cust(w1) + att1(w2) + att2(w3) + att3(w4)$$

The values of w1, w2, etc. are regression coefficients, but these B values do not show how important each predictor variable is. The relative

```
REGRESSION
  /DESCRIPTIVES MEAN STDDEV CORR SIG N
  /MISSING LISTWISE
  /STATISTICS COEFF OUTS R ANOVA
  /CRITERIA=PIN(.05) POUT(.10)
  /NOORIGIN
  /DEPENDENT sales_1
  /METHOD=ENTER cust att1 att2 att3   .
```

Descriptive Statistics

	Mean	Std. Deviation	N
SALES_1	5859.6232	2324.2958	22
Customer visits	50.8182	17.0116	22
ATT1	2.5455	1.1010	22
ATT2	3.0909	.9211	22
ATT3	3.4091	1.1816	22

Correlations

		SALES_1	Cutomer visits	ATT1	ATT2	ATT3
Pearson Correlation	SALES_1	1.000	.727	-.273	-.437	.274
	Customer visits	.727	1.000	-.330	-.516	.269
	ATT1	-.273	-.330	1.000	.700	-.765
	ATT2	-.437	-.516	.700	1.000	-.648
	ATT3	.274	.269	-.765	-.648	1.000
Sig. (1-tailed)	SALES_1	.	.000	.109	.021	.109
	Customer visits	.000	.	.067	.007	.113
	ATT1	.109	.067	.	.000	.000
	ATT2	.021	.007	.000	.	.001
	ATT3	.109	.113	.000	.001	.
N	SALES_1	22	22	22	22	22
	Customer visits	22	22	22	22	22
	ATT1	22	22	22	22	22
	ATT2	22	22	22	22	22
	ATT3	22	22	22	22	22

Continued on facing page

Variables Entered/Removed[b]

Model	Variables Entered	Variables Removed	Method
1	ATT3, Customer visits, ATT2, ATT1[a]		Enter

a. All requested variables entered.

b. Dependent Variable: SALES_1

Model Summary

Model	R	R Square	Adjusted R Square	Std. Error of the Estimate
1	.734[a]	.538	.430	1755.5069

a. Predictors: (Constant), ATT3, Customer visits, ATT2, ATT1

ANOVA[b]

Model		Sum of Squares	df	Mean Square	F	Sig.
1	Regression	61058607	4	15264674	4.953	.008[a]
	Residual	52390676	17	3081804.5		
	Total	1.13E+08	21			

a. Predictors: (Constant), ATT3, Customer visits, ATT2, ATT1

b. Dependent Variable: SALES_1

Coefficients[a]

Model		Unstandardized Coefficients		Standardized Coefficients	t	Sig.
		B	Std. Error	Beta		
1	(Constant)	444.191	4131.189		.108	.916
	Customer visits	94.090	26.412	.689	3.562	.002
	ATT1	188.652	594.575	.089	.317	.755
	ATT2	-186.743	664.803	-.074	-.281	.782
	ATT3	214.419	521.546	.109	.411	.686

a. Dependent Variable: SALES_1

Figure 17.8 *Output from Regression with the Enter method*

importance is shown when the B values have been transformed into standard scores, when they are referred to as beta. These are included in the printout and indicate that cust (with beta = .689) has much more influence on the dependent variable, sales_1, than do att1, att2 or att3. It is worth remembering that the beta coefficients obtained depend on the independent variables which have been used in the analysis, and have no absolute value.

The final columns of the Coefficients table show t values and their probabilities (Sig.). These indicate whether the regression coefficients for each variable are greater than zero. In Figure 17.8, the t values for att1, att2 and att3 are not significant, so one would conclude that these variables do not add to the ability to predict sales_1. The t value for cust is significant ($p = .002$), so this does predict sales_1.

Some idea of the way that the multiple regression method affects the output can be seen by comparing Figure 17.8 with Figure 17.9, which shows the output of analysing the same variables as in Figure 17.8 but

```
REGRESSION
  /MISSING LISTWISE
  /STATISTICS COEFF OUTS R ANOVA
  /CRITERIA=PIN(.05) POUT(.10)
  /NOORIGIN
  /DEPENDENT sales_1
  /METHOD=STEPWISE cust att1 att2 att3    .
```

Variables Entered/Removed[a]

Model	Variables Entered	Variables Removed	Method
1	Customer visits		Stepwise (Criteria: Probability-of-F-to-enter <= .050, Probability-of-F-to-remove >= .100).

a. Dependent Variable: SALES_1

Model Summary

Model	R	R Square	Adjusted R Square	Std. Error of the Estimate
1	.727[a]	.528	.504	1636.2562

a. Predictors: (Constant), Customer visits

ANOVA[b]

Model		Sum of Squares	df	Mean Square	F	Sig.
1	Regression	59902688	1	59902688	22.374	.000[a]
	Residual	53546685	20	2677334.3		
	Total	1.13E+08	21			

a. Predictors: (Constant), Customer visits

b. Dependent Variable: SALES_1

Continued on facing page

Coefficients

Model		Unstandardized Coefficients		Standardized Coefficients	t	Sig.
		B	Std. Error	Beta		
1	(Constant)	814.313	1122.234		.726	.476
	Customer visits	99.282	20.989	.727	4.730	.000

a. Dependent Variable: SALES_1

Excluded Variables

Model		Beta In	t	Sig.	Partial Correlation	Collinearity Statistics
						Tolerance
1	ATT1	-.037[a]	-.224	.825	-.051	.891
	ATT2	-.085[a]	-.466	.647	-.106	.734
	ATT3	.084[a]	.520	.609	.118	.928

a. Predictors in the Model: (Constant), Customer visits
b. Dependent Variable: SALES_1

Figure 17.9   *Output from Regression with the Stepwise method*

using the Stepwise method rather than Enter. The Variables Entered/ Removed table shows that the variable Customer visits (cust) was entered into the regression equation at step 1. The Model Summary table, ANOVA table and Coefficients table are read in a similar way to those in Figure 17.8 except that here only the predictor variable Customer visits has been entered in the regression equation. Those variables not entered are listed in the Excluded Variables table, with the beta values they would have if they were entered. The non-significant t values shown indicate that none of the variables would add to the predictive power of the equation, and so the process terminates without adding them in. Stepwise produces output which is simpler to interpret than Enter. In this example, the two methods produce very similar outcomes: only cust, of the four variables included, predicts sales_1.

18

ANALYSING NOMINAL AND ORDINAL DATA

Summary

- Use non-parametric tests with nominal or rank data, skewed data, or if the groups show unequal variance.
- The chi-square test for independent samples is obtained from the Analyze /Descriptive Statistics /Crosstabs procedure, not from Non-parametric Tests.
- Rank correlation is obtained from Analyze /Correlation.
- All other non-parametric tests are obtained from Analyze /Nonparametric Tests.

18.1 Non-parametric analyses

Non-parametric tests are used when the data does not lend itself to parametric statistical analysis because it is nominal or rank data, or is skewed, or the groups show unequal variance. In this chapter only the more commonly used ones are considered, but others will be found in the same menu as those described here.

It is important to distinguish between dealing with nominal (frequency) data and dealing with ordinal data. If you have counted the number of cases or people who appear in certain categories, the data is nominal and the chi-square test, the binomial test or the McNemar test are appropriate. If the data has been measured on an ordinal scale or consists of ranks, there are a number of tests which allow you to compare the sets of rankings. Section 2.9 gives guidance on deciding which analysis to use.

18.2 Obtaining the non-parametric tests

The chi-square test for independent samples is used when you have a table showing the number of people categorized according to independent variables, such as the number of people who are male and come from the North, who are female from the North, who are male from the South or are female from the South. If the data forms a table like this, with different people appearing in each of the possible categories, then the SPSS procedure needed is Crosstabs with the subcommand for obtaining the chi-square for independent samples. The procedure is described in sections 14.4 and 14.5.

All other non-parametric tests except rank correlation (see section 17.3) are obtained from the menu

```
Analyze
    Nonparametric Tests
```

which offers the options listed below.

- *Chi-square*. Note that this is the one-sample chi-square. The more common chi-square for testing the association between two categorical variables is found under Analyze /Descriptive Statistics /Crosstabs, as described in sections 14.4 and 14.5.
- *Binomial*. The binomial test is used when the data forms two categories (such as male and female), and compares the observed frequency of cases in each category with the frequency expected from the binomial distribution.
- *Runs*. The Runs test examines whether a sequence of two alternative values is in a random order.
- *1 sample K–S*. K–S stands for Kolmogorov–Smirnov. The test is used to determine whether a sample set of scores comes from a specified distribution such as normal or uniform.
- *2 Independent samples*. The dialogue box revealed by selecting this entry offers the Mann–Whitney, Moses extreme reactions, Kolmogorov–Smirnov two sample and Wald–Wolfowitz runs tests.
- *K Independent samples*. This has the Kruskal–Wallis and median tests.
- *2 Related samples*. This includes the Wilcoxon, sign and McNemar tests.
- *K Related samples*. This provides the Friedman and Cochran's Q tests, and Kendall's W (the coefficient of concordance) which is used to measure the relation among three or more sets of rankings. It can be seen as a measure of rank correlation but with three or more sets of data rather than just two. Unlike the correlation coefficient, W can only vary between 0 and 1.

Each set of tests has its own dialogue box in which the particular test is selected and the variables to be analysed are specified in the conventional manner of highlighting the variable name in the source list and clicking on the arrow button. Not all the tests available will be described here, as once you are familiar with the way the system operates and how to use the Help facility, there should be little difficulty in making appropriate decisions for specifying the test required.

The various tests allow you to obtain the mean, standard deviation, lowest and highest scores and number of cases for the variables being analysed, by selecting the Options button and then, in the Statistics area of the dialogue box that appears, selecting Descriptive.

MISSING VALUES IN NONPARAMETRIC TESTS   The Options button of the dialogue box for each test allows you to specify how missing values should be treated. The default is Exclude Cases Test-by-Test, which means that where you have requested a number of tests to be done, as each test is carried out, any cases that have missing values on the variable being analysed are excluded. The alternative is Exclude Cases Listwise: if this is selected, cases with a missing value on any of the variables inserted into the Test Variable List box are excluded from all analyses.

18.3 One-sample chi-square

Do not confuse this with the two-sample chi-square, obtained from the Crosstabs procedure! The one-sample chi-square test is used to test a hypothesis such as 'Suicide rate varies significantly from month to month'. If the hypothesis is false, the suicide rate will be the same for every one of the twelve months. The one-sample chi-square can be used to compare observed suicide rates per month with what would be expected if the rate were equal for all months.

SPSS will assume that you are comparing the observed distribution with an expected distribution in which the cases are spread equally across the categories. This can be altered, using the Values area in the Expected Values part of the dialogue box. So you can compare the observed distribution of suicides with that expected if January had twice as many suicides as August, and all other months had an equal rate midway between the January and August ones. The way to achieve this is to enter a value for each category in the Values text box and click on Add. You must enter the values in the order corresponding to the ascending order of the categories for the variable being tested.

To run this test, select

```
Analyze
     Nonparametric Tests
          Chi-square
```

This opens the appropriate dialogue box. Insert a variable into the Test Variable List box. By default, each value of score on the variable generates its own category, but you can specify the range of values to be used by selecting Use Specified Range and inserting the lower and upper values. In this way you could exclude cases which had a score outside the range you specify.

Figure 18.1 shows the results of applying a one-sample chi-square on the employer variable in salesq, to see whether the number of respondents from all three employers differs from what would be expected if each employer had an equal number. The categories of employer are listed, with the number of cases for each. The expected frequencies which would occur if all employers had had an equal number of cases is shown in the column headed Expected N. The Residual column shows the difference between the observed and the expected values. The Test Statistics table shows the value of chi-square, the degrees of freedom (df) and the probability level. In this example, chi-square is not significant, as the probability (0.834) is larger than 0.05.

```
NPAR TEST
  /CHISQUARE=empl
  /EXPECTED=EQUAL
  /MISSING ANALYSIS.
```

Employer

	Observed N	Expected N	Residual
Jones and Son	8	7.3	.7
Smith and Co	8	7.3	.7
Tomkins	6	7.3	-1.3
Total	??		

Test Statistics

	Employer
Chi-Square[a]	.364
df	2
Asymp. Sig.	.834

a. 0 cells (.0%) have expected frequencies less than 5. The minimum expected cell frequency is 7.3.

Figure 18.1   *Output from the one-sample chi-square test*

18.4 Two matched groups: Wilcoxon test

If you have carried out a within-subjects experiment, and have two scores for each subject, the Wilcoxon test is used to see whether there is a significant difference between the subjects' scores under the two conditions.

It involves calculating the differences between the scores for each subject, and ranking the difference scores, giving rank 1 to the smallest difference etc., but ignoring the sign of the difference. Any subjects where the difference score is 0 are dropped from the analysis. The plus or minus signs of the difference scores are assigned to the rank values, and the sum of the rank-values obtained for the plus- and minus-signed ranks separately.

The Wilcoxon test rests on the argument that if there is no difference between the two sets of scores, the sum of the ranks for plus-differences will be about the same as the sum of the ranks for the minus-differences. If the sums of plus-differences are very dissimilar to the sum of the minus-differences, then it is likely there is a reliable difference between the two sets of scores.

The dialogue box offering the Wilcoxon test also includes the sign test, used to establish that two conditions are different when the two members of each pair can be ranked, and the McNemar test for the significance of changes which is a form of two-sample chi-square for repeated measures.

To obtain the Wilcoxon test, select from the menu

```
Analyze
      Nonparametric Tests
            2 Related Samples
```

In the dialogue box, indicate the two variables to be compared by clicking on each of them; the first one will appear under Current Selections Variable 1:, and the second one will appear as Variable 2. To insert these into the Paired Variables list, click on the right-pointing arrow button: the two variables will then be shown as a linked pair. You can create further pairs in the same way. Figure 18.2 shows the output for a Wilcoxon test to compare the scores on att1 and att2 of the respondents in salesq.

The printout shows how many cases had att2 score less than att1 scores, how many had att2 greater than att1, and how many were tied (i.e. the scores on att1 and att2 were the same). It gives also the mean rank for those situations where the scores were not tied. The test yields a z value, and this together with the relevant probability level is provided in the Test Statistics output. In this instance, probability is less than 0.05, so you can conclude there is a significant difference between the scores on att1 and att2.

18.5 Three or more matched groups: Friedman test

This is used to compare three or more related sets of scores. A table is created where each row is the data for one subject, and the data within each row is ranked. The sum of ranks (T) for each column is calculated. The test is concerned with establishing whether the rank totals of each column differ more than would be expected by chance; if there were no difference between the sets of scores, the rank totals would be more or less the same.

```
NPAR TEST
  /WILCOXON=att1  WITH att2 (PAIRED)
  /MISSING ANALYSIS.
```

Ranks

		N	Mean Rank	Sum of Ranks
ATT2 - ATT1	Negative Ranks	3[a]	8.50	25.50
	Positive Ranks	14[b]	9.11	127.50
	Ties	5[c]		
	Total	22		

a. ATT2 < ATT1

b. ATT2 > ATT1

c. ATT1 = ATT2

Test Statistics[b]

	ATT2 - ATT1
Z	-2.683[a]
Asymp. Sig. (2-tailed)	.007

a. Based on negative ranks.

b. Wilcoxon Signed Ranks Test

Figure 18.2   *Output from the Wilcoxon test*

The test is available by selecting from the menu

```
Analyze
      Nonparametric Tests
          K Related Samples
```

In the dialogue box presented, specify the variables to be compared by clicking on the variable names and then on the right-pointing arrow. The output is shown in Figure 18.3, the test having been used to compare the scores on att1, att2 and att3.

The Friedman test ranks the scores on the variables for each respondent separately, and calculates the mean of these rank score for each variable. These means are shown in the Ranks table; Test Statistics shows the chi-square statistic, degrees of freedom and significance level. In Figure 18.3, the significance value is less than 0.05 and so you would conclude there is a significant difference between the scores on the three variables.

The Cochran Q test, also available from this dialogue box, is used for analysing nominal data from three or more matched groups or repeated measures.

```
NPAR TESTS
  /FRIEDMAN = att1 att2 att3
  /MISSING LISTWISE.
```

Ranks

	Mean Rank
ATT1	1.55
ATT2	2.14
ATT3	2.32

Test Statistics[a]

N	22
Chi-Square	8.316
df	2
Asymp. Sig.	.016

a. Friedman Test

Figure 18.3   *Output from the Friedman test*

18.6 Two independent groups: Mann–Whitney

The Mann–Whitney compares the scores on a specified variable of two independent groups. The scores of the two groups are ranked as one set, the sum of the rank values of each subgroup is found and a U statistic is then calculated. The Mann–Whitney is in the group of tests accessed by selecting from the menu

```
Analyze
    Nonparametric Tests
        2 Independent Samples
```

In the dialogue box, specify the variable to be analysed and then indicate the variable to be used to create the two groups of respondents whose scores are to be compared. This is done by inserting the variable name in the Grouping Variable box and specifying which groups you need by clicking on the Define Groups button. Suppose we want to compare the scores on sales_1 of the respondents in salesq from the employers 1 and 3. Enter the variable name empl into the Grouping Variable box, click the define Groups button, and then enter 1 into the box labelled Group 1, and 3 into the box labelled Group 2.

Figure 18.4 shows the result of using the Mann–Whitney to compare scores on sales_1 for respondents of employer 1 and employer 3. The average rank of each group is shown in the Ranks table. The Test Statistics table shows a value for U and a value for z with the associated two-tailed probability (Sig.). In this example, the probability is less than

0.05, indicating that there is a significant difference between sales_1 scores for employers 1 and 3.

The Mann–Whitney procedure also carries out the Wilcoxon Rank Sum test, and the output shows the value of W.

The Moses extreme reactions, Kolmogorov–Smirnov two-sample and Wald–Wolfowitz runs tests are also available.

```
NPAR TESTS
   /M-W= sales_1   BY empl(1 3)
   /MISSING ANALYSIS.
```

Ranks

	Employer	N	Mean Rank	Sum of Ranks
SALES_1	Jones and Son	8	5.38	43.00
	Tomkins	6	10.33	62.00
	Total	14		

Test Statistics[b]

	SALES_1
Mann-Whitney U	7.000
Wilcoxon W	43.000
Z	-2.195
Asymp. Sig. (2-tailed)	.028
Exact Sig. [2*(1-tailed Sig.)]	.029[a]

a. Not corrected for ties.

b. Grouping Variable: Employer

Figure 18.4 *Output from the Mann–Whitney test*

18.7 Three or more independent groups: Kruskal–Wallis

Kruskal–Wallis is used to compare the scores on a variable of more than two independent groups. It is found under

```
Analyze
     Nonparametric Tests
          K Independent Samples
```

In the dialogue box, specify a grouping variable by selecting a variable from the source list and inserting it in the Grouping Variable box. You then have to define the range of the grouping variable by clicking on the Define Range button which opens a dialogue box in which you enter the values corresponding to the lowest and highest scores on the grouping variable. For example, to compare the scores on cust for the respondents

```
NPAR TESTS
 /K-W=cust   BY empl(1 3)
 /MISSING ANALYSIS.
```

Ranks

	Employer	N	Mean Rank
Cutomer visits	Jones and Son	8	9.00
	Smith and Co	8	8.38
	Tomkins	6	19.00
	Total	22	

Test Statistics [a,b]

	Cutomer visits
Chi-Square	11.055
df	2
Asymp. Sig.	.004

a. Kruskal Wallis Test

b. Grouping Variable: Employer

Figure 18.5   *Output from the Kruskal–Wallis test*

of the three employers in the salesq set of data, remember that the employers were coded as 1, 2 or 3. So in the Several Independent Samples: Define Range box, you would enter 1 as the Minimum and 3 as the Maximum.

The output from the Kruskal–Wallis test is shown in Figure 18.5. The data on customer visits has been ranked, and the mean rank for each employer is given in the Ranks table. A chi-square value is shown in the Test Statistics table, with the df and probability value (Asymp. Sig.). In Figure 18.5 one can see that there is a significant difference between the customer visits of the three employers, as the probability value (.004) is less than 0.05.

The median test which is also available from the dialogue box offering the Kruskal–Wallis is used to test whether three or more independent groups have been drawn from populations with equal medians.

ASSESSING TEST RELIABILITY

Summary

- Reliability refers to the consistency of the results on different items in a test.
- Use the Scale /Reliability procedure to obtain Cronbach's alpha.

19.1 The concept of test reliability

Many studies in the social sciences involve assessing some attribute of the respondents. In the data file salesq, for example, there is data on the sales performance of those who completed the questionnaire and on their responses to three attitude statements. Whenever attributes of people are measured, it is necessary to consider the validity and reliability of the measuring instrument. Validity means 'Does the test measure what it claims to measure?' and is assessed by comparing the test with a 'true' measure of the attribute.

Reliability refers to the consistency of the results. There are a number of types of reliability. Test–retest reliability means that people obtain the same scores if they take the test twice. It can be assessed by giving the test to the same people on two occasions and correlating the two sets of scores. (In practice, to prevent the respondents simply remembering the answers they gave the first time, you may have two versions of the test with slightly different items. The two versions are known as parallel forms.)

Inter-scorer and inter-administrator reliability mean that the test gives the same results whoever is marking or administering it.

Another aspect of reliability is ensuring that all the items measure 'the same thing'. This can be assessed by comparing the scores on any item with the total score on all the items. If one item does not correlate with the total score, it is eliminated so the test has homogeneity of items. Another procedure is to divide the test into two halves and see how far the scores on each half correlate. This 'split-half' reliability indicates the internal consistency of the test.

But there are many ways you can construct the two halves. If you had a test of 40 items, you could take the first 20 and the final 20 or you could take the odd-numbered ones and then the even-numbered ones, or you could take items 1–10 and 21–30 as one half with the others forming the other half and so on. Perhaps the best thing would be to take every possible way of forming two halves, correlate the scores of the halves and then find the average of the correlations. This is essentially what Cronbach's alpha does and is one of the standard ways of expressing a test's reliability.

High reliability in all senses is not always a 'good thing'. High inter-scorer agreement is always desirable, but high item homogeneity is not. If you are measuring intelligence, you want to be sure that all aspects of intelligence are tested, and so you will not want all the items to show a very high correlation with each other.

You may ask what is an acceptable level of reliability, but there is no simple answer. For tests of cognitive ability (such as intelligence tests), reliability coefficients of about 0.8 are usually expected and for ability, tests should not be below 0.7. But tests of personality often have much lower values, partly because personality is a broader construct. The issue of test reliability is complex, and you should consult a text on psycho-metric testing such as Kline (1993).

19.2 Assessing test reliability with SPSS: Reliability

To obtain Cronbach's alpha and other indications of the reliability of a test select

```
Analyze
     Scale
            Reliability Analysis
```

In the dialogue box revealed, identify the items in the test from the list of variables by clicking on them and then on the right-pointing arrow button so the variables appear in the list to the right headed Items. Alternative models for assessing reliability can be chosen from the drop-down menu entitled Model.

An example of the syntax and output can be seen in Figure 19.1, where a reliablility analysis was conducted on the scores for att1, att2 and att3rc. (In the data file salesq, the scores on att3 are negatively related to those on att1 and att2 because of the way the questions are worded. The scores on att3 were recoded into the new variable att3rc, to be consistent with the scoring of att1 and att2, using the recode procedure described in section 12.6.)

Pressing the Statistics button from the original Reliability Analysis dialogue box reveals the box shown in Figure 19.2 from which you can

```
EXECUTE .
RELIABILITY
  /VARIABLES=att1 att2 att3rc
  /FORMAT=NOLABELS
  /SCALE(ALPHA)=ALL/MODEL=ALPHA.

*** Method 1 (space saver) will be used for this analysis ***

R E L I A B I L I T Y   A N A L Y S I S - S C A L E (A L P H A)

Reliability Coefficients
N of Cases =      22.0                    N of Items =  3

Alpha =     .8737
```

Figure 19.1   *Syntax and output from Reliability*

request a number of useful statistics. Figure 19.3 shows the output obtained when Descriptive Statistics for Item, Descriptives for Scale, Inter-item Correlations, and Summaries Means are requested. The first section shows the means and standard deviations on each item and this is followed by the correlations between the items. The figures described as Statistics for Scale show the overall mean score, variance and standard deviation if the scores on the separate items (att1, att2 and att3rc) were added together to make a single scale. Summaries Means gives the mean of the means for the separate items which is shown in the section of

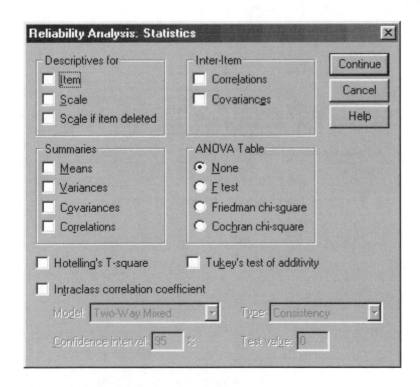

Figure 19.2   *The Reliability Analysis: Statistics dialogue box*

Figure 19.3 headed Item Means. This also prints out the range of the item means, and their variance.

The ANOVA Table section of Figure 19.2 lets you select an analysis of variance to test whether there is a significant difference between the mean scores on the items. The F-test produces a repeated-measures ANOVA table. If the items are in the form of ranks, you can select Friedman chi-square, and if they are all dichotomies you can select Cochran chi-square. Hotelling's *T* square test can be used to test the hypothesis that the item means are equal, while Tukey's test of additivity is used to test the assumption that there is no multiplicative interaction among the items.

```
RELIABILITY
  /VARIABLES=att1 att2 att3rc
  /FORMAT=NOLABELS
  /SCALE(ALPHA)=ALL/MODEL=ALPHA
  /STATISTICS=DESCRIPTIVE SCALE CORR
  /SUMMARY=MEANS .

**Method 2(covariance matrix) will be used for this analysis**

R E L I A B I L I T Y   A N A L Y S I S - S C A L E (A L P H A)

                           Mean        Std Dev      Cases
     1.      ATT1          2.5455       1.1010       22.0
     2.      ATT2          3.0909        .9211       22.0
     3.      ATT3RC        2.5909       1.1816       22.0

                    Correlation Matrix

                  ATT1         ATT2         ATT3RC
     ATT1        1.0000
     ATT2         .7001       1.0000
     ATT3RC       .7654        .6483       1.0000

           N of Cases =        22.0

                                            N of
     Statistics for  Mean    Variance    Std Dev  Variables
          Scale    8.2273     8.2792      2.8774         3

     Item Means    Mean  Minimum  Maximum Range  Max/Min   Variance
                  2.7424   2.5455   3.0909 .5455   1.2143     .0916

     Reliability Coefficients     3 items

     Alpha =    .8737          Standardized item alpha =    .8774
```

Figure 19.3 *Example of statistics obtained using Reliability Statistics*

FACTOR ANALYSIS

Summary

- For factor analysis the number of respondents should not be less than 100, and there should be at least twice as many respondents as variables. The respondents should be heterogeneous on the abilities or measures being studied.
- Perform a principal components analysis first. The number of factors to extract can be determined from a scree plot.
- Then run a common factor analysis with the number of factors set to the value obtained from the principal components analysis.
- To obtain an orthogonal simple structure rotation use Varimax. If an oblique rotation is needed, use Direct Oblimin.

20.1 Basic principles of factor analysis

Factor analysis is a technique or more accurately a family of techniques which aim to simplify complex sets of data by analysing the correlations between them. The underlying principles are explained in texts such as Stevens (1996) or Tabachnick and Fidell (1996). A simple coverage is provided by Kline (1994), and this chapter relies heavily on his exposition.

Given a set of scores on a number of variables, the correlation between each of the variables can be calculated and yields a correlation matrix such as is shown in the upper part of Figure 20.3. In the example data used in this chapter, 300 respondents answered 10 questions labelled att1 to att10. In Figure 20.3, the correlations between the responses to each question are shown: for example, the correlation between att1 and att2 is .368, and the correlation between att2 and att3 is .748.

Factor analysis is designed to simplify the correlation matrix and reveal the small number of factors which can explain the correlations. A component or a factor explains the variance in the intercorrelation matrix, and the amount of variance explained is known as the eigenvalue for the factor.

A factor loading is the correlation of a variable with a factor. A loading of 0.3 or more is frequently taken as meaningful when interpreting a factor. So when deciding what a factor signifies, one looks to see which variables have loadings of 0.3 or above. Communality is the proportion of the variance in each variable which the factors explain; the higher it is, the more the factors explain the variable's variance.

Exploratory factor analysis is employed to identify the main constructs which will explain the intercorrelation matrix, and is the most common usage. Confirmatory factor analysis is where one tests whether hypothesized factor loadings fit an observed intercorrelation matrix.

There are a number of considerations to bear in mind before carrying out factor analysis. First, the outcome depends on the variables which have been measured and the respondents who yielded the data. Secondly, the number of respondents should not be less than 100, and there should be at least twice as many respondents as variables. So if you are measuring 60 variables you need at least 120 respondents. Both the number of respondents and the ratio of respondents to variables should be as large as possible. Thirdly, the respondents should be heterogeneous on the abilities or measures being studied.

As mentioned above, there are many different types of factor analysis and you should have previously decided which particular procedures you mean to follow. (Those described in this chapter are only an illustration and not necessarily those relevant to your specific problem.)

In carrying out exploratory factor analysis, Kline recommends that one should first of all perform a principal components analysis. This is a form of analysis which derives as many components as there are variables, although the amount of variance explained by each component will decrease as more components are extracted. It is a consequence of the nature of principal components analysis that it will yield a large general factor first. The components obtained in a principal components analysis are uncorrelated and emerge in decreasing order of the amount of variance explained. Although one initially obtains as many components as there are variables, the aim of factor analysis is to explain the matrix with as few factors as possible. The number to extract can be determined if one obtains a scree plot; an example is shown in Figure 20.4. A scree plot shows the eigenvalues plotted against the number of the components. One looks at the plot to find where the line changes slope, where the 'elbow' is. In Figure 20.4 it is between the factor numbers 2 and 3, so one would take 2 as the number of factors to be extracted.

Once the principal components analysis has indicated the number of factors to extract, a common factor analysis is run with the number of factors set to the value obtained from the principal components analysis. There are many alternative types of analysis which can be chosen; 'In general principal factor analysis is an adequate method' (Kline, 1994: 54). Kline recommends running the analysis with rotation of factors; again, there are alternative methods of rotation but he recommends using the Varimax method: 'where an orthogonal simple structure rotation is desired, Varimax should be applied' (1994: 68).

However, it is not necessary for the factors to be orthogonal, and there can be advantages in having oblique or correlated factors. 'If an oblique rotation gives a better simple structure then the Direct Oblimin package is the one to use' (Kline, 1994: 76).

20.2 Obtaining a factor analysis

From the menu select

```
Analyze
     Data Reduction
          Factor
```

This opens the dialogue box shown in Figure 20.1. Identify the variables to be included in the analysis by selecting them and pressing the button with the right arrow. Clicking the Extraction button reveals another

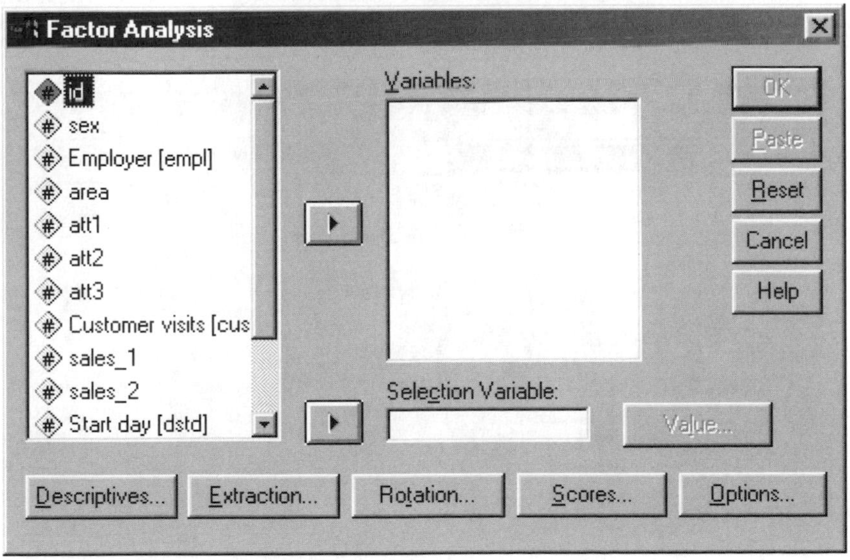

Figure 20.1   *Dialogue box for Factor Analysis*

dialogue box, shown in Figure 20.2, in which you can choose from the drop-down menu the method to use; principal components is the default. A scree plot is requested by clicking on the check box. If you want the correlation matrix shown in Figure 20.3, press the Descriptives button of Figure 20.1 and check the box labelled Coefficients in the area headed Correlation Matrix.

The syntax and output from a principal components analysis is illustrated in Figure 20.3. The first section of output illustrates the intercorrelations between the scores on each of the variables, requested via the Descriptives button of Figure 20.1. Principal components will begin with the same number of components as variables. The left-hand part of the Total Variance Explained table shows the eigenvalues and percentage of variance explained by each of the initial factors. The total of the eigenvalues equals the number of variables, and the percentage of variance explained is calculated from the eigenvalues: the eigenvalue for the factor is divided by the sum of the eigenvalues and multiplied by 100. The right-hand part of the Total Variance Explained table shows the percentage of variance explained just for those factors with an eigenvalue greater than 1.00.

The Component Matrix table shows the loading of each of the variables on each of the two factors which were extracted.

The principal components analysis indicated that two factors underlie the scores on variables att1 to att10, so a simple factor analysis with two factors to be extracted was run. From the dialogue box of Figure 20.2, the Principal-axis method was selected from the Method drop-down menu and the Number of Factors to Extract was set at 2 by clicking the radio

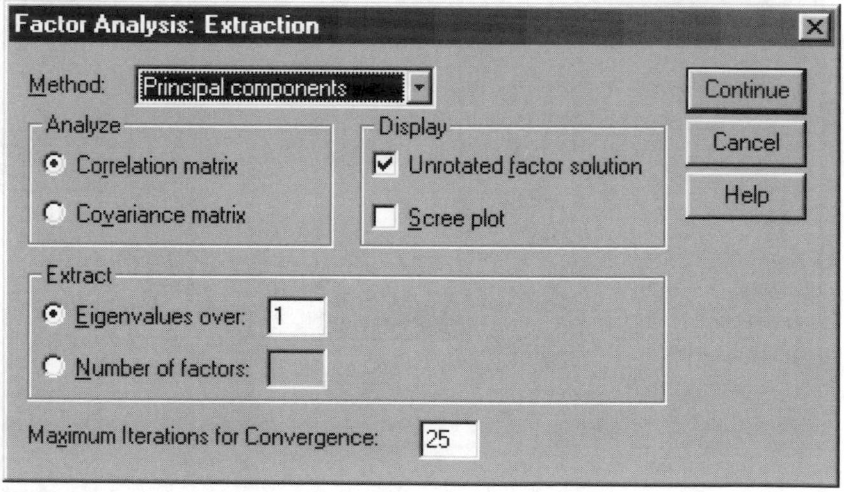

Figure 20.2   *The Factor Analysis: Extraction dialogue box*

```
FACTOR
 /VARIABLES att1 att2 att3 att4 att5 att6 att7 att8 att9 att10  /MISSING
 LISTWISE /ANALYSIS att1 att2 att3 att4 att5 att6 att7 att8 att9 att10
 /PRINT INITIAL CORRELATION EXTRACTION
 /CRITERIA MINEIGEN(1) ITERATE(25)
 /EXTRACTION PC
 /ROTATION NOROTATE
 /METHOD=CORRELATION .
```

Correlation Matrix

		ATT1	ATT2	ATT3	ATT4	ATT5	ATT6	ATT7	ATT8	ATT9	ATT10
Correlation	ATT1	1.000	.368	.327	.350	.431	.389	.369	.356	.340	.476
	ATT2	.368	1.000	.748	.759	.411	.841	.248	.275	.714	.707
	ATT3	.327	.748	1.000	.627	.420	.680	.273	.355	.711	.677
	ATT4	.350	.759	.627	1.000	.413	.748	.280	.238	.672	.684
	ATT5	.431	.411	.420	.413	1.000	.403	.521	.425	.369	.486
	ATT6	.389	.841	.680	.748	.403	1.000	.266	.310	.721	.710
	ATT7	.369	.248	.273	.280	.521	.266	1.000	.320	.351	.345
	ATT8	.356	.275	.355	.238	.425	.310	.320	1.000	.355	.276
	ATT9	.340	.714	.711	.672	.369	.721	.351	.355	1.000	.748
	ATT10	.476	.707	.677	.684	.486	.710	.345	.276	.748	1.000

Communalities

	Initial	Extraction
ATT1	1.000	.493
ATT2	1.000	.844
ATT3	1.000	.711
ATT4	1.000	.739
ATT5	1.000	.655
ATT6	1.000	.813
ATT7	1.000	.604
ATT8	1.000	.481
ATT9	1.000	.746
ATT10	1.000	.750

Extraction Method: Principal Component Analysis.

Total Variance Explained

	Initial Eigenvalues			Extraction Sums of Squared Loadings		
Component	Total	% of Variance	Cumulative %	Total	% of Variance	Cumulative %
1	5.484	54.844	54.844	5.484	54.844	54.844
2	1.352	13.517	68.361	1.352	13.517	68.361
3	.718	7.182	75.543			
4	.653	6.530	82.073			
5	.486	4.863	86.936			
6	.388	3.876	90.812			
7	.322	3.218	94.030			
8	.253	2.531	96.561			
9	.201	2.008	98.569			
10	.143	1.431	100.000			

Extraction Method: Principal Component Analysis.

Component Matrix[a]

	Component	
	1	2
ATT1	.564	.418
ATT2	.869	-.299
ATT3	.822	-.188
ATT4	.821	-.253
ATT5	.629	.509
ATT6	.864	-.259
ATT7	.486	.606
ATT8	.481	.500
ATT9	.845	-.181
ATT10	.859	-.107

Extraction Method: Principal Component Analysis.

a. 2 components extracted.

Figure 20.3   *Output from the principal components analysis*

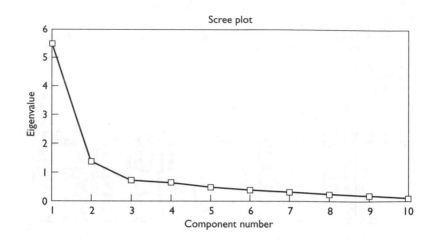

Figure 20.4   *Example of a scree plot*

button and typing 2 into the text box. From the dialogue box shown in
Figure 20.1 the Rotation button was used to reveal a box allowing
various rotation methods to be chosen, and Varimax was selected. The
syntax and output is shown in Figure 20.5.

The output is similar to that from principal components (Figure 20.3).
(The principal axis method of factor analysis is identical to principal
components analysis with one exception. In principal components, a
value of 1 is inserted in the diagonal of the intercorrelation matrix but in
the principal axis method an estimate of communality is used.) This is
why the Initial Eigenvalues section of the Total Variance Explained tables
of Figure 20.3 and Figure 20.5 are identical. In Figure 20.5 the result of
the Varimax rotation is presented, showing the loading on each of the
factors for each of the variables in the table headed Rotated Factor
Matrix.

If oblique rather than orthogonal factor rotation is used, you select
Direct Oblimin instead of Varimax in the dialogue box revealed by
selecting the Rotation button of Figure 20.1. The syntax and output
following oblimin rotation is shown in Figure 20.6. The Table headed
Pattern Matrix shows the coefficients used to express standardized
observed variables in terms of the factors, but the Table headed Structure
Matrix is the correlation between variables and factors and is used to
interpret the factors. The Factor Correlation matrix shows the correlation
between the factors.

In deciding whether to use orthogonal or oblique factor rotation, one
can apply orthogonal rotation and see whether it provides a simple
structure solution. Kline (1994: 65) maintains that the overriding criterion
of simple structure is that each factor should have a few high loadings
with the rest being zero or close to zero. On this criterion, the solution

shown in Figure 20.5 is superior to that shown in Figure 20.6. In Figure 20.5, those variables which load at 0.7 or above on factor 1 (att2, att3, att4, att6, att9 and att10) all load less than 0.4 on factor 2 whereas the variables that have low loadings on factor 1 (att 1, att 5, att 7 and att 8) all

```
FACTOR
  /VARIABLES att1 att2 att3 att4 att5 att6 att7 att8 att9 att10  /MISSING
  LISTWISE /ANALYSIS att1 att2 att3 att4 att5 att6 att7 att8 att9 att10
  /PRINT INITIAL EXTRACTION ROTATION
  /CRITERIA FACTORS(2) ITERATE(25)
  /EXTRACTION PAF
  /CRITERIA ITERATE(25)
  /ROTATION VARIMAX
  /METHOD=CORRELATION .
```

Communalities

	Initial	Extraction
ATT1	.334	.355
ATT2	.790	.835
ATT3	.646	.648
ATT4	.650	.672
ATT5	.459	.597
ATT6	.760	.788
ATT7	.333	.426
ATT8	.293	.292
ATT9	.699	.695
ATT10	.699	.707

Extraction Method: Principal Axis Factoring.

Total Variance Explained

Factor	Initial Eigenvalues			Extraction Sums of Squared Loadings			Rotation Sums of Squared Loadings		
	Total	% of Variance	Cumulative %	Total	% of Variance	Cumulative %	Total	% of Variance	Cumulative %
1	5.484	54.844	54.844	5.153	51.533	51.533	4.021	40.214	40.214
2	1.352	13.517	68.361	.001	8.612	60.145	1.993	19.930	60.145
3	.718	7.182	75.543						
4	.653	6.530	82.073						
5	.486	4.863	86.936						
6	.388	3.876	90.812						
7	.322	3.218	94.030						
8	.253	2.531	96.561						
9	.201	2.008	98.569						
10	.143	1.431	100.000						

Extraction Method: Principal Axis Factoring.

Factor Matrix[a]

	Factor	
	1	2
ATT1	.510	.308
ATT2	.873	-.271
ATT3	.795	-.123
ATT4	.800	-.182
ATT5	.596	.492
ATT6	.860	-.221
ATT7	.444	.478
ATT8	.428	.329
ATT9	.824	-.123
ATT10	.840	-3.96E-02

Extraction Method: Principal Axis Factoring.
a. 2 factors extracted. 8 iterations required.

Continued on next page

Rotated Factor Matrix[a]

	Factor	
	1	2
ATT1	.280	.526
ATT2	.888	.216
ATT3	.745	.303
ATT4	.779	.255
ATT5	.259	.728
ATT6	.851	.251
ATT7	.136	.639
ATT8	.198	.502
ATT9	.770	.318
ATT10	.741	.397

Extraction Method: Principal Axis Factoring.
Rotation Method: Varimax with Kaiser Normalization.
a. Rotation converged in 3 iterations.

Factor Transformation Matrix

Factor	1	2
1	.858	.514
2	-.514	.858

Extraction Method: Principal Axis Factoring.
Rotation Method: Varimax with Kaiser Normalization.

Figure 20.5   *Syntax and output for factor analysis with varimax rotation*

have quite high loadings (above 0.5) on factor 2. In Figure 20.6, however, the loadings shown in the Structure Matrix table are less clear-cut: all items are loading over 0.3 on both factors. In this instance, therefore, one would stop at the orthogonal, varimax procedure.

20.3 Adding factor scores to the data file

It is possible to have the factor scores for each case added to the active data file by pressing the Scores button of Figure 20.1 and checking the Save as Variables option. There are alternative ways in which the factor scores are calculated: use the Help button to gain information about them. If you use this procedure, a new variable for each factor is added to the data in the data window. To preserve these factor scores it is necessary to save the modified data file to disk.

```
FACTOR
  /VARIABLES att1 att2 att3 att4 att5 att6 att7 att8 att9 att10  /MISSING
  LISTWISE /ANALYSIS att1 att2 att3 att4 att5 att6 att7 att8 att9 att10
  /PRINT INITIAL EXTRACTION ROTATION
  /CRITERIA FACTORS(2) ITERATE(25)
  /EXTRACTION PAF
  /CRITERIA ITERATE(25) DELTA(0)
  /ROTATION OBLIMIN
  /METHOD=CORRELATION .
```

Pattern Matrix[a]

	Factor	
	1	2
ATT1	.128	.510
ATT2	.970	-.101
ATT3	.767	5.980E-02
ATT4	.827	-1.14E-02
ATT5	2.441E-02	.758
ATT6	.913	-4.40E-02
ATT7	-8.68E-02	.701
ATT8	4.025E-02	.515
ATT9	.792	6.675E-02
ATT10	.726	.173

Extraction Method: Principal Axis Factoring.
Rotation Method: Oblimin with Kaiser Normalization.
   a. Rotation converged in 4 iterations.

Structure Matrix

	Factor	
	1	2
ATT1	.434	.587
ATT2	.910	.481
ATT3	.803	.520
ATT4	.820	.484
ATT5	.479	.773
ATT6	.887	.504
ATT7	.334	.649
ATT8	.349	.539
ATT9	.832	.541
ATT10	.829	.608

Extraction Method. Principal Axis Factoring.
Rotation Method: Oblimin with Kaiser Normalization.

Factor Correlation Matrix

Factor	1	2
1	1.000	.599
2	.599	1.000

Extraction Method: Principal Axis Factoring.
Rotation Method: Oblimin with Kaiser Normalization.

Figure 20.6   *Syntax and excerpt of the output for factor analysis with oblimin rotation*

OBTAINING NEAT PRINTOUTS AND TABLES

Summary

- To obtain a clean version of the output, create a perfect syntax file and run it into a new, empty output file.
- The Tables procedure allows you to obtain tables of results laid out according to your specifications.

There are two situations when you want a clean version of the output. The first is when you have carried out statistical analyses, probably making some mistakes on the way, and need a clean version with all indications of your past errors removed to include in your report of the research. Ways to achieve a cleaned copy of the output are described in section 21.1.

The other situation is when you need tables summarizing the data from the data file. You might, for example, want a neat table showing the mean scores on specific variables for the male and female respondents. There are a number of ways of obtaining such tables, and these are briefly explained in sections 21.2 to 21.4.

21.1 Obtaining a clean output (.spo) file

If you wish to use the .spo file for presenting the results of your analysis, you will need a 'clean' version of the file, containing just the results you want. There are various ways of obtaining a clean .spo file. The simplest way is to start with a syntax file which is perfect so that it runs without error, then open a new output file (File /New /Output) and run the commands in the syntax file. A clean version of the output will be placed in the output window. (This is one of the reasons why the creation of a syntax file is recommended.) An alternative is to edit the .spo file, either within SPSS or by importing it into a word processor as described in section 7.12.

21.2 Generating tables using OLAP Cubes

The OLAP Cubes procedure, which was Layered Reports in version 8 of SPSS, calculates totals, means, and other univariate statistics for continuous summary variables within categories of one or more categorical grouping variables. (OLAP stands for Online Analytical Processing.) A separate layer in the table is created for each category of each grouping variable. The procedure is accessed by selecting

```
Analyze
        Reports
                OLAP Cubes
```

Specify the summary variable and the grouping variables by selecting them from the variable list and pressing the arrow key to enter them in the appropriate list. The Statistics button allows you to select the statistics you want displayed. An example of the output obtained when cust was the summary variable and area the categorical variable is given in Figure 21.1.

The output does not appear to provide separate layers for each category of the categorical variable, but this is misleading. Only one layer of the table is visible at a time, but you can view other layers after the table is displayed in the Viewer by double-clicking the table. A drop-down list, shown in Figure 21.2, will become available and you use it to select which of the subgroup's data to display.

```
OLAP CUBES
    cust   BY area
    /CELLS=SUM COUNT MEAN STDDEV SPCT NPCT
    /TITLE='OLAP Cubes'.
```

Case Processing Summary

	Cases					
	Included		Excluded		Total	
	N	Percent	N	Percent	N	Percent
Customer visits * AREA	22	100.0%	0	.0%	22	100.0%

OLAP Cubes

AREA: Total

	Sum	N	Mean	Std. Deviation	% of Total Sum	% of Total N
Customer visits	1118.00	22	50.8182	17.0116	100.0%	100.0%

Figure 21.1   *Initial output from OLAP Cubes*

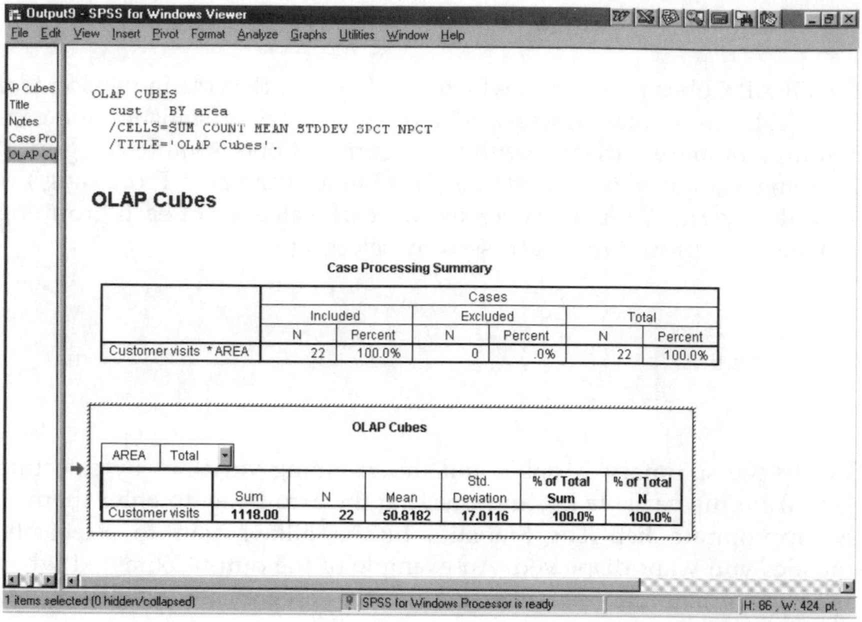

Figure 21.2   *Output from OLAP Cubes showing that alternative views are available*

21.3 Generating tables using Case Summaries

Tables showing a list of the scores on specific variables for cases subdivided by a category (such as respondent's sex), as shown in Figure 21.3, can be obtained by selecting

```
Analyze
     Reports
           Case summaries
```

The Summarize procedure calculates subgroup statistics for variables within categories and across all categories, the particular statistics to be shown being selected by pressing the Statistics button and selecting from the list of possibilities presented. For Figure 21.3, a table showing mean scores, standard deviations and *n* on the variable cust for subgroups of area was requested. The table in Figure 21.3 includes a listing of all the cases in each subgroup, but this can be suppressed by unchecking Display Cases in the Summarize Cases window. The result of doing this is shown in Figure 21.4 where subgroups of sex and area were requested.

The Analyze /Reports menu also includes the entries Report Summaries in Rows and Report Summaries in Columns. These invoke a procedure called Report which is of such complexity that few will have bothered to use it. The output from the Report procedure has not been updated and is in a text format. The procedure is now obsolete and

```
SUMMARIZE
  /TABLES=cust  BY area
  /FORMAT=VALIDLIST NOCASENUM TOTAL LIMIT=100
  /TITLE='Case Summaries'
  /MISSING=VARIABLE
  /CELLS=COUNT MEAN STDDEV .
```

Summarize

Case Summaries[a]

				Customer visits
AREA	North	1		43.00
		2		83.00
		3		41.00
		4		39.00
		5		30.00
		6		79.00
		7		48.00
		8		58.00
		9		40.00
		Total	N	9
			Mean	51.2222
			Std. Deviation	18.4917
	South	1		46.00
		2		48.00
		3		71.00
		4		72.00
		5		42.00
		6		28.00
		7		76.00
		8		68.00
		9		33.00
		10		36.00
		11		38.00
		12		60.00
		13		39.00
		Total	N	13
			Mean	50.5385
			Std. Deviation	16.6814
	Total	N		22
		Mean		50.8182
		Std. Deviation		17.0116

a. Limited to first 100 cases.

Figure 21.3 *Example of output from Case Summaries*

```
SUMMARIZE
  /TABLES=cust  BY area BY sex
  /FORMAT=NOLIST TOTAL
  /TITLE='Case Summaries' /FOOTNOTE ''
  /MISSING=VARIABLE
  /CELLS=COUNT MEAN STDDEV .
```

Case Summaries

Cutomer visits

AREA	SEX	N	Mean	Std. Deviation
North	male	3	51.3333	27.9702
	female	6	51.1667	15.3025
	Total	9	51.2222	18.4917
South	male	7	49.0000	17.1367
	female	5	48.6000	16.7571
	Total	12	48.8333	16.1967
Total	male	10	49.7000	19.2588
	female	11	50.0000	15.2053
	Total	21	49.8571	16.8086

Figure 21.4   *Example of output from Case Summaries with Display Cases suppressed*

redundant since far neater tables are obtained using the Table procedure.

21.4 Generating tables using Custom Tables

Sophisticated tables of the data can be obtained using Custom Tables, which is obtained from

```
Analyze
      Custom Tables
```

If Basic Tables is selected, the dialogue box shown in Figure 21.5 is presented. Specify which variables are to be shown in the tables by selecting variables from the list in the left hand box and inserting them into the Summaries box by clicking on the right-pointing arrow. The variables to be used to form subgroups are specified in a similar way. The Statistics button allows you to request a number of alternative statistics. The Layout, Totals, Format, and Titles buttons provide access to further options for the appearance of the table.

An example of a Basic Table is shown in Figure 21.6, where the mean and standard deviation on the variables cust and sales_1 were requested. Count indicates the number of cases, usually denoted by *n*.

In Figure 21.7, overall statistics are also shown; these are obtained by selecting the Totals button from Figure 21.5 and checking the option Totals over Each Group Variable.

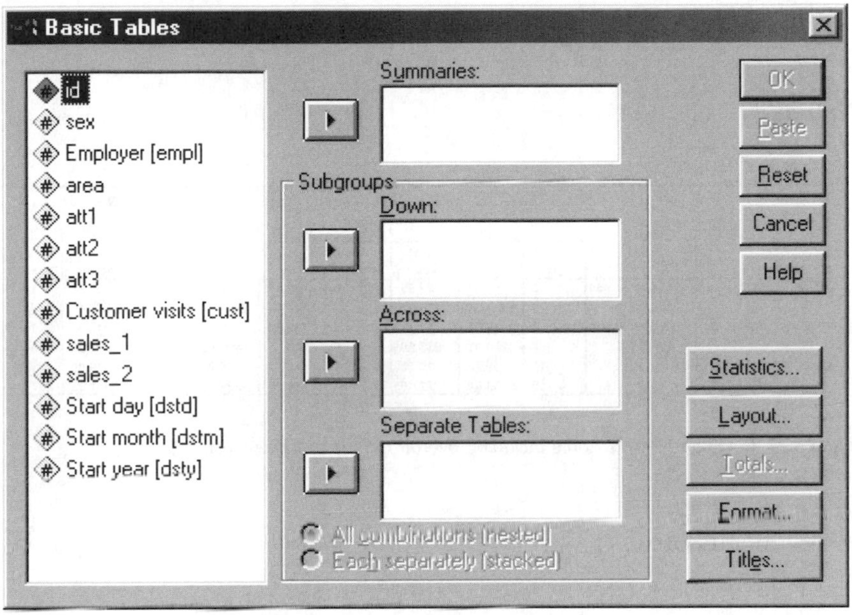

Figure 21.5 *The Basic Tables dialogue box*

```
* Basic Tables.
TABLES
  /FORMAT BLANK MISSING('.')
  /OBSERVATION cust sales_1
  /TABLES area > (cust + sales_1)
  BY sex > (STATISTICS)
  /STATISTICS
  count( ( F5.0 ))
  mean( )
  stddev( ).
```

Tables

			SEX					
			male			female		
			Count	Mean	Std Deviation	Count	Mean	Std Deviation
AREA	North	Customer visits	3	51.33	27.97	6	51.17	15.30
		SALES_1	3	5321.34	3134.37	6	6577.05	2284.41
	South	Customer visits	7	49.00	17.14	5	48.60	16.76
		SALES_1	7	6220.33	2823.50	5	4700.33	1409.68

Figure 21.6 *Example of a table obtained using Basic Tables*

```
TABLES
  /FORMAT BLANK MISSING('.')
  /OBSERVATION cust sales_1
  /FTOTAL $t 'Group Total'
  /TABLES (area > (cust + sales_1) +  $t )
  BY (sex > (STATISTICS) +  $t )
  /STATISTICS
  count( ( F5.0 ))
  mean( )
  stddev( ).
```

Tables

			SEX						Group Total		
			male			female					
			Count	Mean	Std Deviation	Count	Mean	Std Deviation	Count	Mean	Std Deviation
AREA	North	Customer visits	3	51.33	27.97	6	51.17	15.30	9	51.22	18.49
		SALES_1	3	5321.34	3134.37	6	6577.05	2284.41	9	6158.48	2472.22
	South	Customer visits	7	49.00	17.14	5	48.60	16.76	12	48.83	16.20
		SALES_1	7	6220.33	2823.50	5	4700.33	1409.68	12	5587.00	2384.05
Group Tota	Customer visits		10	49.70	19.26	11	50.00	15.21	21	49.86	16.81
	SALES_1		10	5950.64	2772.46	11	5724.00	2089.19	21	5831.92	2377.97

Figure 21.7   *Example of a table including overall means, obtained using Basic Tables*

The menu entry

```
Analyze
      Custom Tables
            General Tables
```

allows more complex tables than are available from Basic Tables. In Basic Tables, the same summary statistics are given for all the variables being summarized, but General Tables allows different statistics to be shown for different variables. An example of such a table is shown in Figure 21.8. It was created by having cust and sales_1 as row variables, and ensuring for each one that the option Selected Variable is Summarized was checked. Then Edit Statistics was used to select the statistics required (mean for cust and median for sales_1). The variable sex was entered as a column variable and the variable area was entered as a layer variable.

Different subgroups can form separate layers of the table, but only one layer of the table is visible at a time. To view other layers of the table, double-click it so that a drop-down list similar to that shown in Figure 21.2 is presented.

The Tables of Frequencies option of the Analyze /Custom Tables menu allows you to produce tables that contain multiple variables with the same values. By default, the variables form columns and the categories form rows, as shown in Figure 21.9. Each cell displays the number of cases in that category. In Figure 21.9, the table shows the number of

```
TABLES
  /FORMAT BLANK MISSING('.')
  /OBSERVATION= cust sales_1
  /GBASE=CASES
  /TABLE=cust + sales_1  BY sex  BY area
  /STATISTICS
  mean( cust)
  median( sales_1).
```

Tables

AREA North

		SEX	
		male	female
Customer visits	Mean	51.33	51.17
SALES_1	Median	5723.52	6884.50

Figure 21.8   *Example of a table obtained using General Tables showing different summary statistics for different variables*

males and females who made each possible response on the three variables att1, att2 and att3.

Different subgroups can form separate layers of the table, but only one layer of the table is visible at a time. To view other layers of the table, double-click it so that a drop-down list similar to that shown in Figure 21.2 is presented.

```
TABLES
  /FORMAT BLANK MISSING('.') /TABLES
  (LABELS)  BY
  sex > ( att1 + att2 + att3 )
  /STATISTICS COUNT ((F5.0) 'Count' ) .
```

	SEX					
	male			female		
	ATT1	ATT2	ATT3	ATT1	ATT2	ATT3
	Count	Count	Count	Count	Count	Count
1.00	1			2		3
2.00	5	2		4	3	
3.00	2	4	4	2	6	3
4.00	2	3	4	2	1	4
5.00		1	2	1	1	1

Figure 21.9   *Example of a table obtained using Tables of Frequencies*

REFERENCES

Hinton, P.R. (1995) *Statistics Explained*. London: Routledge.

Howell, D.C. (1992) *Statistical Methods for Psychology*. 3rd edn. Belmont, CA: Duxbury.

Kline, P. (1993) *The Handbook of Psychological Testing*. London: Routledge.

Kline, P. (1994) *An Easy Guide to Factor Analysis*. London: Routledge.

Stevens, J. (1996) *Applied Multivariate Statistics for the Social Sciences*. 3rd edn. Mahwah, NJ: Erlbaum.

Tabachnick, B.G. and Fidell, L.S. (1996) *Using Multivariate Statistics*. 3rd edn. New York: HarperCollins.

INDEX